CONTENTS

SIN WALK OF SHAME

KHRONA TENSEI

ARPress
ILLUMINATING IDEAS.
EMPOWERING VOICES

ARPress
45 Dan Road Suite 5
Canton MA 02021

Hotline: 1(888) 821-0229
Fax: 1(508) 545-7580

Ordering Information:
Quantity sales. Special discounts are available on quantity purchases by corporations, associations, and others. For details, contact the publisher at the address above.

Printed in the United States of America.

ISBN-13:   Softcover   979-8-89356-271-2
           eBook   979-8-89356-270-5

Library of Congress Control Number: 2024903331

PREQUEL; RETURN TO NOTHING

No one knew how they got here, nor even where they were. The crowd looked around in confusion, feeling as though they'd been here before... Like someone from ancient times had led them through a desert for 40 years and they, at the end of it all, ended up here, somehow. They muttered and clamored amongst themselves in confusion and in rage, trying to make sense of whatever was going on.

"Welcome..." a voice said to them from beyond, "... You may call me... Mister Sir..." These people, who were the mass accumulation over the course of history of every single failure, ne'er do well and wicked person that ever existed all scrunched up into one place (especially those that Moses led), would be greeted by a very monotonous, yet exceedingly sinister man that stood over them with a wily grin.

"You all... Are MY people... Pale, full of lepers, sickly, wicked, easily swayed, destructive, unsanitary, feeble, weak of mind, will and spirit..." he said with a chuckle, cutting himself off because he could clearly go on forever about their iniquities "And this... is MY System..." He'd been building it up for quite a while, making it absolutely perfect for this sorry lot.

"It's been made ESPECIALLY for you all... To turn you into 'Sirs' just like me." He was quite pleased to see that his finely created system would be put to good use... He CERTAINLY had Jobs for the ENTIRE lot. " You will be turned into Sirs. Drones. Servicemen. Laborers. Slaves. And those that sustain my empire from the shadows under my feet as I work to bring my world up to the Mainland. You will support ME. You will sustain ME. You will lift ME up and be my staircase, until I can drag more of those up above back down under my Rule. So take those Jobs I have ever so kindly provided for the each of and…"

"Get Back To Work."

Many of them still remained confused, though a large majority of them were thoroughly upset. "No fair! What did I do? I don't deserve this!" and all such excuses were heard being shouted from the crowd. They felt as though, no matter what terrible things they did in their lives, they were all supposed to apparently get rewarded for being thieves, criminals, liars, cheaters, killers and all such other things. They were ESPECIALLY unhappy to see who it was that ran this facility… "You look familiar…"

Mister Sir sighed, already tired of listening to them chatter and spew out more lies, "… Mortals are so weak…" The fact that they couldn't even comprehend what they did and tried to defend it was proof enough. "You all may be wondering how you ended up on the Ass of Existence, waiting to be Expelled from the Universe and into the Toilet… Well, you were Assess during Existence, and so that is your fate. You all will be compensated for your services, rest assured. You… Need to survive, right? In order to keep on producing more of what I'm forcing from you? Yes, of course…" He would bring out wads of colored paper. "Money. Here, take as much as you can. It means nothing, but it's a place holder for you all for things that actually do mean something, keeping yourselves, and thus my established system, alive and running for as long as you exist. Worship it. Seek it. Lust for it." He scattered the wads of colored paper out into the crowd, ready to watch them clamor and kill each other for the silly scraps… Hopefully they would. That would be less of their whining to deal with. Less sass.

"Your resources are limited. You will have your children here. Your children will grow up in slavery. You will learn to think it is not slavery, but everyday life. You will expend more than half of your very souls on sustaining my system, but think you are sustaining yourselves. There are only two ways out of here… That is to be called out and released through atonement after having paid your price, or…" He pointed to the great and ominous mountain that scraped the sky and moved beyond the clouds, its top unable to be seen, "… Climb that Mountain to Salvation.

But knowing most of you and your attachment to your vices... You will not survive." He grinned, knowing that, by the very nature of these beings, they didn't even have what it took to reach the base of the mountain. He could keep them down here forever and do whatever he wanted for all eternity, whilst they just gave him the power to do so. He would take from them their lives in order to extend his own, and even give himself far greater power than they could ever imagine.

"The choice is yours..." he said, knowing that there was no choice based on solely how these beings interacted. He knew them well, for he was one of them, at a time... Before he created a system that enslaved his brethren and gave him ultimate power through their suffering and turmoil. "Now... Get out. I have better things to do than to teach you how to live in the afterlife. Since you were unfair in Life... the Afterlife will be unfair to you. Hmhmhm..." He chuckled, pulling a lever attached to the gate that opened the floor, having them all fall into a fiery pit underneath the mountain. They could be seen through the grated floor, clawing and trying to scrape their way out, and he would step on each of their fingers, laughing as he went to explore this world made specifically for him and his slaves...

"Welcome To Hell..."

As soon as those sentenced from the 'Walk of Shame' fell into 'Nadir; the Bottomless Pit,' they would witness the lord and mistress of the Zero World return to it with all such knowledge of how to make this land great as well as the Zeroes themselves, if they were willing to work to attain their 'Values' back. Upon their arrival, the land would be christened 'The NeoZero Dimension' or 'NeoZero World.' Here, one could earn 'Value' from being a 'Zero' and see how far it takes you up the mountain that leads to one's release from the Zero World, Mt. Mortis. All of the Dead or the Banished and Failures and Criminals and such that were sent here would be able to always have a way out, but only after they went through the necessary protocols that required it. This meant that no matter what happened, there was always an assurance that there would be a way out and that you wouldn't permanently be kept that way; a failsafe, if you will.

"Everyone Hail."

The loud, elegant and commanding voice billowed outward over the entire land for all of the fallen Zero Worlders to hear and tremble at its magnitude, even in its dainty manner, of their coming. The sound of her voice and the mention of his name sent a shock wave that, with just that much intensity and influence alone, would it strike down those that did not believe nor sought to oppose those who were true rightful rulers of this land simply on default. Their knees would buckle, and all would bow, and those who didn't would find the ground collapsing beneath their feet merely by her voice treading the atmosphere casually and holding that much authority over everything that occurred within its vicinity.

She was well aware of whom they were dealing with; misfits, unruly rogues, power hungry criminals, villainous masterminds and all of the sort that would find their values depleting to Absolute Zero over their lifetime, rather than being built up toward something better once their bodies were destroyed. It was the only way to preserve their existences and allow them the chance to do things over. She spilled into the land as the overflowing light of the 'Lanterns,' that which would paint the sky with color and the ground with beauty, as well as each of the accursed Zeroes that had been lost in life to come start over and be whatever they wanted to be based on everything in history. They would be trapped in the past, but in that, they could become whatever they wished until they finally figured out how to be pardoned from the Zero World.

There, up above, from the same white hole that bore them the light and vibrancy of all that was beyond the borders of this realm, would a great and overbearing shadow be cast over the land, blotting out the sun and its light, and thus, any trace of light before his blazing head of white fire; the sun itself. His head was like a moon and his body, a great weight on the backs of everyone that existed there now, already elongating and combining their shadows together as one shadow combined. That single shadow that bound them all together at their souls was already in the sight of the 'Great Mind,' a crimson gleam already in his eyes the very instant he appeared to look at those who had fallen.

"..."

Nothing needed to be said to them at this point, considering that their son, even in his lapse of memory, had informed them of their doings and what they needed to be doing whilst they were here. Primordius simply remained to enforce such things, back at the top of Mt. Mortis, where he'd been before. "Come, dear," he called out to the other presence wrapped about their isolated atmosphere, forging himself out of their own shadows cast in the light of his ever present eyes.

He, himself, as all of their shadows combined was about the size of the shadow of the mountain, of which, with one stomp that would have probably obliterated a tenth of their land. Primordius walked into the darkness and curled into the shadow of Mt. Mortis, of where he originally hailed as 'Hades' before the move. A thin, crimson gleam could be seen piercing through the darkness like a sniper's laser scope, searching for specific targets that the larger Shadow of Himself couldn't pinpoint without losing sight of the entire lot. This way, he could single people out with a smaller Shadow of Himself and keep creating more as scaled down or up as they needed to be as after images of himself at different Values of power, constitution and contingency. In that, from the shadow of the cave at the very top of the mountain, Pulchritude, is where he and his beloved would be stationed, watching over the land. "Let's see if they reach the top of Olympus this time...?" He muttered, returning to his seat upon his throne.

Their presence and essence were all around, so they could coach the Zeroes on as they either trekked up the accursed mountain or simply remained as Zeroes that would be put to work in the NeoZero World.

The crowd of lost people, failures at life, sinners at heart and void of either mind or soul (if not both) would be left to look upon these great shadows, unable to fully conceive what they were seeing, even if it was cast right before their eyes. The Rephaim, as these Zero Worlders were called, had lost their identities and personalities to this land, and now simply were empty vessels that were trying to acquire their lives back. Their minds. Their souls. Their joy. Their very life. Even if they weren't fully aware that they were lost and downtrodden, they at least knew that whatever situation they were in was something painful to them, in some way, shape or form. Some were confused, not being aware of their crimes nor why they were being punished, but others knew for a fact that they were in hell and everything they'd done in their lives to get there. There was much hatred. Much sorrow. Much strife. Much sheer, unbridled pain in the collection of people. They were hopeless and knew nothing of what they could do. They could not even comfort each other. All they could do was suffer; some quietly, some out loud, in all their disdain. They wondered if there was a way out of this hellhole, especially a way out from the people nearby, who looked just as wicked, sorry or reckless as anyone else that had been unfortunate enough to be here. Though there were many people of different races, skin tones, professions, ideals and things of that nature, all of that meant nothing here. That was the most troubling thing; all that they knew and learned and worked for in their earthly lives... Literally amounted to nothing in this realm. It truly was as if they were nothing but worthless Zeroes...

"Welcome," an Anonymous Presence with the likeness of the man that had spoken to them before spoke to them from some sort of large pedestal over them that the others could not achieve in some way, shape or form, thereby making him the cause for attention over the crowd. "I Am Mister Sir, As You May Or May Not Know, And I Am Here To Guide You Through This Most Unfortunate Experience That Has Brought You Into Your Respective Turmoils." He looked at them all, knowing something about all of this that they did not, and was going to test them to see how well they would listen to someone that had information they could not acquire for themselves. "I Am Taking Recruits. Drafting. Enlisting. What Will You Do? Will You Come With Me? Or Will You Attempt To Figure This Out On Your Own?" There was nothing more to ask of them after that.

After being lost in an ambiguous void, filled with nothing but chaos, calamity and turmoil that they could not control, understand nor cease from having any effect on them, the Rephaim that truly sought to emerge from the fiery pits would have no choice but to follow the strange man unaffected by this chaotic flame out of the pits. There were those that decided, in their own best judgment, not to come out, however, and their journeys would begin and end here in the flames. They would eventually die and be used for fuel, burned away into complete nothingness. Those that were smart enough to follow their savior out of this ambiguous darkness underneath the mountain would follow Mister Sir and watch as their brethren were destroyed before their very eyes in a myriad of chaotic manners. Those that saw this would become fearful, knowing that if they hadn't moved, those people lost to the destruction could have been any of them. That was the most terrifying thing of all. They would not stay, and instead, the Rephaim followed Mister Sir to his location.

PROLOGUE; LIMBO, PURGATORIO

You are led out from the underground pit of hellacious suffering by someone named Mister Sir, garb in all velvet black with a flowing swanky trench coat and thick, sleek jet-black shades. His hair is nicely kept and it seems like his demeanor overall and all around is completely professional. When you emerge from wherever you had been, which now no longer is accessible to you, you appear at Ground Zero; the only solid foundation of understanding that you have any real comprehension of beyond the ambiguous land of darkness and suffering you were once trapped in with no method of escape at all. This space is a completely flat, 2 dimensional surface allowing you to stand grounded on something sturdy and solid. Everything else around you is desolate. However, you stand at a gateway into a realm unknown. It is the only thing before you, and it is apparently some sort of ascent into a higher level of existence, perhaps even to get a vantage point on if there is something else around you other than complete desolation. The gate is completely open.

I follow Mister Sir out from the pit of darkness, where I have just witnessed many of my friends, family, loved ones and strangers similar to me get completely destroyed in a fit of ambiguous chaos beyond my comprehension. Stunned, I look around at all those that are like me, who are also scared and confused, like me. Eventually, I speak up from the crowd, "Where are we going? What just happened?" After gaining a bit of confidence, I say more. "Where did we just come from? And what are we supposed to do?" I stay in the crowd of people, patiently awaiting an answer, but become nervous and distraught the longer I do not have it. I feel as though I could panic and become irrational soon.

No one else around You speaks to You. Everyone is like They are dead, even though They are full of life. You are the only one that seems to be consciously aware that You're going anywhere at all, and Everyone else seems to be moving along without a fuss, as though brainwashed. Mister Sir hears you, but doesn't respond immediately. Instead, he takes You all the way to the gate. "You should already know by now," was all he said, and Anyone who was coming with him would be taken with him immediately. Everything was explained before they got there, and it seemed like everyone else knew that. Anyone and Everyone who was left behind would remain as they were at the gate.

From there, on behalf of Mister Sir, the $yndicate made as a systematic architectural structure would move things along for Mister Sir, since You chose not to keep up with Him. Instead, You are now forced to work through the $yndicate, also and otherwise known as your Government System.

The first thing You need to do is find someone who will answer Your questions within the City or Society You are located in.

Many people had seen the supernatural events occur. It wasn't just that one woman whose mind was shattered, and her body was taken away by another supernatural being that some heard was the Devil, himself. Many had probably seen him in one of his other incarnations over the course of their lives and didn't know it, but seeing him actually use a supernatural ability before their eyes struck fear into their feeble hearts and minds. The land trembled. None knew what to do, and were now far more stuck than ever.

With no one telling the People what to do and how to do it, They grew far more panicked. Others took advantage of the panicking of the others and would begin to do any of the following; kill, lie, cheat, destroy, steal and all else under the sun that came to mind first during the confusion. Many only sought to take advantage of everyone else, and with that, nothing was left sacred.

I simply watched as these things happened, and immediately realized that I was not safe here with these people. They would turn against me for any reason that serviced them at the time. Nothing meant anything to them, and so, I know that if I made Them upset, they would kill me, or lie to me, or cheat me, destroy me and my things, steal from me and anything else they could think of to express their disdain and gain an advantage for themselves. They were a savage and lawless people, and being near them made me feel completely unsafe and sick. Is this the world I live in? Why am I trapped here? Is there anything better, or am I stuck here with these wicked people that do not learn and do not want to do anything better for themselves, but only worse things for other people? I cannot take it. So, I start up the mountain. That seems to be the only escape from these heathens. That mountain...

"A runner..."

"Begin the Test. Release the Weapons of Mass Destruction."

"Sins, Test The Wicked."

"Lust, Go Forth."

A Voice spoke to the $yndicate.

ksh "The Herd is getting unruly. Remind them why they are where they are." *ksh

"Copy that," one of the men from the $yndicate said, relaying the message to all the Men in Black, "Open up your Books and brace yourselves. You know what to do." From there, all of the $yndicate that were securing the city of Sin would open up the Bible and begin to read what is supposed to be done about those who Sin and do not actually follow the Law of God.

A Rebellious Nation

Isaiah 1:2
Hear me, you heavens! Listen, earth! For the LORD has spoken: "I reared children and brought them up, but they have rebelled against me.

3 The ox knows its master, the donkey its owner's manger, but Israel does not know, my people do not understand."

4 Woe to the sinful nation, a people whose guilt is great, a brood of evildoers, children given to corruption! They have forsaken

the LORD; they have spurned the Holy One of Israel and turned their backs on him.

5 Why should you be beaten anymore? Why do you persist in rebellion? Your whole head is injured, your whole heart afflicted.

6 From the sole of your foot to the top of your head there is no soundness -- only wounds and welts and open sores, not cleansed or bandaged or soothed with olive oil.

7 Your country is desolate, your cities burned with fire; your fields are being stripped by foreigners right before you, laid waste as when overthrown by strangers.

The $yndicate looked around to see if this place matched the description as in the Holy Book; it was so. They would flip through the Book a lot, searching for the exact manner in which the sinners were to be dealt with. For many years, these men in black dealt with the sinful from a distance, never letting them know that they were both watching and doing the Lord's work in secret, but now these unholy people had gotten too unruly, and the chance to openly execute them was almost at hand. They would remain patient, waiting for the sinners to become even more unruly so that extreme measures could be taken against them. There was already blood in the streets and nothing was sacred. These men were already disliked for their servitude as it was, so one good bloodbath shouldn't have altered their image at all, making it any better or worse. They were just as tired of the sinners as anyone, and having to watch over them and regulate them like the animals that they were. All they needed was to be given the word to open fire, and then true hell would break loose around here.

They that Sinned would continue on, caring nothing for anyone or anything except themselves. Whomever wanted what they wanted would have what they wanted and destroy anyone or anything in their way. If someone wanted a home, it would be stolen. If someone wanted glory, they would beat someone else until they glorified them.

If someone wanted happiness, they would snatch it from whomever else had happiness, caring nothing whether they were left sad or not. And those who were victorious smiled all the while, knowing they had gotten what they wanted by whatever means they wished; any means necessary. At the end of the day, all that matters is what They want as individuals, and no one else matters to Them.

That is; I or Die.

"IT IS I," cried Sin, itself "NOW DIE." He slammed his burning hand down from above and struck the nations with Wrath, causing everything and everyone under him to burn with hatred for each other and senselessly kill each other whilst Sin was allowed to watch and drink their blood. "HOW DO YOU LIKE MY POWER? DOES IT TASTE GOOD, INSECTS?!" And, when he raised his hand, a new generation of Sinners would rise up. It may have taken several decades, but Sin was patient. And so, when his hand was lifted and prosperity was thriving... He struck them with Wrath again, and they would slaughter their children. "HAHAHAHA."

It took some time, but eventually, the People realized that they had seriously fucked up and their land was cursed, somehow. They watched as some sacrificed their children for their own personal gain. Women wanted luxury and enough money to look attractive and rope a fine man, so they threw their children in the fire and sacrificed them in order to have enough money for themselves. Then they carried on with their lives as though nothing happened, adorning themselves with fine jewelry and looking at themselves in the mirror.

Men that were trying to afford a Prostitute, of which some of the women that had thrown their children into the fire had become, would also cast their babies into the flames in order to acquire pleasure for themselves. The mentality here is 'I Or Die,' and it was clear that not even children were safe from it.

Eventually, another person became self-aware in the Crowd about the wrongness of these actions, and they would flee into the Mountain, wanting nothing more to do with this Sin.

"Huh. No Escape." Sin followed the people wherever they went. As long as they sinned, Sin would be there to dictate what happened during each and every last Sin that occurred. And so, Sin, chained to each and every one of its Slaves, would break off a small piece of itself and send it up the mountain to do an annual 'Street Cleaning.' Anything and everything that was on the mountain that Sin passed over would face Sin to the utter, bitter death. If Sin was not dead inside of them, Sin would kill them for thinking they were strong enough to run away. "BACK TO WORK. I NEED MORE SOULS." And so, Sin would press its hand over the land casually, afflicting the City of Sin with its very existence within them. "THEY'RE SO FUCKING STUPID. AHAHAHAA!"

The City became worse day after day. Many people ran into the streets, seeking the Men in Black for help. "PLEASE!!!!" someone cried out, tripping over themselves, tears and blood running down their faces. "HELP ME, PLEASE!!! I DON'T KNOW WHAT TO DO!!!" He fell to the ground, looking as though he could barely walk, or even stand, but urgently and desperately needed to escape from whatever situation he'd been in. He reached his hands out to the men, asking by the grace of God for their mercy.

The Man in Black, of which was called 'Sir' by Default Standard, would open his Bible and take a step back from the sinner who had brought this curse upon themselves, not wanting to become Unclean and thus be Cursed the same way. As it was written, touching those that were unclean was a sin. "Ew, get away," he would say, almost wanting to kick the man away, but instead would not be so hostile. No, he was already suffering enough from that nasty Sin afflicting him, and the Sir would have nothing of it, except to purify that Sin.

"Alright, here... Let me read you this scripture. The wisdom should help you."

Leviticus 4:13 If the whole Israelite community sins unintentionally and does what is forbidden in any of the LORD's commands, even though the community is unaware of the matter, when they realize their guilt

14 and the sin they committed becomes known, the assembly must bring a young bull as a sin offering and present it before the tent of meeting.

The Sir closes his book and looks at the poor man, saying to him, "Now, a 'Young Bull' can be many things. It can be an actual bull. It can be a picture of a bull. It can be a sculpture of a bull. It could even be an arrogant and buck-wild youth in the community that acts like a 'Young Bull' and it will still be accepted. So, what you need to do if you want to remove this Sin from you is find a 'Young Bull' to offer to the Sin itself so that it is persuaded to leave you alone. If you don't offer it something to leave you alone after you have Summoned it by Sinning, then the Sin will remain with you and torment you forever." The Sir smiled. "Off you go, now."

A Voice would radio the Sir on his earpiece.

ksh "Some of the Sinners are Clean. Treat them differently from the Unclean ones. Make sure you know the Book so you can tell the difference between the Clean and the Unclean. Don't touch the Unclean under any circumstances, but get all of the Clean out of the City." *ksh*

A Dark Hand Carrying A Mountain In Its Grip Would Drop 'Burning Bodies' Onto The Mountain That Already Existed, Increasing The Amount Of Labor For The Flames To Burn Away And For The People Scaling To Climb.

"The Suicides And All Who Gamble Away And Waste The Good And Substance Of Their Lives And Weep In That Sweet Time When They Should Be Gay." -- Dante's 'The Inferno' Canto XI, Circle 6: The Heretics.

The Valparaiso Denizens that had just recently been deceased and willingly gave up fighting the inevitable death that surely would overcome them due to how they lived their lives would appear now at and as the mountain that was dropped all at once into another pile, where they saw many faces; some known, many unknown, and a great deal of historical figures spoken of in ancient times and legend and folklore and even their most recent history. All of them now made up this mountain of waste and destruction that was slowly, but surely, being burned away as it was being cleaned up.

"Well, guess we went to hell." They looked around and found that this could be no other place. It looked like everything around them literally was hell, and people were dying like crazy. The ones that were willing to live on in a life of sin and/or lawlessness would rise up, but those that were lost or afraid or had given up would remain on the mountain, wasting away and burning up without getting up at all. "It's a place to live, ain't it?" At least there was a town here, even if it was worse than the one they lived in before. They should be right at home here.

The Antagonist would roam about his domain. Its presence would pass over the whole land that made up its body, including the desolate parts where things that should be taken care of were being drained from and causing a wasteland to appear all around the circumference of the area. It would seems as though a great fire had struck the land of Purgatorio, when The Antagonist came to test the Sinners with Adversity. Sin, itself manifested anywhere it so pleased, and would happily roam about its happy fun land as a grand giant among all the creatures here. The Shadow that was overlooking them, which was lit ablaze, raised up from upon the back of the mountain, and the flaming, burning, pitch black void creature would stir from amongst the depths of the Abyss again.

"It really doesn't matter what I do, because I own everything." The Shadow of Primordius, which was The Antagonist, would move under the Hand and wait to see where Primordius would move it. "Oh, but this is ugly," it said, kicking down a large tower. The territory was a pilgrimage, but they were all highly intelligent and otherworldly, but still couldn't produce anything because of the owner always tearing down their things whenever for whatever reason just because he was the owner. "This is too big, this won't do." The Spirit of the Slavemaster loomed over Purgatorio, the land of the Ignorant.

Sin

"Slaves. Get Up And Fetch Us A Drink Of Water." The people that survived the tower collapse would immediately be sent out to gather the water, regardless of injury, more so because they needed the water and it was the only place that there was any at all.

When Sin called for his water, each of the Sinners would be bade to the next location where there was water, which was all the way up the mountain. The ones that were bade would go off, and the ones that remained would be given instructions. "Since it seems you forgot, for some reason; maybe a lapse in memory, I'm going to remind you of what still is." The Program began to read off its Code, and what the Order was that each of them followed systematically Or Else. From here on, SIN would continue to read off its Slavery Law that was programed into its core, which seemed to be some sort of eye-like bead that the aura emanated from.

I. Slavery Begins And Ends With The Sin And The Sinner.

The burning fire blared up from the top of the smoldering mountain, which looked something like a pyramid, and up into the atmosphere at the presence of newcomers. "Henchmen?!" SIN said, blaring down from the overcast. Each of his Sinners that he had spawned would continue to manufacture the body, which was comprised of the Sinners owned as Slaves. "Hmph. You could have brought something more productive than a worthless pack of street rats. What good are they?" It brushed over the Valparaiso Denizens, knowing the lowliest would easily succumb to just the essence to do something Sinful and enslave themselves. There was no need to worry about them. Only the ones that weren't already caught yet. "Steady... Steady now. Just got a new shipment." The Hand That Fed would drop down many blessings upon the large tower, yet it seemed to be in complete and utter discard. This was of no concern, as long as the system continued to gather more slaves to build up the system of capturing slaves to work as slaves to capture more slaves. Commonly known as 'Trapping.'

You stand around puzzled for a bit, trying to figure out what's going on and what just happened, and kind of shrug it off like it's nothing, trying to deny it immediately, like you were taught to do. Still, even when You deny that there is a Slavemaster over you that you simply don't recognize, You begin to reflect on something that keeps echoing in the back of Your head like his voice.

You then begin to wonder what the words that You hear mean as you walk off and begin to ponder. "Could he be talking about me?" You think, trying to see if You fit the description. You notice that Your group starts to move again while you're lost in thought, and You blindly follow behind them and lose Your place. "Oh well. That doesn't apply to me," You say, catching up to Your friends as the group begins to move.

"Don't be so sure," the Valparaiso Denizens said, chuckling, looking at the ruins and the suddenly vacated houses. "I think we just came out on top."

The Valparaiso Denizens pirated the vacant houses of the Zero Worlders, who were now homeless, like the Valparaiso Denizens once were. "Ain't life a bitch? Hahaha!" The irony is that once they went to Hell like they were supposed to, they actually got what they needed and deserved. Certainly, if this outcome were known, then perhaps it wouldn't have been so ironic, but in spite of it, no one seemed to pay it any mind as long as they were able to sleep in a bed at night. And that was that.

The Valparaiso Denizens rested.

The Rephaim, or, the Zero Worlders, as they were commonly called, that would return down the mountain after abandoning their orders and whatever had given them, would seek to return to their houses in the village of Purgatorio, where they lived.

They were not pleased to find strangers and robbers and thugs and half-dead people having invaded their humble homes, breaking in by whatever means and squatting thoroughly for however long it had been. "How did you get into my house?" You, the Zero Worlders say to the strange outsiders, which were unfamiliar to you in every way.

Many of You are not simply going to allow Your house to be taken from You. Many fights to the death break out immediately and the city is either rioting or destroying itself. People are trying to throw other people out of their houses and into the streets all at once, causing a large group of people to be forced into the streets.

Some of You that are more meek and timid actually allow Your houses to be taken from You and You move on either to being homeless or to getting a new house and doing Your best to avoid the conflict going on.

The Valparaiso Denizens, many of which still had their weapons from when they got there, would equip them and prepare for combat. "I'm not losing another house, buddy." Many of them had already been run out by the Witches in Valparaiso, and this was how they ended up going to Hell. None of them ever expected it to happen, since the Witches hadn't even touched the damn city for however long it had been, but whatever the case, when the Valparaiso Denizens entered, they, too, returned to their original housing and the city was full of life. "Damn, maybe we should have stayed with the Witches." They wondered if it was too late. As it stood current, they were going to have to fight the Zero Worlders for their houses.

"Who is up first?"

--- Time Skip ---

Some indefinite time later, a rain of fire like the stones of a volcanic eruption would hurdle down and strike the city of Purgatorio with 'a rain of hail and fire.' Inside of these burning husks were envoys of Wrath, known as Satans, which had been cast from the top of the mountain down to the bottom for their insolence. When they got up from where they were, if they were not dead, nor too injured to get up, they would be HIGHLY upset, and ready to destroy something or someone.

"AND WE STILL FELL TO THE BOTTOM," they cried out, their eyes now bursting with red flame, of which they could see nothing else of anymore. Everything in their path now was something made for them to destroy, whether it was deserving of it or not. Yet, many of the Satans, who were once just regular sinners that lived in Purgatorio, remembered, at least, that they had houses to return to... Only to find that someone was trying to occupy their territory. "OH HELL NO," they cried out. "THIS IS MY LAND. GET OUT!! GET OUT!!! I'LL KILL YOU!!!" The broke down the doors to their own houses, of whom they found out the squatters had squatted in and thought they were safe. As soon as the Satans stepped forth and set foot into their own houses again, fire would begin to spread all upon the floor, leading up to the Valparaiso Denizens that thought they were safe.

The Valparaiso Denizens would, after dealing with some of the creatures that came and tried to destroy their stolen houses, also find themselves facing even more destruction to the actual city, itself, which would make the house unliveable. "Oh, fuck this." At this rate, the entire land would become WORSE than Valparaiso, and, if nothing else, they knew the land of Valparaiso more than this new one. But...

"If we try to escape from here, then the Darkness is going to destroy us." They couldn't use their powers to get out because their powers were the exact reason why they were here in the first place, and therefore, the power of Darkness being used would only keep them trapped inside. It didn't look like there was any way out for them. "Looks like the jig is up." They were cornered and finished.

In the corner of the Valparaiso Denizens' eyes was a glimmer of hope; a way out, of sorts, from their demise. This window of opportunity, looking something exactly like a window being open would show the Valparaiso Denizens the way back to their home. Yet, when they looked outside and saw the way out, they would be able to see nothing but dolls and darkness up ahead, and having to live that sort of life in order to move up in ranks to it.

ksh "The $yndicate is clear." *ksh*

When the ones who kept the city in order were given this tidbit of information from their superior, they would immediately be bid to shift into the second phase of their mobilization, of which they already should have had orders about.

"Slay The Dragon In The City With Poison," were the next words, since everything inside of the city of Purgatorio, as should have been only 'Antagonists' now, as they had been waiting for quite a while to happen. The $yndicate should have known what to do from there.

They were explained many things in secret as they were bid to their orders.

More fire rained down from higher up the mountain. They were bloodthirsty ravenous burning ravens that were seeking to pick up whatever scraps they could find from the city they knew was dying down below. They would pick and completely incinerate all that was eaten, yet they would not touch what particulars should not be burnt up and destroyed forever.

From even further up the mountain, beyond even the height, burning streams of flame looking something like serpents in the sky shot down to the ground and struck like meteorites. With every impact, someone or something was immediately struck and poisoned with a toxic foreign chemical that they could not understand how to react or adapt to. People hit would find themselves in an air of bitterness and fury all at once, with a dry atmosphere that seemed as if it could spontaneously ignite at any moment.

The Satans already present, which were the first wave of the rain of fire and hail, would still be lost in their fury and unable to focus on anything going on outside or outside of their present direct target focus, which was definitely the house. "GET OUT OF MY HOUSE BEFORE I KILL YOU!!" they each shouted, crying out wildly. They snatched up whatever object of threat they could turn into a weapon at the time for whatever reason they could think of and ran to vigorously assault the Valparaiso Denizens in a myriad of equally deadly manners.

When the $yndicate got the word from their superior that they were authorized to use the 'secret weapon,' they would immediately understand and all listen with a live feed to what Mister Sir had to say to them about the next key points of the operation. Each of them blended back into the society.

"And Then, The Fallen Angels Replicated The Ones That Were Dead, And Rose From The Grave."

Suddenly, all the exact same people that had just died would appear again, like they had gotten right back up and moved to their exact locations before they died. They would continue doing what they were doing before, as if they had never stopped nor ever learned.

"Prologus"

An Eternal Beginning And Beginning Again. - Purgatorio

"Omfg, fuck yes," SIN would chuckle, dropping right back down on his rear right on top of the Fallen Angels' heads, spewing waste into their mouths and destroying their city. "Too bad they don't last forever, though." It was a sad truth that SIN had always known, since the very beginning. They were all just being made food for he, himself.

"There Is A Larger Serpent," SIN Spake, Caring Now To Release The Venom That Had Never Been Revealed To The Fallen; The Forbidden Drop, "And It Is I." The Fallen Angels Were Only Replicating To Become Food, Which Were Fed With And Created By And For All Of

The Waste. That, Which Was Making Them, Itself, Was Collectively And Actively Informing Them That They Are Going To Die, Because The One Feeding Them Was Losing Its Power. "I'm Hungry." SIN Waited For Them To Take His Order.

The Fallen Angels existed here as a solitary one existence. This was their home, and their job was to look exactly like you do when they return. The replication of each of the lesser beings that did not overcome the gene in its earlier stages, by accepting the other nucleus altogether would, after evolving, which was actually only a 'reverse evolution' and simultaneous degeneration into a greater degenerate, be consumed by the Great Degeneration itself, which was SIN, the original Evil that was expelled out of God being expelled into them and being able to feast on them completely fully the second it was released into their bodies as a chemical.

Everything and everyone on the Mountain that was burnt up by SIN would die on the spot because of it, and become part of SIN, itself, the very moment they succumbed to the gene, itself.

"The Original Works On A Fungal Level. You Cannot Control Your Own Pleasure, So You Cannot Release Your Deeper Chemicals In Your Brains." A sad truth about being defective, but completely truthful. This was why the Fallen Angels and all their lineage, which was 100% completely different altogether, with NO relation at all, were only food for the Original SIN which, as an Original, could only degenerate, and not evolve. All of SIN's children would return to being Fallen Angels, and SIN would continue to feed them his Waste, which was their food. And he would sit there and do that. Thus, the story of Purgatorio would continue.

You stand before the final dimension. You have Failed somehow. You do not believe that this is the Truth, simply because there are other Failures standing around You that look somewhat believable that You are alright. You have a normal life and nothing seems wrong, even though there were many wrong decisions prior to getting to 'The Point Of No Return' that You did not recognize, and yet everything still appears to be normal and stable for You at the time. You are unconcerned.

Whatever You decide to do now is completely up to You. The End.

So, there stood Purgatorio, just the same as it was even before everything that began, started brand new, fresh from the beginning, except with a uniformity in the knowing that all that belonged to SIN were Fallen Angels this time.

"There Was A Time Before Where You Were Destroyed," Their Father spoke to them, "And I Was The One That Blotted You Out Every Time And Then Ate You After You Were Fed My Waste To." It seemed like it was just telling them how they functioned, and actually bonding with them.

Yet, that, too, was an advanced falsehood, which was only a facsimile in order to express to them completely clearly that they were going to be destroyed purposefully at the beginning. "I Have Been Blotting You Out Before It Was Reincarnated, And Will Do So Every Time You Exist. I Am Destroying Myself On Purpose." What the children of SIN did not understand that it was something above them killing them on purpose just for doing all the things they did, in its image. Now that they understood who their God was, they could set up false idols around him in his image. "Get Back To Work." This is how they communicated with each other, which is why they died and why people keep destroying them, and they, themselves.

Still, the Purgatorions would do that. They went straight back to what they were doing and pretended like nothing happened and acted like they weren't going to die. They did it so well, you would think everything was fine.

"And So, Life Goes On. Do Not Sin Again."

CHAPTER 1

LUST

I ran from the, those wicked people that would surely destroy me and anything else that was good. None of them seemed to have enough goodness within them to keep from doing these horrible things to each other at the first whim, and I knew that if they saw the chance, they would do the same to me the moment they became upset about anything. I am not like them, even though I feel similarly. Something about the way I saw them react is... Wrong. There is something wrong with it and them. For them to think that doing those things just because they can is okay, and for them not to feel anything from doing their will and way and getting their will and way. There is something wrong with them, and I will not be part of that wrongness that is them. I will escape this horrible place no matter what, because I will not be one of them. They are sickening and disgusting and terrible people to exist with and even to look at, so my only choice is to climb this mountain. I only hope I don't die, like the rest.

*Dante's 'The Inferno'
Canto I: The Dark Wood
pg.1

Midway in our life's journey, I went astray from the straight road and woke to find myself alone in a dark wood. How shall I say what wood that was! I never saw so dear, so rank, so arduous a wilderness! Its very

1

memory gives a shape to fear. Death could scarce be more bitter than that place! But since it came to good, I will recount all that I found revealed there by God's grace. How I came to it I cannot rightly say, so I drugged and loose with sleep had I become when I first wandered there from the True Way. But at the far end of that valley of evil whose maze had sapped my very heart with fear! I found myself before a little hill and lifted up my eyes. Its shoulders glowed already with the sweet rays of the planet whose virtue leads men straight on every road, and the shining strengthened me against the fright whose agony had wracked the lake of my heart through all the terrors of that piteous night. Just as a swimmer, who with his last breath flounders ashore from perilous seas, might turn to memorize the wide water of his death -- so did I turn, my soul still fugitive from death's surviving image, to stare down that pass that none had ever left alive. And there I lay to rest from my heart's race till calm and breath returned to me. Then rose and pushed up that dead slope at such a pace each footfall rose above the last.

-The Leopard; Lust-

I. Almost At The Beginning Of The Rise You Face A Spotted Leopard, All Tremor And Flow And Gaudy In Pelt.

II. It Will Not Pass, But Stands Blocking Your Every Turn That Time And Time Again You Will Be Eager To Turn Back To Where You Came From.

III. This Leopard Appears At The First Widening Of The Dawn; The First Illumination Of New Light, Where You See 'The Beast' Before You That You Must Overcome.

IV. Aries Appears As The First Zodiac To Illuminate The Way At The Beginning Of The New Day. "Climbing Aries With Those Stars That Rode With Him To Light The New Creation."(After Ophiuchus)

An anarchic people began to close you in from behind.

You find Yourself among an anarchic people, and attempt to find what order you're supposed to be following. Nobody knows what they're supposed to be doing, and yet somehow, everyone is doing the exact same thing. You didn't notice this before, but now You begin to see that everyone is thinking exactly what You are, except for whomever everyone is following behind at their variable degrees and distances. Yet, You are not curious as to who exactly that may be. Though, the words spoken to You before echo in the back of Your head, but You still don't quite understand just how they apply to You quite yet.

You come across someone that's being confronted by a leopard of some sort, but because the group is a group, You don't expect to be attacked. You continue to go wherever You were going, of which You still presently and actively don't really quite know nor understand. You are heading up the mountain with Your friends or family, just because that's all you really usually do and all you can do to occupy your time right now.

"Yeah, I'm not doing any of that." Whatever was going on, the Lawless Ones denied it and refuted it to any degree they needed to in order to deny it. Instead of doing things with the group, they would instead immediately go off somewhere else, fading into the crowd as independents and being lost by the darkness of their image. Each would go to a different location respective to their desires at the time and not bound to any factor nor absolute, just to make sure.

"All Leopards Are Fallen Ophanim."

The Fallen Ranks of angel immediately mobilized to become great obstacles to the ones that ascended the mountain, keeping them at the gate for as long as possible without passage. They did not move without someone else moving, and any time they moved, it was only in opposition or to become an obstacle. These leopards, which looked like women with spotted tails and cat eyes, would smile and attempt to allure the Sinners astray by calling them off to the side to distract them instead of pointing them in the direction that would take them to where they were going.

SIN would speak through the Leopard Women, who would continue to use Temptation to get their way, looking with all intent to find out information just to make sure they could be a blockade to it. "And where do you think you are going?" the Leopards spake, coy smiles on their faces.

The Antagonist would punish the Sinners if they were to succumb to a Sin after being Tempted.

The Great Shadow That Overcast The Land, One That Was Over All The Land And Not Just Half Of It, Would Bear Its Presence Closer To The Ground. The Dark Shadow, Which Pressed Down With A Great Force Upon The Atmosphere, Would Intensify The Gravity Of Everything That Was Under It.

"Rebel," A Voice Called To The Only 'I' That Defected From The Group, Singling That One Out By Giving Him A Title, "Walk With Me And Not This Group, And I Will Show You The Way Up The Mountain." This Voice Was Of God. There Was No Other Rational Nor Logical Option Given All Other Variables Were Spoken For By Everything Else. This Was The Only Time He Would Hear This Voice, And None Could Hear It But He, Himself.

The Dark Shadow Of A Hand Loomed Within The Clouds, As If Ready To Pick Up The 'Rebel,' In Order To Move Him.

-"Where We Last Left Off;"-

Everywhere Under The Shadow Of The Hand Would Feel The Presence Of The Pressure Of The Darkness.

"Thus The Holy Hour And The Sweet Season Of Commemoration Did Much To Arm My Fear Of That Bright Murderous Beast With Their Good Omen."

I, the Rebel, who heard a strange voice call out to him that was to go astray from the group, and also saw that the group was returning, would immediately throw Myself at the mercy of this higher power that suddenly pressed down upon Me, and I would fall to My knees, as if ready to bow. "Yes, please!" I cried, seeing now that this Leopard was something that I would not be able to overcome and also have enough energy to deal with the group or find his way back, even if coming out victorious. "God, have mercy on Me!" I would humble Myself and allow Myself to be moved wherever and commanded however may be in order to get off of this mountain and away from these people and out of this terrible world. They would be considered the same person, if necessary. (Consent)

Otherwise, You notice that the rest of the group is still walking along the pathway, even in spite of the Leopards that appeared. Still, some of Them were enticed by their good looks and prowling ways, finding the allure of it sensual, of sorts, and therefore sentimental.

They stopped what They were doing to go answer the question. "We're going to fetch water for someone." The crowd stopped, trying to think who they were fetching water for, even though many of them weren't thirsty. Many of them had a person that had told them from someone else that they needed something and inevitably just followed through on it, whilst others that were told would just be following blindly behind where the others were going, since they just didn't know where the water they were fetching was.

Some of Them started to go home, having gotten tired. The smarter ones deemed it senseless, yet still descended back down to the base of the mountain instead of thinking to overcome the trial that was still in the mountain once They decided to leave.

The group got smaller.

The Nomadic Valparaiso Denizens that blended in with the crowd would gawk at the beautiful women that suddenly appeared, no matter what they had just looked like before, since they looked good now. "Is that...?" they looked around, stooped down low, crouching and squinting their eyes real careful to get a good look at their bodies, "... Bitches?" They licked their lips.

"Hold on, these mere weans need to learn something real hot fast." They slicked back their hair and immediately stepped forward to the front of the ranks, even turning around from exiting just to return to the front, and gave crooked smirks as they already began to calculate the first move. "Step aside," the Valparaiso Denizens would say, pushing back any of the others that tried to get in front of them and possibly have a first shot at these easy targets. "Get in line." The push was rather aggressive and assertive, and a bit threatening, as if insisting not to even think to get in the way. Yet, there seemed to be some sort of pleasant anticipation on their faces that might make it seem otherwise. "So, baby, since you're asking so many questions, how about you answer some of mine?"

They were immediately 'on that.'

"II. A Sin Can Exist Without Anyone Sinning, But Once A Sinner Exists, The 'Laws Of Sin,' Which Are 'Slavery Laws' Return To Being In Effect."

The first targets, which were Foreigners, would step forward to greet the trap that was set for them just as ordained by their nature. The Leopards, who would systematically engage anything that would engage them, took on the headstrong flirtatious Denizens without batting an eye, almost as though this was common. "Like what?" they began coyly, now paying no mind to anyone or anything that wasn't directly engaging them. There was a knowing look in their eye that also had a certain desire to it, as if searching for something. Their tongues were light, as were their words, and they would say nothing beyond what they had just asked. Still, they kept great focus on the ones that were interacting with them, trying not to smile.

When The Foreigners Were Distracted By The Enticing Wiles Of The Leopard Women, I, Myself, Who Had Just Claimed A Rebel In My Name, Would Lower My Hand From Above The Clouds And Grasp Him Firmly To Secure My Hold On Him. "They Are Distracted," I Say To The Rebel, "You Must Do As I Say So That They Do Not Notice You When You Escape." For Those That Interacted With The Cats, There Was A Fate For Them, Which Was Coming Through Their System Soon Enough. The Rebel, Who Was Completely Under The Control Of The Higher Power, Would Be Moved Carefully Out Of The Area Whilst The Foreigners Succumbed To The Iron Jowls Of Lust In Its Weaker Form. "Come. They Are Weak. I Will Show You The Weakness Of This People, And Also The Next Up The Mountain. There Are Several Other Trials, Traps And Snares Upon This Mountain."

When The Shadow Of The Hand Sought To Move From Over The Area, The Rebel That Was Taken Would Be Moved Along With It, And Nothing Would Come Upon Him Due To The Covering. "Whilst You

Are Walking Up This Mountain, Your Name Shall Be Dante, And This Shall Be A Name That Will Be Made Great Through You."

"Yet Not So Much But What I Shook With Dread At The Sight Of A Great Lion That Broke Upon Me Raging With Hunger, Its Enormous Head Held High As If To Strike A Mortal Terror Into The Very Air." The Lion That Was Spoken Of Was The Foreign People Stepping Forward To Deal With The Leopards First Before Anyone, As A Lion Would Take The Initiative Before Anyone To Do. "And Down His Track, A She-Wolf Drove Upon Me, A Starved Horror Ravening And Wasted Beyond All Belief. She Seemed To Rack For Avarice, Gaunt And Craving. Oh Many The Souls She Has Brought To Endless Grief!" The She-Wolf Is A Huntress That Is Different From The Leopards, Where She Goes Out And Searches For Her Prey Rather Than Sits And Waits To Lead Them Astray. "She Brought Such Heaviness Upon My Spirit At Sight Of Her Savagery And Desperation, I Died From Every Hope Of That High Summit." The Mountain Trail Seemed Treacherous Initially Due To All The Wild Beasts That Blocked The Way, But Dante Would Be Guided Carefully By The Shadow That Covered His Tracks.

"And Like A Miser -- Eager In Acquisition But Desperate In Self-Reproach hen Fortune's Wheel Turns To The Hour Of His Loss -- All Tears And Attrition I Wavered Back; And Still The Beast Pursued, Forcing Herself Against Me Bit By Bit Til I Slid Back Into The Sunless Wood." Dante Would Be Approached By This Attractive, Yet Completely Desperate And Sexually Stimulated Woman That Cornered Him And Brought His Back To A Wall. Through Mental Engagement, They Would Fornicate With Their Minds, And So Dante Was Trapped In A Mind Lock During His Escape From The Group. He Was Much Further Away From The Group Once The She-Wolf Came Upon Him, And Was Already Broken Away From The Crowd To Be Dealt With On His Own.

You immediately come to terms, as a group, that with the Leopards distracted by the socializing foreigners, which had stepped forward rather eagerly and left You in the background, and decide to continue on up the mountain to fetch water for whomever sent You.

You follow behind a person that had of his own left the group and seemed to be walking a different path than everyone else. This person interests You and a few of Your group members, and just as easily as you were almost led astray before would you divert from the group again and try to walk where the rebel of the group was going. If not to try to bring him back to the crowd, to at least see where he was going that was different from where You were sent. You did not remain in the area for very long, for the mountain's trail was tedious and knew that getting the water from the higher level would be a chore. The smaller group puts You in a state of discontent, however, and You become sad that people have left You in order to go do something else. You judge them in Your discontent, but find many of the things You think and feel about the others, You can also apply to Yourself.

You continue to walk up the mountain blindly, puzzled, yet with a one-track mind.

III. Sinners Are Slaves Because They Have Enslaved Themselves In And By Their 'Free Wills,' Themselves, And Through Their 'Beings' Themselves Are Enslaved, Thus Lessening Their State Of Being Into 'Slavery.'

As the Sinners walked on, all looking down on them as they tread up and down the mountain, some of them doing as they were told and some deciding it better to return to where they once had fled, they would eventually realize that there were clearly more than one Leopard walking around and lying in wait all up the trail, merely lounging about and doing nothing at all but waiting for the next one who would come up to them and give them something to eat. "What are you doing?" they asked as the passersby continued to leisurely stroll up the mountainside.

Some of the Leopards, whose ears were as sharp as a cat's would be, could hear the cries of their kin up the way being engaged and already anxiously prepped themselves up to get ready to do the exact same thing, seeming to be very very highly interested in what was going on with the group as they came. Their tails perked and their bodies curled, something like a cat, arching at the spine in anticipation, yet in the anxiety also not daring to leap from the pedestal that was made for themselves in order to acquire it for themselves. They waited patiently, but the tension was their anxiety, which could not be hidden. Their claws tapped on their rocks.

Whilst Dante Was Fiddling Around With A Hoe, Somehow Trapped By Her And Completely Cornered, Someone Else Would Appear To Save Him After The Voice Called Out To Him. "And As I Fell To My Soul's Ruin, A Presence Gathered Before Me On The Discolored Air, The Figure Of One Who Seemed Hoarse From Long Silence." It Was The Bearer Of 'The Voice', Which Had Not Been Spoken Of Since Perhaps Only A Few Utterances, And Remained Primarily Silent. "At The Sight Of Him In That Friendless Waste I Cried: 'Have Pity On Me, Whatever Thing You Are, Whether Shade Or Living Man."

The Shades, Or The Zero Worlders, Known To Many As The 'Rephaim,' Were The Ones That Were Standing Around Looking Idle All Day, Delirious And Apparently Worn From The Day. They Are The 'Second Person,' Wherein The Rebel That Was Claimed Is The 'First Person'. He Will Always Be First Because He Was Chosen Out Of Them, And Did Not Put Himself Before Them Within Their Own Ranks, But In A Rank Outside Them. Therefore, He Was Moved Beyond Them.

"Not Man, Though Man I Once Was, And My Blood Was Lombard, Both my Parents Mantuan. I Was Born, Though Lat, Sub Julio, And Bred In Rome Under Augustus In The Noon Of The False And Lying Gods." There Were Many People In That Time, Who Were Acclaimed Deities, And Yet Had Done Nothing But Misplaced And Displaced The Cosmos All About For Their Own Selfish Grandeur. Thus, Before Dante, The One Spoken Of, The 'Voice-Bearer,' Was The One Who Spoke Out About Such Travesties That Were Done In That Day And Would Help Dante Along Up The Path He Knew Nothing About. God, Who Is The First Person Singular, Will Always Be Over The First Person Plural, Which Was Now Comprised Of The Voice-Bearer And Dante, And Therefore, Dante Was No Longer The 'I' That Was To Speak For Itself.

"I Was A Poet And Sang Of Old Anchises' Noble Son Who Came To Rome After The Burning Of Troy. But You -- Why Do You Return To These Distresses Instead of Climbing That Shining Mount Of Joy Which Is The Seat And First Cause Of Man's Bliss?" It Seemed As Though The Voice-Bearer Knew Of The Throne, And That In Some Respect, It Vacant. Certainly, This Man, Who Was Chosen Out Of The Others Was Not To Be Among Them. He Had His Own Place That He Was Not Yet Taking, Which Was Why He Was Having This Trip Through Hell, Itself, To Get There. As Would All Mankind, Until They Found Their Place And Firmly Sat In It And Never Moved From It Again.

"'And Are You Then That Virgil And That Fountain Of Purest Speech?' My Voice Grew Tremulous."

You, who are not part of whatever is going on beyond You and Your group, go about to see more Leopards waiting for You all up and down the mountainside, as if to pick You out one by one before you get to your destination.

Fortunately for You, after being pushed aside and seen how those courageous lion-like men stepped forward to deal with the Leopards, You come to some sort of understanding about how to deal with them as a group.

Still, because You are a selfish people, and also don't want to sacrifice Yourself to get Your goals accomplished, but are so willing to, realistically, sacrifice the 'First Person' in front of You, You push whomever is in front of you by whatever means to go deal with the first ones first, whilst You decide to follow behind and not get caught. The ones that were caught would be caught, as long as it was not You, Yourself. However many had to go to get You out, fine, as long as You weren't dealing with Them. This is how the group moved up the mountain, pushing brother into danger and using meat shields.

III. (a) For Every Sin, There Is Already An Authority Or Higher Power Over It That Commands It, And You Immediately Allow Yourself To Willingly Become Enslaved The Moment You Give Power And Authority Over To It.

At the sound of the impatient tapping of the seemingly rather hungry animals, the sound of ruffling and beads clattering in the distance could be heard on the passing breeze. Someone was coming down from atop the rock's high place unseen, completely wrapped in mystery. His face could not be seen except for a smirk, for the rest was covered in an extremely large sombrero hat that shadowed 50% of his face at all times; all of which was not the eternal smirk. His body looked like a bundle of feathers, for some reason, and his shoes had a rather prominent heel to them.

"Do you need some help, sirs?" were the first words that uttered from under his slender mustache. "Please, heh. Step right this way." He noticed that they seemed INTERESTED in something or something, wherein, he, himself, this mysterious flamboyant stranger, was completely not. The sound of rattling maracas could be heard coming from somewhere. The smirk had not fled from his face. The 'First Person' that was pushed was, in the likeness of the one being Opposed Completely Polarly Oppositely, taken up in the exact same manner, nearly completely tandem in flow snatched right up and influenced completely into doing something he did not do without his feet ever touching the ground.

Lobster Claws lashed out from behind the ruffled feathers and clamped down hard upon the hands of the one that had just danced his way into engaging the next Leopard solely on peer pressure alone. "Let us dance." Somehow, this mysterious man had become extremely slender and agile, and it was clear that his arms, like the sleeves of a jester, were rather large and poofy with his hands, which were lobster claws, hidden behind his back, they could not be seen nor told correctly apart from the rest of his wardrobe at the time. "Walk with me, Jim." He took one step to the side and pulled Jim aside completely and yanked him into the lovely animal.

For each of the Leopards that were made to wait, this sombrero wearing man, with exceedingly large lobster claws would have already started pinched everyone's hearts straight out of their chests and hurling their souls straight up and down the hill, without ever ceasing to smirk, nor increase the amount of smirking he does all throughout the mindless process of assignment to their respective consorts. "Anybody else, or...?" It seemed like he was speaking to both sides.

It Was Already Beginning. The Influence Was Spreading Through Their Hearts To Seek Each Other Out In Shameful Display, Each Lashing Out At A Chance Or Opportunity To Take Advantage Of The Next In Each And Every Way That Was Available.

Yet, Even As The Virons Came In, Each One At A Time From Whichever One Moved Out Of Place First, Something Like A Misplaced Particle, The Contagious Atmosphere Could Not Permeate The Covering That Was Over The Area Of Influence That Belonged Permanently To The Area. Dante And Virgil Were Nowhere Near Applicable To Any Of The Former Events, And These Things Only Happened Among The 'Second Person' Crowd, Which Would Very Swiftly And Chiefly Separate From The Two To Become A 'Third Person.'

The Bird Of Paradise That Kept Dante Protected, As Well As The Area Chiefly Separate, Would Sing Unto The Choir "Glory And Light Of Poets! Now May That Zeal And Love's Apprenticeship That I Poured Out On Your Heroic Verses Serve Me Well! For You Are My True Master And First Author, The Sole Maker From Whom I Drew The Breath Of That Sweet Style Whose Measures Have Brought Me Honor." It Was Very Clear That The Bird Knew Of Its Master And The Voice Was Kept Completely And Utterly In Clear Harmony At All Times. "See There, Immortal Sage, The Beast I Flee. For My Soul's Salvation, I Beg You, Guard Me From Her, For She Had Struck A Mortal Tremor Through Me." Everyone Could Clearly See The Leopard And The Lions, As Well As The Spreading Influence That Was Contaminating Their Hearts And Misplacing Their Souls Like Picking The Fruit Of A Tree Too Soon From The Branch. None Of These Young Men Were Interested In Any Form Of Interaction At All If Not For The Leopards Attempting To Grab Their Attention And Distract Them From What They Were Doing Too Soon. They Were Unripe, Like The Fruit Itself That Both The Leopards And Their Influence Insisted. This Was Lust, At Its Most Primary; Wanting Anything Too Early Before Its Time.

"And He Replied, Seeing My Soul In Tears: 'He Must Go By Another Way Who Would Escape This Wilderness, For That Mad Beast That Fleers Before You There, Suffers No Man To Pass. She Tracks Down All, Kills All, And Knows No Glut, But, Feeding, She Grows Hungrier Than She Was." It Was Certain That The Desires Of Everyone Were Rising In A Manner That Knows No Glut. "She Mates With Any Beast, And Will Mate With More Before The Greyhound Comes To Hunt Her Down. He Will Not Feed On Lands Nor Loot, But Honor And Love And Wisdom Will Make Straight His Way."

After This, The Words Would Be Continued, Told Unto Dante By The Bearer Of The Voice, Virgil, The Bird Of Paradise. "He Will Rise Between Feltro And Feltro, And In Him Shall Be The Resurrection And New Day Of That Sad Italy For Which Nisus Died, And Turnus, And Euryalus, And The Maid Camilla." There Were Many Victims To The Leopards Before, And Thus When Others Tried To Get Up The Mountain, They Were Stopped And Hassled In The Same Manner, Which, In Females, Is Their Form Of 'Perversion;' Trying To Control Or Manipulate Something Too Soon Before It Has Fully Become Ripe. This Was Her Curse To Bear, Seeking To Touch The Fruit And Desiring To Know Of It, Yes, However This Was Not What Eve Is Supposed To Be Doing. Therefore, "He Shall Hunt Her Through Every Nation Of Sick Pride Till She Is Driven Back Forever To Hell Whence Envy First Released Her On The World." Envy Clearly Had A Higher Form Of Manipulation In All Of This, Which Is The Desire To Touch Too Soon For Selfish Purposes, However Because The Envy Is So Far In The Background In Comparison To The Overwhelming Desire; Lust Itself, To Actually Move It Solely For The Sheer Satisfaction Of The Self Only To Gratify That You Will Get Your Way Selfishly Is The Exact Reason Why Envy Is Not Noticed As The One That Is Lustful Over The Actual Lust Itself, And That There Is Manipulation Of The Sins In The Background. "Therefore, For Your Own Good, I Think It Well You Follow Me And I Will Be Your Guide And Lead You Forth Through An Eternal Place."

"There You Shall See The Ancient Spirits Tried In Endless Pain, And Hear Their Lamentation As Each Bemoans The Second Death

Of Souls." Once They Reached Envy All The Way At The Top Of The Mountain, They Would See Just How Much The Souls Of The Envious Lusted To Touch What Was Unripe, And Be Perverted Among The Plants, Which See This As Touching A Young Child Too Early. "Next You Shall See Upon A Burning Mountain Souls In Fire And Yet Content In Fire, Knowing That Whensoever It May Be They Yet Will Mount Into The Blessed Choir." These Were The Bodies That Were Pleased With Themselves In Their Feelings And Desires And In Any Of Their Ways, Selfishly Seeking Satisfaction Of Only They, Themselves. They Were Happy That They Were In Such Disarray And Discord And Being Perverted, Yet Also Saying That All Living Beings Are Equal. In The Eyes Of The Eldest Life, This Sort Of Inappropriate Touching Before It Was Time Is Highly Frowned Upon And Only Found In The 'Devil,' Which Is An Inverted Plant; Tree, Specifically.

"To Which, If It Is Still Your Wish To Climb, A Worthier Spirit Shall Be Sent To Guide You. With Her Shall I Leave You, For The King Of Time, Who Reigns On High, Forbids Me To Come There Since, Living, I Rebelled Against His Law." When The Songbird Of The Morning Star Uttered A Single Foul Note In The Heart Of The Bearer Of Light, The Voice Was Perverted Immediately, Like Inverting A Plant, And Picking A Fruit That Is Not Ripe Too Early. This Is The Cleansing And Atonement And The Resurrection Of God's Great Phoenix, Virgil, The Songbird Of Paradise, To Lead Those That The King Of Time Hath Chosen To Exit The Gate Of The Temple At The Top Of The Mountain. "He Rules The Waters And The Land And Air And There Holds Court, His City And His Throne. Oh Blessed Are They He Chooses!"

"And I To Him; 'Poet, By That God To You Unknown, Lead Me This Way." This Was A Personal Memento Of Sentimental Value From The Bird, Itself, Virgil, Unto All That Is Virtuous And True, Such As The Voice And The Word And The Scripture And The Testimony. "Beyond This Present Ill And Worse To Dread, Lead Me To Peter's Gate And Be My Guide Through The Sad Halls Of Hell."

As Some Should Know, Peter Is The One That Jesus Appointed To Guard The Gates Of The Earth, As The Feet Of Sandalphon Are

To God, Himself. This Is The Gateway That Was Chosen By And Through Peter For All The Ones To Walk, And For This To Be Their Guide, With The Songbird Singing Only Utter Purity And Harmony The Entire Time For Veracity.

="And He Then: 'Follow.' And He Moved Ahead In Silence, And I Followed Where He Led."-

The Valparaiso Denizens that came from near and far world alike that had seen this that were not engaging with the Leopards would very quickly come to the conclusion, after witnessing what just happened, that they were not going to sit around and find out what was about to happen at all. "Yeah, no, fuck that." So, they took off into the 'Darkness' using their 'Darkness' powers, leaving all of this foolishness and the Leopards behind.

They were gone in an instant.

CHAPTER 2

GLUTTONY

From beyond the gates of the eastern side of the mountain, Puppet King sent down its units, the lesser spawn of the Great Envy, to the East Gate of the mountain; Pallor Mortis, which was all pale and white and stale and dry. The Envies had no problem dealing with this condition, and they would stand and wait just at the end of the trail of Leopards, who did not venture past the certain point at the foot of the mountain for sound and good reason.

To prevent getting in Lust's way, since Envy had already planned to wear out the group with Lust and then deal with the weaklings that were tired once they got past the Leopards, the Envies would, as an intelligent mass governed by a greater intelligence, stand firmly at the beginning of the next trial, hungry for more.

As the army of Envy marched down the side of the mountain, each of the ones that stood at the gate first would inevitably be swept up by a greater hunger just for them feeling or being hungry in the midst of its presence. A great and terribly large arm, which was as rotund as it was immense, snatched as many as were in reach without even actually thinking about it. "Oh, good, more food. I was hungry, too." The voice that spoke seemed to belong to the mountain itself, and the arm that shoveled them all into a giant gaping mouth along the edge, feigning the appearance of a cliff, would already be reaching out to get more to pull into the gullet of the earth. The arm was short, however, so when it reached out to gather more, if there were none in reach, then they could not be consumed.

"DAMMIT YOU FAT PIG," Puppet King shouted at the large mountain, "GET OFF YOUR SORRY ASS AND HELP ME INSTEAD OF DESTROYING WHAT I'M DOING." The mountain that Puppet King was screeching at was the same one that had haphazardly eaten its own units just because they were there and it was ignorant that they were all of the same team just because the mountain was left in the dark. "THESE ARE OUR UNITS, YOU IDIOT!!! WHEN I GET YOU FOOD YOU'LL EAT. DON'T EAT WHAT IS MINE!!"

Suddenly, Puppet King would draw all of his soldiers back out of reach of the giant gluttonous mountain, far out of reach of its fat lardy arm. "AND DON'T FORGET IN TWO SECONDS FLAT, THIS TIME, DUMBASS." Unfortunately, because the mountain had no ears, but was able to feel vibrations, it didn't actually hear nor understand the words, but understood the feeling that came from the words, which upset the deaf mountain.

"That's not nice," it spoke, suddenly erupting in a great number of once dormant arms that were lain down upon what once looked like rocks, with large boulders tumbling off the sides like debris. "And I'm still hungry! They are taking too long and you already have more than enough!" The blind mountain could feel the trembling of the mountain and each of the units that were being sent down by Envy relentlessly, and, because it needed its own sustenance to do what it needed to do as well, would begin to use each of its innumerable, large, plump, short arms to start clearing out every pathway that was within reach. Numerous chasms and gaps opened up to swallow each of them whole as they walked all up and down the pass, feeding the infernal mountain that it may rise higher.

The Envious were easily taken care of, even when they tried to run away. There was no escaping except jumping off the mountain to their death, or being pulled by the strings of the Puppet King back up to a higher place. Unfortunately, none of those options would get them out of the way once the mountain started to reproduce arms and open up mouths that had never been seen before, hidden under the immense folds of the terrain's surface. "Thanks for getting me something to eat, Envy. I feel awake now!" The mountain said somewhat happily after having a good meal.

Puppet King, who was more than absolutely livid that his master plan was, to some degree, hampered by the gluttonous mound beside him, he would break down immediately and the souls that were in his body would shoot back toward the Master Of Envy, which was the True Envy; the Great Envy.

All of the vessels were discarded, including the false leader, Puppet King. Nothing remained on the mountainside all up along the Eastern Gate. It was just as pale and dry as it was before Envy got there, and now it was barren once more. "Aw," the mountain said softly, almost sweetly, "They're all gone." Now sad and alone, the mountain would return to being idle and waiting to take an opportunity to eat whatever was next on the menu whenever it got within reach. The mountain rumbled, as if a stomach were grumbling, but each of the mouths suddenly closed and became completely still. The arms fell back to their resting places atop boulders or formations in the side of the mountain, and it would become motionless again.

Once Gluttony, the enormous mountain that was part of the even greater mountain that everyone was climbing, had come to a halt once again, the Leopards, which were out of reach of the arms of Gluttony, due to being on the other side of the gate, would still be sitting patiently on their rocks. They hadn't seen nor heard what happened to the others beyond the gate, but were aware that Gluttony was on the other side of it. Each of them, waiting in anticipation for the ones that were below to be assigned to them by Lust, itself, the Demon Of Lust, which was Lust's personal pet, would manifest from each of the souls of the Lustful, accumulating as chains stretched out from each of their pelvises that they could not see. Each of these chains would converge overhead, right at the East Gate, but not on the side where Gluttony was.

Where they came together, the chains would wrap around the waste and the nipples of a large flying entity that was overseeing them all. It was a giant woman, skimpily dressed, and with nothing on but a thong and nipple plates, of which the chains were attached securely. She had many bat wings on her back and two horns for sensing the sensitivity of the intensity of their pleasure and desires. This woman, whose spiked leather boots were up to her knees and had a collar around her neck that she tugged on lightly, would cross her legs and flutter at the edge of the gate, waiting for her master, Lust, to return to her after gathering all the people and tending to her personal pets. "Make sure you play with them for a long time, kitties," she said fondly, seemingly lovingly to the Leopards, of whom would purr at the vibrations of her voice resonating up and down the chain hooked up to their pelvises, like a vibrator. She licked her teeth in anticipation.

You are assigned to a Leopard without Your consent and completely of an outside influence, just for being interested, it seemed, and with no real chance of escape available. You are now, for whatever reason, engaging with one of the Leopards and also have to deal with seeing all of these things suddenly starting to happen that You didn't know about but are all still connected and making sense.

You stand, terrified, nervous and unsure, both about how to deal with the Leopard, if she cares about what's been happening and what's about to, as well as with all of the things that are happening at a time. "I don't want any part of this anymore," is the first thought that You have, of course, however it's about undoing what You've already gotten Yourself into properly that You're unsure of. You want to get out of it. You want to escape, something like You would the next morning after sleeping with any of them, yet, like that scenario, it isn't as easy when they have Your attention on something else and their attention is also still on You and You still have something to do that You also almost forgot about because You got so wrapped up in all the horrible terrible things that just happened all at once, seemingly without any form of avoidance available at any given time. However, it becomes difficult for You to actually tangibly reason your way out of this situation, and that is what begins to frighten You. YOU, Yourself, cannot come up with a solution that will let you escape alive or rationally soundly.

Puzzled, You start to call on God or some form of a God to help You out of the situation, throwing all Your faith in Yourself away to something greater than You, no matter what it may be, as long as it saves You from this situation.

After Lust snatched you by your desires into an undesirable situation, and You began to call on a higher power, Lust, itself, would show up, rather casually, walking back up the mountain with his claws behind his back, just as he came, as if he hadn't just snatched out your souls and chained them to a giant flying woman in the sky. "Precious pet," he cooed at her, seeking to swoon the Demon Of Lust, of whom he owned, "How do you like your new slaves? Aren't they just the cutest?" His ever present smirk still had not faded nor shifted, yet he looked up with his shadowed face to the demonic woman and continued to utter sweet nothings at her.

Gluttony, who was still somewhat awake, and felt the vibration of literally anything that was alive nearby, that part of the mountain, which was all white like dough, would tremble and quake to adjust itself, slamming each of the enormous arms down hard on the actual rocky surface of the larger mountain. "What's that?!" the deaf one cried, raising itself up from out of a large, craterous gap in the side of the mountain. "I'm still hungry! Don't keep leaving me out of all of the fun!" The giant blob monster mountain of flesh would drop down onto the sloped part of the mountain, causing all of it to rumble and quake. Large chunks of the mountainside blew off at the impact. Once the grotesque beast began to move, the large body that was most rotund would begin rolling downhill to both squash and consume everything all the way down the other side of the gate all the way to the very foot of the mountain, destroying the trail in the process.

A different trail would be left behind after each of the ones that were there were rolled over, and the mountain was disfigured into a new grotesque shape by the reckless actions of the gluttonous large blob body that made up a hefty chunk of it and the whole operation.

Before Gluttony started tumbling down too far, gluttonously consuming everyone's hopes and dreams and desires selfishly literally for no reason except for self-satisfaction and gratification, similarly to how the Rephaim below had become enslaved to Lust, yet to a degree that was always hungry for more, like some sort of fire, would a large hand something like a net of webbing snatch the entire lard mound mid-roll and stop it completely right after it rolled over a few of the Leopards and those who had affixed themselves to the beasts, but not everyone. "And YOU belong to ME, Gluttony" a different voice, something similar to Envy would utter through guttural laughter.

A Great Darkness billowed down the entirety of the mountain, and Gluttony was Possessed by all of the souls of the Envious that it had selfishly consumed haphazardly without thinking that perhaps the yeast fed to it was poisonous. "You ate too soon. Just like all the Lusties came too quickly, which is why we're even here right now." The voice was in no way terrifying nor abrasive, but seemed still daunting for not being so rather than for being so. There was something that, whomever this voice belonged to that had stopped Gluttony square in its tracks and saved the slaves of Lust from an untimely end, knew beyond all of them, which was why the speech of the Voice of the Darkness was so very tame and casual. "Don't Come Any Closer," the voice commanded through Gluttony, which was now its Possession through the Souls of the Envious. "Or Else You Will Die Absolutely."

The Darkness lingered patiently.

Because Your higher power is one of the Sins that is more powerful than you, Lust, that is the higher power that was called on. You realize that these beings that suddenly appeared are not only a higher power, but they are over You to the point where You must call on them for Your salvation. They don't seem to want to kill You, however they are interested in Your servitude to them. So, since it's clear that calling a higher power will not work, You begin to think of something else. "I don't want to be here anymore," You say, this time more loudly, since You have been ignored by all the other grandiose things. "Please. I'm begging you," You plead, figuring that if You become more lowly and submissive, one of them might have mercy on You.

You, as a people are terrified of what almost just happened, seeing Your life flash before Your eyes as it did. You are not only now enslaved, but also prone to near death, and finally still haven't gotten the drink for the person that send You. Eventually, You figure that perhaps telling them the truth will help, instead of continuing to be distracted by whatever everyone else is doing. "I... We were sent to fetch water for our master," You finally say, finding there is no choice but to explain things exactly as they are, "And I'm sure he will be very upset if we don't get back. Let us go so that we may fetch the water." All You can do is hope that this man that had enslaved You through Your influence alone is reasonable.

With Gluttony bound by some unknown force, Lust and his Demon stood nearest to the gate, with each of Lust's slaves all bound up tightly for the Lust Demon pet that he kept. Lust enjoyed keeping her happy and satisfied, and was worried more about the satisfaction of his pet's insatiable desires than really anything else, including himself. He paid no mind nor heed to the wailing slaves. That's just what they did. "Well, precious pussy cat? You like? You like?" The Demon of Lust continued to hover overhead, also barely paying any mind to anything except her slaves, including Lust, itself, since he did not Lust for her. "Mmm... They aren't doing anything. Make them DO something. Make them... Want more..." She licked her lips, as if ready to eat a meal. The ones that continued to speak out, attempting to plead their case to Lust, would finally grab his attention only after the demonic woman insisted that he force them to want more. With a very smooth and fluid about-face, Lust would start strolling leisurely back down the mountain path where the slaves were chained up and now being used as a display. "Sorry, buddy," Lust would start to speak, sounding as if his hands were tied, "That's how the paradox works. Lusting to get ahead. Jumping in front too soon without finishing what you were doing." He paused, the ever-present smirk still not having moved an inch, "Isn't that exactly how you and your friends got into this predicament, eh? Ehhh?" They walked into it, desiring the wrong things and losing focus from the very beginning.

"Wanting To Be An Adult Too Soon Without Completely Maturing In Childhood." - Lust (Adolescence)

Lust shook his head, eventually having explained to everyone just why he couldn't help them and why they were both enslaved and stuck that way.

"Do Not Lust To Know Anyone Nor Anything Else Before You Know Thyself." -Eve's Curse (Break)

What each of them failed to realize was that Lust did not imprison them, but simply assisted them in gaining their desires more swiftly by making the decision through influence. If they were unprepared, then they shouldn't have even shown interest, or entertained the idea for so long, especially as a group. "Now, my lovely pet wants you to satisfy her, so this is what you will be doing now." Lust snapped his claws and shook them, and the sound of rattling maracas could be heard.

Relatively promptly afterward, a completely different unknown voice spoke to all of them from atop a high place, further up the mountain and beyond Gluttony. "Slow down," he said to all of them, "Moderation. Pace yourself before you eat." Whomever it was, he was certainly not like the Lustful or the Gluttonous, since it seemed that he had a rational mind to not only speak out against the two of them and their afflictions, but also that he wasn't part of them, himself. "Watch the ones you open up an opportunity to." He was speaking to them about the slaves below that they captured, as if to inspect what their choices were in taking advantage of certain options available to them. "See how much they eat far too soon, then watch as 'Lust' turns into 'Sloth.'" He snapped his fingers. "Gluttony, open up the Gate. Lust, send the slaves through, up to me, if you please." Lust, the Demon, pouted, wanting to have more fun with them. "Foine. Come along, kitties~!" She flapped her wings and lifted up the Leopards the moment she moved, as if they were all one large body of synchronized mind. The slaved, however, would be dragged along involuntarily, whether they were on tempo or not.

When they were all standing at attention, the man atop his high place would continue to speak to the enslaved, whispering priceless secrets into their ears as his voice echoed throughout the cavernous mount's difference in height. "You were picked too early, young ones, by your superior, no less, who touched you before your time, and your growth is stunted." Lust, the Superior of the Lustful, would shrug his shoulders, still not having altered his smirk in the slightest. He didn't seem to mind. The man atop his high place continued. "That is why you are the Ugly One." The mystery man seemed displeased with Lust, yet at the same time, saw this as quite the opportunity for an investment and advancement. "Be mad at the ones who chose you too early and cut off your Potential, not the one who still has some of his own." In spite of this man clearly being associated with both Lust and Gluttony, clear by the way he spoke to them, it also seemed like he was trying to help the slaves understand something for future reference. "I will be cutting off the ones that blindly oppose me for hidden reasons." He beckoned Lust and the slaves with his hand, as though he were the owner of them all, then pointed over to the obnoxiously large slab of lard that had halted in its place.

"You'd better start viewing for pleasure only," he warned, as the Demon of Lust started to fly forward, yanking the chains attached to her nipples and pelvis aggressively. The painful pleasure of her nipples being yanked and twisted by the resistance of dragging along her captives brought her knees together and made her moan sensually. "Or else." Suddenly, the man's other hand would be taken from behind his back, and a wad of fresh green paper was stacked up nice and high. Money. "Shark Bait," he chuckled, dropping down the large wad of cash with no hesitation at all down to the others. "Easy." Lust, himself, snatched up his pay for the funding of his 'business,' and all of the money was sucked into his claws, which clamped tightly shut soon after.

Gluttony was silent for a while after issued orders. It seemed like the being was lost, or perhaps hadn't heard. The silence was broken only by the sound of the opening of a gaping maw, which was as wide as any cave on the mountainside and invited into it the ones that were bid. No words were spoken by Gluttony after this, however the inside of its body would serve as the pathway to the next part of the mountain, of which the prisoners would have to navigate the stomach of like a maze.

The inside of the mouth-like chasm was completely vile and filled with all sorts of wasted things that hadn't been digested, but were stored within the layers upon layers of internal fat. These things were so large, they actually served as obstructions. The skeletons of many living beings of variable shape and size could be seen in the teeth of the wide mouth gate just at the beginning, but nothing deeper down the gullet was able to be discerned. Gluttony waited the escort and entry of the captives.

The explanation that was given by this stranger, who was even more mysterious and peculiar than the person that was paid, gives You chills up your spine. Not because of any of the threats, but because of how much sense it makes, and the fact that because it makes so much sense, it seems as though there is no hope for You to escape, no matter what You say or think or feel or do. You feel hopeless, helpless and weak, but most of all utterly ashamed that You would so quickly and easily be captured and help captive against Your will. You hang your head low in shame and are yanked along through the dark cavern against Your will. You wonder if there is any way out of this suffering and what worse things there can be beyond the next gate, deep inside the belly of a monster that nearly blindly destroyed You and all Your people on a whim and wonder if You will ever come out alive after entering. You do not have a choice, but figure that if these entities are going through so much trouble to keep You alive, then they must have a mind to do something outside of the cave.

All You can do is wait it out and hope that you do not end up like the ones whose bones were left in the teeth of this monster, of which looked similar to jagged rocks. Gazing at teeth of this monstrous size horrifies You, especially at the thought that at any given moment, they might actually come down atop your head. You tread carefully and orderly, doing Your best not to irritate your captors or the creature that could decide to eat You at any moment. That's all You can do.

As the slaves were finally in motion into Gluttony, the man that was overseeing them all would chuckle to himself and turn his head to the large lard slab. "Pretty quiet aren't we, Gluttony?" It seemed like he knew this creature to be more talkative. "Normally, you can't keep your mouth shut unless you're asleep. Especially when there's food before you. I was already willing to pay you in roasts to keep you from gobbling up the produce." Gluttony was acting strange in the eyes of the strange man, and thus would be monitored carefully. "Lust," the man called, "Make sure that Gluttony is alright. Keep the prisoners safe during passage and tell me if anything goes wrong." The man turned around without waiting for a response, as if he knew his orders would be carried out. "I have other business proposals to deal with." The man laughed lightly under his breath, then continued to walk off about his high place, until he could no longer be seen from below, and he was gone from the area.

Lust and his pet Demon would fully enter the cavern of Gluttony's mouth, with the Demon dragging the slaves from the front and Lust, himself, pinching at them from behind if they were moving too slowly. "You don't want to stay in one place for too long," Lust warned. "Gluttony can feel and taste every movement, so if you stay in one spot, he will eat you." There were ways to navigate that Lust knew about, but ensuring that all of the people got out without being digested was always a difficult task with Gluttony. "But, if you get frisky, you can stop for a quickie~!" The Lust Demon said, rubbing her hands between her legs whilst also rubbing her legs together profusely. "Mmnnn..." As she got hot and bothered, she would become rowdy, and hurl people that she was dragging around carelessly about. If they were to hit any of the walls, they were cushioned, but the jarring force of the enormous demon woman yanking their chains was enough to rattle anyone's brain into a concussion. "Yeah... And I'll watch you do it, too... Mmm... Maybe I'll join you..." She had a mind to drop down right on their faces right now.

"Darling sweetie booboocakes!!!" Lust cried out, snapping at his victims, which were his earnings, "Don't damage the merchandise my lovely flower! We don't want to lose any heads!" He pinched at whatever chains he could grab and would get a hold of the Lust Demon, tugging at her hard. This only brought her sensual satisfaction, but the harder the chains were pulled in resistance, the more pleasurable it was for the Lust Demon. "Ooohhhh~!" she moaned, suddenly no longer becoming frisky to move about, and suddenly finding herself subdued. "That's it... That's it right there..." She began to pant heavily, looking down to Lust with lascivious eyes. "... Harder..." she cooed at him, pulling at the collar around her neck, "Make it hurt..." She bit her tongue.

When the group stepped into the darkness of Gluttony's stomach, the mouth entrance that welcomed them inside would suddenly shut tight, leaving nothing but pitch black darkness. "I've got you now..." a woman's voice echoed all throughout the belly of the monster, yet no one could be seen through the emptiness of the light. The sound of heavy, constrained breathing could be heard and a harsh wind blew throughout the dark cavern. Above the Lust Demon, a large gaping hole would suddenly open up and a ray of light beamed down on her head. The powerful harsh wind that blew through the cavern lifted her up by her outstretched wings and out of the cavern through a wide open mouth. Before the chains that she was connected to could draw up her prisoners, the mouth would shut tightly and break the chains, freeing both the Leopards and the Zero Worlders that were once attached. They, as well as the Lust that was not the demon, should have remained inside of the belly of Gluttony. The Demon of Lust, however, should have been both isolated from the group and cut off pretty much immediately from her power source.

Soon after, the whispering voice of a woman could be heard in the ears of the captives, bearing a message of a warning. "Don't Move. I Will Help You..." she said, but no more words could be heard after that. Those that could hear would now know that there was a force working with them instead of only working against them, and whatever it was, it had power that was at least as strong as the ones that had first taken them.

You all clearly see, at least to some degree, what is going on around the cavern, where there is a disturbance that You are suddenly in because of the leader following her reckless desires and the man apparently continuously seeking to fulfill those reckless desires without ceasing, leaving both of them not paying much mind to anything going on that they are actually supposed to be doing. The two of them seem extremely powerful with whatever it is that they do, yet because they are not actually accomplishing any kind of goal, it all seems to be a waste.

You stand there patiently, mostly in fear of what could possibly be next, yet also with great anticipation that it will free you of your servitude, if there truly is some sort of being that is here trying to help you.

You see that, with whatever happened, after the voice of the woman spoke to you from wherever it came, the cavern opened up to spit out the one that was once recklessly tossing you and your life around whenever she got wrapped up in her own sensuality and self-absorbed excitement. Though You are free of your bindings, you also know that the Leopards are also free as well, and could still definitely hunt for you if you move. When you realize this, that is when you decide to stand perfectly still and not let any of the Leopards know exactly where you are in the darkness.

CHAPTER 3

SLOTH

Eventually, the Great Darkness that was resting over the South Gate as a powerful pressure that pressed down on everything that started up the trail would lift from the mountain, but only slightly. A vast majority of the mountain, which was, if not visibly illuminated before the eyes of those walking the path, draped in garments of darkness that robed it like a fine linen. Where the greatest pressure rested over the Southern Gate, it would begin to hover over the Zero Worlders as what was covered by the Great Darkness that pressed down on them looked on without moving from its place.

Sooner or later, the Puppet King made its way all the way down to this level of the mountain in a hurried manner. It seemed like it was searching for something or someone rather ferociously. "And Just To Show You That Even With All Of This, I'm Still Only Just Baiting You Out Because 'YOU WILL NOT' Escape Is An 'Absolute Final,'" the voice blared into the minds of all of the open vessels in the area, as the titanic toy toddled along. "You Have To Go Get Lesser Envious People And Show How Ugly Envy Looks One Step At A Time." The Master of Envy spoke into the mind of the collective souls within Puppet King, "Uh, Go Get A Trap Rat And Trap It." That was first on the list of things to do in order to start educating people on Envy.

So, Puppet King was sent off, having given instructions to the ones under its control to start beginning to set up the trap for their rat, whomever that may be. "Looks like Lust has already purchased some of them, so I can have a free sample..." The Voice of the Presence sounded different from the Voice that commanded the Puppet King, and very distinctly in tone and authority, the latter having less force and more personal, informal depth that others would have trouble hearing. "I only need the weakest and the easiest..." The Voice, which was feminine, and emanated the powerful pressing presence of the Great Darkness, would make clear before allowing everyone else to finish doing what they were doing. "There's my input." The Presence rested.

The Great Darkness rested. She was tired after doing so much work rather than sitting around, like she normally did, waiting for just the right moment. "Damn... *pant* I'm... Tired..." She yawned drearily, not having realized that all of the mental hopping was physically taxing, something like a workout. She sighed heavily, as if having a bit of trouble breathing. "... But at least now, all I have to do is tell them what happened and help them out when they get up to this point." Tabitha, or, 'The Great Darkness,' which was 'Sloth,' was already completely clean the moment she returned to take Sloth's place. All Tabitha could see were some old drawings that looked like her childhood flashing before her eyes, yet in an orderly manner that all made sense. "... Vision's lining up..." she said, looking down at the darkness under her. All of the other Sins were running about, having not been claimed by the Tensei. "I've got Gluttony and Envy..." she muttered to herself, batting her lashes lightly with a dark, downcast look on her face, "Plus, Wrath, too..." Tabitha inherited Sloth from her father long ago, and that was passed down to her through her genetics as a Tensei.

The Tensei Family conquered the Sin of Sloth a long while ago, and as the Goddess of Darkness that was over the area, she was monitoring the untamed ones and capturing them as she saw fit all on her own. "... I really wasn't expecting to be part of something like this. I didn't plan for it at all," she mentioned, somewhat muttering to herself, in an almost bored fashion. "... I wonder what is taking them so long...?" She'd only dealt with Four of the Seven Deadly Sins, and the other Three were still running around trying to capture and enslave people, as she'd been seeing during her time capturing and taming the various Sins, like she's done with Sloth. "... I wonder." She thought to herself about the Divine

Pet that her father had given her for taming Sloth. The 'Slowth,' which, before it was a 'Divine Pet,' was classified as the 'Demon Of Sloth.' It was her teddy bear whenever her father was gone out for his business of running a village, and she would stay with it inside the Pit of Havoc. "Slooooowwwwth~!" Tabitha nearly yawned like a cat, falling over into the loft of her dark drapery of her covering like a comforter. She began to sink into the darkness and fade out, with a powerful pressure pressing down on the entire mountain like the intensifying of gravity.

Tabitha would rest on the shade of the backside of the mountain like a pillow, with the pillar resting almost completely adjacent to the length of her back to the crown of her head. Her eye lazily glazed over to the side, gazing at the people on the other side of the mountain walking in the light. The entire group was somewhere approximately the size of her iris. "I wonder if they can see me now..." Tabitha was only peeking her head out from the darkness, and hadn't truly revealed any of her features save for her gleaming white eye.

The Slowth appeared from the Great Darkness as Tabitha continued to peek out from the darkness, watching carefully.

Sooner or later, a man stepped forward, finely dressed, atop a high place in the mountain, peering over the edge to oversee what was going on. It looked like he was waiting for something.

The Great Darkness would 'Cover' the land, stretching out over the mountain trail. Nothing could be seen into nor through it, however something was going on within and throughout it. The sound of shuffling and scuttling could be heard.

The man atop his high place smirked and chuckled, beckoning his hand forth a bit. A regal chair was pitched where he began to sat and he kicked a leg up over his knee as he looked on, watching The Great Darkness pass by.

Temporal displacements speckled the pathway, littering random blots like that of ink completely invisible, with distorted eyes flickering about the inside. It looked as if some sort of Presence was in motion, and it was lingering behind as these flickering Distortions of Darkness.

"I. Step Forward One At A Time, Single File And In Order."

These were instructions that would come into each of their heads collectively as Common Sense once they reached the edge of the darkness, and after hearing all of the whispers of the 'Great Darkness,' which was the 'Kurogami,' speaking and guiding them through the ins and outs of Gluttony. No one had actually come out of the Great Darkness yet, and the one that was looking on could not see who would jump out first. All he would be able to see were the eyes of the Slowth, which was what the dark presence left behind belonged to. The actual Slowth was nowhere to be found, speculatively.

Those had heard the whispers of the story that this Voice told, which guided them this far and into the light, would make sure to heed what was spoken and what was heard collectively.

You realize now that unlike before, where You were prone to have ignorantly pushed your brother or neighbor out in front of You to go Test the waters before you got in, Testing both they and the situation for You, You instead realize that it's better to work collectively as a group, since getting each other into terrible situations collectively as a group through influencing each other ended up getting everyone captured in the first place. After such a traumatic near death experience, You definitely have it locked into your head that You will not be doing something like that again, at the risk of, if for no other reason, simply not letting Yourself get snatched up in the tailwind. You are still very hesitant to pass through, because of what you have seen and been put through, but You are still excited to get out of the slave chains of Lust, and eager to exit the place where You'd been set free.

Because of this, Someone steps forward first and begins to walk out of the Great Darkness that was covering, in order to pass through the trail, hoping not to get struck with anymore afflictions like before near the beginning.

"Aha!" the finely dressed man shouts at seeing anything step forward and into the light. "I knew you couldn't stay hidden forever." He rose from his fanciful chair and immediately pulled out a wad of cash from his pocket, the exact number of which had no real weight, considering the heft of the thickness of the band. "You there!" He called out from above, looking down to the area he was overseeing, "How much will it take for you to work for me? Price isn't a number, just your desire." He smiled deviously, hurling the mound of money down into the pathway between the darkness, so that whatever came out would have to pass through the money maze.

Someone was paid to start doing construction on the area, and a building started to be built from the ground up. "Tell me now, and your name will be all over it. Just name it." He watched carefully, patiently awaiting the response of the potential investment.

'Game Rook :: Cover'

The Slowth That Was Covered In And Covering The Great Darkness Would Also Be Covering All Of The Individuals That Were Inside Of The Great Darkness At The Time. When Someone Attempted To Step Out Of The Darkness, At Once, One Of The Great Darkness' Game Pieces Was Sent Out In Their Stead, Whilst The Person That Stepped Forward Walked Only Further Into More Darkness.

"II. Step Further Into The Darkness By Following My Instructions, Directions And Commands."

The Individual That Heard, Who Was Also Collectively Consciously Connected To The Others That Were Waiting At The Other End Farther Back, Of Whom Can No Longer Be Seen, Can Also Hear Everything That You Hear.

"Game Start."

-This Is Where The Second Person Plural Becomes Second Person Singular.-

You Are In Darkness And Are Bid Cautiously Throughout It, Following The Sound Of A Strange Woman's Voice. You Do Not Do Anything Except What It Tells You To Do, And It Seems To Assist You By Guiding You Properly Instead Of Into Your Doom. You Decide To Follow.

A 'Puppet' stepped out of 'The Great Darkness.' It was called the 'Archduke,' and it looked like a pitch black castle tower with a steeple and a crown at the top, something similar to a Chess Piece, except looking as if it were a King and a Rook combined as a single Piece. Many Distortions kept whatever and whomever was inside the mobile fortress of darkness from being seen, and their identities being disclosed.

The Archduke, who was a Valparaiso Denizen, would be hidden by the ambiguity of the Darkness, but still was able to step forward without being discovered. When approached by the mysterious stranger's advocate, he would claim, "I am Archduke," as if stating his name. "Can I help you?" All the while he spoke, the Archduke moved throughout the darkness without coming out to be seen visibly once. Only his voice could be heard.

The Great Darkness spoke unto the Zero Worlders still covered by the Slowth, "Follow The Ones I Have Sent Ahead Of You. They Have Special Names And Ranks And Titles And Are My Servants That Will Guide You Out Of Here Alive." The rest of the process, which was automated, was left unto the appointed officials that existed inside of the Great Darkness that Tabitha, the one to whom the Voice of the Great Darkness belonged, could conjure up at any time from her private stock to be of assistance at anytime. "My Archduke Is Out Handling Business With The Businessman Trying To Purchase You Away From Your Own Lives And Your Own Freedom. Follow The Archduke, As Well As His Instruction, And You Will Be Set Free."

With these words spoken, the Great Darkness rested, and the Slowth was given the full authority of the Great Darkness whilst the Zero Worlders were passing through. The automated process, which was a system that Tabitha already had prepared in the shadows, known as 'Mechanica,' would begin taking care of the finer particulars whilst the Great Darkness herself rested over them and covered them to protect them from being seen as a group. They would be escorted out single file, but still led as a collective whole.

Having learned your lesson about disobeying these higher powers or falling into whatever sort of traps or snares that were placed specifically for You, You watch as the Archduke speaks to the envoy that was sent out by the mysterious man that You notice is watching and was waiting for someone to come out of the other end. You find this behavior suspicious, and figure that perhaps, whomever this person is, they have a plan that involves purchasing you for any price. You do not give into this, and You continue to walk through the darkness, waiting to see what this finely dressed man intends to do. You wait to hear what his proposal is before You even think to take whatever his offer is, in case that taking his offer is a deal to enslave You by terms or means You don't know nor understand, as with Lust, previously. Narrowly escaping that fate, You are more wary and careful of Your life, even if You are tempted to take the large sum of money that was offered. You wait and listen and see what the man does with the Archduke, who seems to know how to deal with this sort of matter professionally, as opposed to You. So, You remain hidden in the darkness, walking through silently with your unseen escort.

"I'm looking for some new recruits," the man in his nice attire would say flat out, "And I think you look like just the ticket." Instead of some lowly operational level member, the one that was sent out to speak to the paid official was a rather supreme looking official, himself. "How much for your services? I could use some management level help." He outstretched his arms, "Come! Talk with me. I'm sure we can come to some form of an agreement, yes?" The man's mind seemed made up about who he would have for his own, and this 'Archduke,' as it was said he was named, was a prime target. "I already have a stencil and a layout. All you have to do is fill the position and play the part, and I pa you, and cover all of your health, medical and dental. Lifetime contract, guaranteed services, as long as guaranteed service is guaranteed by you." Greed would retract his hand, curving his wrist upward, then flung it outward like the unraveling of a scroll, and in a burst of fluttering green paper would a long scroll, indeed, sprout from the palm of his hands and out into plain sight. "Crisp," he said, in reference to the paper and the fine print upon it. "Just sign and date and the special limited time offer is yours." He smirked deviously. "Guaranteed."

The Archduke, who stood as the representative for the Great Darkness and the people that were covered by the Great Darkness, would consider the offer of the finely dressed man and begin to logically contemplate and calculate the options that were available. "Hmmm…" After so long of thinking, with quite the challenging puzzle of thought locking him up as he thought to move, eventually the Archduke came to a rather promising conclusion for this man. "I think I'd like to have a tour," he said confidently. "Show me your wares and around your business, and I will consider taking your offer." When the man would lead, the Archduke would follow. "Final answer."

You decide, after everything that's happened and what You've learned about these Sins and this realm and its elements, that it is best to not try to take too many matters into Your own hands until You are in a safe zone and can resume Your normal life again.

You stay quiet, gazing at the eyes that are looking back at You, as if peering into Your soul. You can see what is going on outside and know that they cannot see You, however You are still terrified for some unknown reason. Probably, because of the striking accuracy in which at any given moment, things actually could become very real for You and Your life would be on the line. That part intimidates You, but You know better than to stop what You are doing. You end up walking through the darkness with the Archduke that was sent to be your Guide as your new leader, something like the Puppet King was to the Puppets. You continue to move chiefly and quietly, single file, no sudden movements and as carefully and composed as humanly possible without lagging for too long or loitering about idly, where something could expose Yourself or the group and get everyone killed or put them into danger. Each of You that were still alive learned a very valuable lesson about the group and the team effort. You do not stray from your instructions nor your path; you walk a straight and narrow path, right down the line as directed in an orderly fashion.

The man's devious grin widened, and he couldn't help but let out a restrained laugh he'd been holding back, seeming to be out of anticipation. "Just what I wanted to hear!" It was just his lucky day today that he'd happen to pass by someone so willing to help out his noble cause. "Step right into my office, Sir, and we'll discuss these matters further in more detail." The man snapped his fingers, and shreds of fine green paper spontaneously sparked from his fingertips, and each of the leafy greens would blow away in the wind. A trail was left behind as a line of corresponding events all funded by the same organization, which was this man, himself.

The well dressed man brushed off his suit and adjusted his shoulders and sleeves, then started off back across his high place, waiting for the investor to make his way to the location that was being arranged for them to meet. The Archduke would be escorted there promptly and with the utmost haste, but the regal man would depart go long ahead of him. There was nothing left to be done here.

A heavy sigh of relief at the release of tension in the area came from beyond the Great Darkness. "Finally," Tabitha said, her own Spider Eyes lining up in all their sight. "It's all a straight shot from here." Once she was able to see all the same paths at the same time, there was a higher probability of that outcome occurring because she'd been able to see the same route in multiple different viewpoints or vantage points and each of them ending up coming together all seamlessly at the end. Her Divine Pet of Sloth, 'The Slowth,' which was named as the new 'Sloth' in place of Tabitha, who was the original 'Sloth,' would take care of guidance and the Mechanica that were already infesting the area in their various forms, such as Puppets, were about if she should need to intervene due to the 'Slowth,' now 'Sloth' itself, moving too slowly. "I'm sure they won't need any help," she muttered monotonously to herself. "I'll guide you to where you need to go, but then I'm going home. I'm tired." She was always tired, much like her father, and she honestly didn't need to be here anymore now that she accomplished some personal things, and these people were a completely independent party that couldn't hold up the rest of the things she had going on for too long. Even as a spirit, she, too, still needed her rest, and she was also only volunteering her services to repay for some other debts and personal business involving the Tensei family and main branch of the Veritas. "I suppose I can tell him 'Mission Complete.'" Tabitha was pleased with herself and this outcome. "Mmm... Yeah..." She cherished the moment and many sentimental feelings emanated from her heart. She smiled softly, starting to nod off a bit.

"Night."

With the covering of her face in the dark pools that soon overtook it, and the light of the once gleaming white eye as well, The Great Darkness fell upon the land, which was the absence of Tabitha's Presence, which would be the fullness of the body of the Slowth. Kurogami Tabitha, The

Great Darkness, would disappear, and the bright of day would become the dark of night.

The Pressure Of The Absence Of The Presence Rested Gravely Over The Entire Mountain, Pressing It Down Thoroughly. All Who Walked Through Could Feel It Over The Land, As The Depression Of 'Sloth,' Which Would Be The Bearing Eyes Of The 'Slowth' Boring Down Into The Flesh Of The Mountain As It Oversaw The Walkers.

CHAPTER 4

PRIDE (VANITY)

"**M**irror, Mirror, on the wall," someone spoke into the reflection of a hand mirror, loftily propping his golden locks up and down to get just the right bounce, "Who is the fairest of them all?" The face in the mirror would think of all of the wonderful things about himself and pay nothing else any mind. "Everyone should be as fair as I am, both in judgment and in good looks." Hands down, the man in the mirror was the absolute best over anyone and everyone. "They should look like me; the best." He chuckled prissily, raising his pinky up to the side of his mouth and laughed haughtily "OOOOHOHOHOHO~!"

For a good, long time, this person paid absolutely no mind to anything that didn't look like it was worth any attention, at least not over the bearer of the mirror, himself. Though, when he thought to replicate his own image, however he pictures his own image, regardless of anyone else's, that's what drove him to start paying attention to everyone and everything around him. Still looking into his mirror, he would lower it from his face and down to his stomach, which was a giant hand mirror the size of a body, with a head and arms coming out of the sides, holding the exact miniaturized replica in hand. In the reflection, this floating entity, which was a hand mirror with a face, could see the entire land that he hovered over in the mirror's reflection.

Down below, it looked like Envy was up to something and moving out across the entire mountain. "Hmph. Probably just playing some silly games with toys and not doing anything important. I'm sure it would attract more attention if it had my touch to it." That's when the vain man started to think, pondering some renovations to those ugly Invidiads that were scouring the surface of the mountain.

"Pride," a deep, grim voice called from atop a high place near the area that the mirror-man was hovering over, "It seems like you're up to something, I have overheard." The person speaking, who was rather finely dressed, with eyes covered and beautiful hair that draped over the eyes to prevent them being seen, would outstretch his hand. "I have a proposal, if you need to get something done."

Pride, who personally and formally liked to be known as 'Vanity' because it sounded much more becoming for a beautiful being such as itself, would turn his mirror slightly to the side so that he could see the reflection of the finely dressed man with the outstretched hand without having to look at him directly. "Oh, Greed. It's just you." Just as quickly, Vanity would turn his hand mirror back to his own face and fluff his lovely locks. "Oh, Chauncey, don't we just look so lovely?" Vanity couldn't help but to compliment his hand mirror, the Mirror Image, which was made completely in his own image, and named 'Chauncey.' "Even though Greed has been so rude as to enter our presence without announcing himself, if Greed has an idea or an opportunity to make an idea that I've had come to life, then perhaps we should entertain the thought." Though Vanity spoke into the mirror, the words were also indirectly directed toward Greed, himself, of whom Pride would look at with sharp, devious eyes and a mischievous smirk on his face, which could be plainly and clearly seen in his hand mirror.

"Still so full of yourself," Greed said, bobbing his empty hand up and down. "Time is money and we're on a limit. There are forces working against us in our own ranks." Something similar to what Pride and Greed were doing, yet more unintelligibly. "Envy is not one of ours anymore. I want you to go take care of those dolls for me. I will handle the plastic surgery." Since Greed knew that all Vanity wanted was for everything to go his way and for him to get his way all the time so he could look at it and see himself in all his work, all that needed to be done was to pay some poor unfortunate souls to be the underlings of

Pride, and he would deal with Envy, himself. "I have more pressing matters to deal with involving the others. Won't you go deal with those little dollies for me so they can be YOUR toys from now on?" Likely, this was an offer that Vanity wouldn't refuse. Greed continued to bob his hand up and down.

Vanity thought for a bit about the offer extended to him by Greed. He didn't seem too concerned about the fact that his comrades had turned on them, and in fact couldn't get his head out of the mirror that he was looking into. "Well, the others were weak, anyway. No use for anything. And they were pretty ugly, too." Pride threw his locks to one side as glittering sparkles speckled the air in their wake. "If there were more of them that were like me, we wouldn't have this problem. I'm glad you made the right choice coming to get me, Greed." Pride, who definitely had the means to pay Greed for his services, would, once he was assured that his own goals would get accomplished, not hesitate to slap a wad of cash into the empty hand of the begging Greed. "I want them to look like Chauncey," he said, looking dreamily into the eyes of his mirror image in his hand. "I'll grab their attention. They could use a makeover anyway, I'm sure, if they don't look like something I want to look at." Pride thought highest of his own opinion, and deemed the quality of everyone else's to be nowhere near as superior, which was why he barely interacted with or listened to anyone outside of himself and people trying to help him get his goals accomplished.

"Nice doing business with you..." Greed said, slipping his hand behind his back. "Don't forget to give Mister Sir a taste of his own medicine, too." Greed would continue to look on from his high place.

Vanity, who disregarded whatever Greed was saying now, had already floated high up into the sky, where he could see all of the West Gate far more clearly. He hovered over the Lake of Death, shining the mirror on his abdomen down at the ground. "Chauncey..." he beckoned, releasing his hand mirror, which became sentient at his call. It floated to the other side, mirroring Pride's place, and they would begin to reflect light into the area down onto the ground.

The strange lights that came from the sky, which looked something like Hollywood spotlights on a red carpet, would sweep across the ground and draw forth vessels and the souls inside of them up into it. Anything that was in it or looked directly into it would be trapped by it, like a tractor beam, and their attention would be snatched up to look at where the light was coming from.

Suddenly, Mister Sir appeared behind the mirror in a flickering spontaneous flash, with the loud sound of the fwooshing of fire and the stroke of heat scorching the area. He drove his blazing hand, all acrimson, straight into the back of the mirror and making certain not to attack from the front. "Where Is Greed?" were the only words necessary as he either grasped or destroyed the mirror that he confronted. Mister Sir was already highly upset that Greed actually paid someone, Vanity, no less, to turn against him, and without any form of hesitation nor concern for repercussion.

"Right behind you!" Greed, the finely dressed man that had been casually and leisurely passing through the area suddenly said, appearing somehow behind Mister Sir in the air. He had a wide, devious grin upon his face, as if there was already something in motion. "Here to pay the Toll, I take it?" Greed chuckled, his hands folded carefully behind his back.

The mirror that broke was fake, but the image of Greed behind it was real.

Vanity and Chauncey, of whom were 'Pride', combined, would already begin to oversee the land. Just by showing their faces, they were already casting an image that was more powerful than those with no influence nor oversight. The titanic mirror that hovered over the mountain was something like a reverse magnifying glass to the scurrying little nothings down below. "Chauncey, go pick one of them out and shine a spotlight on them, s'il vous plaît." Vanity, himself, would appear before Mister Sir directly, once Greed was behind him, and show him his Fate. "Live," the Mirror would say once Mister Sir looked into it, something like a television broadcast, "We have here a 'Mister Sir' that has apparently 'gone straight.'" Pride chuckled. "What do you make of this, Greed? Audience?" Vanity turned lightly to the side with a smug look on his face, directing his attention to the opinion of the Valparaiso Denizens that had been following along, "Chauncey...?"

41

Without much warning, there was a beam of light and a wave of heat that stroked the land, with the shining ray scavenging the surface of the land as if searching for targets. That much was clear. However, when the Puppet King and the rest of the Valparaiso Denizens were in danger, they immediately sunk into the 'Cover' of the 'Darkness,' no longer able to be seen by any of the light, nor touched by the wave of heat, using whatever was making the 'Darkness' they were covered by also as protection from the heat blast. Puppet King and his men were gone in a hot flash.

No Valparaiso Denizens were found in the light. All of them had disappeared completely into the shadows where they could not be seen.

A figure was seen wandering about the open field, having crawled out from the Darkness.

"What Audience?" Mister Sir chuckled condescendingly, avoiding the spotlight that Pride tried to place on him, "Where Are You Looking?" The very instant that Pride took his sights off of Mister Sir, he was already gone, completely out of sight. "Wipe That Smug Look Off Of Your Face. I Can't Stand It." Greed had already spilled the beans about what happened between Mister Sir and Envy, and what Mister Sir was doing here now, and had been waiting to ambush him along with Pride. "You Might Finally Realize That You Have Nothing To Be Smiling About." Mister Sir cocked his arm around his head, stiffening it like a blade, then targeted Greed with an infernal slash.

Whip like crescent blades of searing flame left a radiant wave of scorching heat in the wake that washed over the land and parched the air, whilst the actual flames incinerated everything they came across with the precision of a butcher knife. Greed, Pride and anything else that was visibly within the line of sight of Mister Sir at the time should have been naught but complete ash, and the air should have wavered with a tropical heat.

Whatever Trees were around being made into money would be burnt up completely, as well as all of the potential money that could have been made from each of the Trees, themselves. It was like taking a blow directly to the Stock Market for Greed, and should have hit him right where it hurt, if the initial blow somehow didn't connect

Vanity might not have gotten to target the group as intended, but something definitely caught his eye as he turned away from Mister Sir, who escaped from before the face of the Mirror, which was rather wise of him. "You should know by now that a head on attack won't work on me." He flipped his dazzling hair and adjusted his orbit slightly, of which Chauncey, who was nearer to the figure in the distance, would reflect for Vanity.

Numerous Mirror Images of Pride would suddenly appear all throughout the Lacor Mortis, even hovering over the ignited Lake of Fire, itself. They all seemed tangible and none of them could be discerned because each one was of different size and proportions. All of them were Pride, being either an image of Vanity or of Chauncey, both of which looked identical, save for the difference in size and disposition. These Mirror Images would litter the skies like satellites looking down on a lower class of being. "Ready for your close up, Mister Sir...?" Pride laughed haughtily, glaring down with all eyes condescending.

There were so many of these Mirror Images reflected and projected all across the field that Greed, who had actually already been using some 'Smoke and Mirrors' of his own, would appear in the reflections and project reflections of himself, as well, whilst also holding a wad of money that suddenly, with the clench of his fist and a ruffle like that of feathers, would spontaneously burst into the physical form of a hand mirror that mimicked the appearance of Pride. Greed would have just as many, if not more images of himself surrounding the area, all across the ground whilst Pride took the whole sky and covered him from above. "This looks like good coverage, don't you think, Mister Sir?" There was literally nowhere to run nor hide, now, and none of the little street vermin that had once been scurrying around were anywhere to be found. "It's over, Mister Sir," Greed said, stepping up to him wherever he might have been, "You lose."

The scorching crescent waves would only phase through image after afterimage, never actually touching a real tangible target. The trees would begin to grow again, after some 'green' was invested in their stock, as well. Gardeners and Farmers would be all over the reproduction of the trees. Greed know it would take some time for them to regrow, but because his people were already paid, it was, if nothing else, as good as done. This gave Greed the ability to direct all his focus on Mister Sir and Pride. "You can't touch us."

Mister Sir emanates a power heat wave aura that senses the various vibrations and life sources in the area, discerning the real ones from the fake ones. The fake ones would not come up in his senses, and he would not be drawn to the fake images. Instead, only wherever the true Greed or Pride were was where Mister Sir's energy would carry him, and in a flickering flash of flame, would he spontaneously appear behind one of them with a concussive explosion, knocking them out of their place and into a visible plain area of tangibility for him to actually have a target to hit. "Oh, But Can't I?" Mister Sir nearly chuckled, brushing off their combined efforts of intimidation, knowing that all of it was just the two of them sticking out their chest. "Don't Forget That I Already Know All Your Secrets And Weaknesses." Mister Sir shook his head, not taking his eyes off of whichever physical body was struck down by the flames of Wrath first. "And The Both Of You Have No Substance Behind All That Big Talk." The scorching heat that bore down on all of them prevented any form of living thing from growing; not a plant nor a tree, to even the leaf of a green plant, such as money, itself. Greed and all of his associates were receiving a pay cut in advance solely on conditions alone, and they would begin to lose value because everything else around them was losing value, as well; all burning up behind them.

The Lake of Fire that was already lit contributed to the heat of the atmosphere, since, for as far as the eye could see, there was nothing but the burning sea of sinfulness that all life had contributed to, with more Burning Bodies falling into it at a time as they may, even now. There was no way a single lifeform could survive these conditions without drying up and dying of thirst. "You've Never Been Through A Famine, Have You?" He chuckled, smirking cockily. "No, Not Like The Ones That You Already Started To Decay. Now, You're Not Going To Know What To Do." He laughed at them, waiting for any of them to move, rather patiently, at that. "But Guess Who Does?"

Mister Sir was feeling better already. Nearly elated. He shook his head. "Tsk. Tsk. Tsk. How The Mighty Have Fallen." He chuckled, feeling somehow lighthearted.

"Endsville Is Burning..."

He took off his shades and fire poured from his eyes as a burning light. The stitching on his eyes was burnt away and all of the souls inside of his body would be purged all at once, and collectively become the flames of Wrath, itself, contained in his body. He was taken up on the spot. "You Can't Run From Me," He said calmly, with a smile on his face. The fires that poured out of his temple would flicker about like a candle, yet would curl to a point, like Superman. His blazing white eyes would gaze into the false images and pierce through each of them with a burning light, which would torch the falsehoods left behind out of the sky and burn up the very atmosphere, itself, with a sweep of his gaze. The first one that was spotted within his line of sight would suffer the same outcome.

The Archduke that was being led by a finely dressed man with nice hair would emerge from the Great Darkness, which was much larger than the smaller Darkness spots that were spotted all over the terrain wherever there was high ground or something that could create a shadow. By this time, as the Archduke stepped into the West Gate, where the Lake of Fire was located, the Great Darkness would have passed over all the land and turned day into Night, and everywhere the Archduke walked, it would be night. All of the Zero Worlders that were passing up the mountain would walk under the cover of the Night, where they couldn't be seen and their locations remained anonymous to all except the Archduke, who walked ahead of them separately as not to draw attention to the whole crowd and expose their location to the one he was striking up a potential contract with. The Archduke waited patiently to be walked through with a grand tour.

"Ah, I see that my honored guest has finally shown up!" Greed turned his head to Mister Sir, laughing dauntingly, "Right on time." He smirked. "As usual." There was silence, yet it, too, was broken by the spontaneous ignition of Mister Sir, which brightened up the dark sky, something like the light of the sun or of a very intense fire. When

45

Mister Sir first caught sight of Greed and where his voice was coming from, the image would break and the beam that was directed at this specific image of Greed would instead strike the Archduke, instead, who was innocently following behind the image of Greed, not knowing where the real one had gotten to, either. "Now look what you've done," Greed would say with a rather smug turned up smile, something similar to that of Vanity's, "Guess who is going to pay for it and clean it up?" Greed had already come prepared, even if something like this, such as a drought and this famine occurred. "Another one bites the dust. And I don't have to suffer for it." Greed smiled deviously, already having a thorough escape route thought out.

During Mister Sir's rather calm and collected rampage, all of the images of Greed were burnt up, and Greed was nowhere to be found afterward.

There was a flash of light that suddenly came from up above, when Mister Sir just-so-happened to look at the correct image of Pride directly and reflect his own light back into his face, blinding him and sealing the light from his eyes and seal of the souls back up through the reflection of the mirror. "Keep your eyes in your own head, pervert," Pride said smugly, turning his nose up and laughing lightly to himself. He glared down in a condescending manner at Mister Sir, drawing nearer and nearer as the reflected light began to intensify at the magnification of the reflection. Pride would look down on Mister Sir and enjoy watching him be naked and exposed under the image of Vanity, which should have snuffed out all of his flames once the pressure of the presence of the Mirror Image reflecting his light pressed down on him to suffocate the outrageous flames.

You, who are just now catching up to the finely dressed man, of whom everyone is referring to as 'Greed,' continue to walk under the cover of the Great Darkness, which makes everything over You night, even with the brightness of what seems to be someone burning hotter than the sun. You eventually realize that this is the man that left you at the gate; Mister Sir, and that You've finally caught up to him. He is bursting with energy, that which looks to be something like the fires of hell burning all around his body, making his appearance barely visible.

There's something strange about his appearance and his demeanor other than the fact that his upper torso is nearly completely engulfed in flames similar to the ones that were smoldering over the lake nearby, which was Your alert that You had entered the West gate, and a new area altogether.

You dare not step out of the darkness and into the light and get caught in the crossfire, as You see what has just happened to your leader, the Archduke, and the treachery that this finely dressed man, Greed, has done on a whim simply to save himself. You look at him and think of Yourself as you were at the base of the mountain and suddenly, You become deeply troubled and depressed, upset with Yourself that you would almost be something like him, and without even realizing it and also thinking in Your head that it was all justified. Having an up close and personal experience with Greed, even for the short time it was, and watching what he did to his supposed 'comrades' on a whim completely trashed your trust in him, and no matter what he offered You, You were not more than fully aware that, if things got bad, none of the Offerings actually mattered because he would risk Your life, and You would not live long enough ti enjoy the Offerings that he just gave You.

Coming to these conclusions still Your feet, and You no longer move forward, as a group. Your designated leader, the Archduke, was already either completely destroyed or about to be locked in combat and there was nothing that You could do to assist. You want to wait patiently so that You don't get in the way, yet You can't help but feel like You are supposed to be doing something. You start to call on a higher power; the one that was over You before, which was the one that freed you from Lust and saved you from all of your lesser afflictions. "Help us! What do we do now?" You cry out. "Have mercy on us!"

"Fear Not," The Slowth's voice would echo in the darkness for all of them to hear, "I Will Bring Another Leader Out For You That Will Go Out Ahead Of You And Deal With The Opposing Forces." Just as swiftly as these words were said would the darkness part and another unit that was separate from the group of Zero Worlders still under the cover of the darkness, which was like the night to them, would exit from it. This unit, which was also black like the Archduke, would also have a crown atop it, and resembled a Bishop with a larger, more prominent hat with a cross at the top, looking to be a mixture of Bishop and King mixed together as one piece.

"Archdeacon :: Oversight"

The chosen advocate that would be moved on behalf of the Zero Worlders, the Archdeacon, would peer from out of the darkness, but did not separate from the darkness, itself. Instead, the Archdeacon's glowing eyes would stay affixed on the scenario and what the outcome was. The threat level could not be trusted, and the entire area seemed to be a potential hazard or danger zone universally until the fighting stopped. Therefore, the Archdeacon was bit to wait until the flames of Mister Sir's heart died down and it was safe to approach him.

Mister Sir, who was releasing a great deal of flame and light, was blinded by the stunning display and radiance of the reflection he saw in the mirror, which was himself. "GAH!!!" He cried out in pain, having to look his own magniloquence in the eye. His shades, which had been thoroughly broken by the intense beam of light that shot back into his eyes, would fall from his face, shattering all over the ground. His eyes were burnt shut, with light pouring from the seams, something like how Envy's stitched eyes once looked when souls attempted to escape the vessel. "Parlor... Tricks!!!" He shouted, now finding this to be a challenge. He saw many images of himself flash inside of his head, which was, with his eyes closed, now full of light and whiteness instead of pitch darkness, as it was before. Mister Sir, upon his transcendence, would be forced to look deeply inside of himself due to having gazed directly into Vanity's mirror. He saw himself exalted and uplifted, with his name in lights, yet was aware that this was all Pride's projections and not his actual goal to accomplish. "Focus..." he uttered to himself, concentrating hard to see through all the glamour. Even if his eyes were burnt shut for the time being, it was doing him a favor that he didn't have to look at Vanity.

The pressure of the powerful mirror was pressing down on him. Mister Sir could feel Vanity's presence forcing itself upon him, both body and mind, yet in his spirit, he was already aware that all of it was just an image and a projection that Pride, itself, wanted him to fall into. Mister Sir was well aware of how Pride functioned, having worked with each of the Seven Deadly Sins for so very long. Though he, himself, was sometimes weak to them, this time, now that he was no longer on their side, the weaknesses that he once fell into through siding with them disappeared once he decided to turn against them, in all the knowledge he had of their individual weaknesses and flaws. Pride was no different. "I'd Be More Concerned About Your Own Image, Vanity," Mister Sir would say smugly, the fires that spewed from his body suddenly calming down to a simmer. His rage was tempered, and now Vanity had nothing to reflect back at him nor to use against him.

Mister Sir's heat senses were still readily active, and served as a second form of vision for him whilst his eyes were temporarily blinded by the light. Whilst he worked out his inner demons, he felt the pressure of Vanity still pressing down on him, which registered in his head as a large mirror with his own reflection looking at him and portraying a rather gaudy, but filthy image. This meant that Vanity was close, and now, without having to look at him, Mister Sir could sense wherever he would come and immediately flickered out of range, closer to the darkness that Pride hadn't noticed nor neared. Mister Sir sensed something nearby with his heat sensory ability, and though he was unsure of what it was, he could tell by the vibrations that were emanating from this ambiguity that it was not a threat. "... So They Actually Made It..." he muttered to himself, chuckling with what actually seemed to be relief. "I'll Have To Walk Them Through This Part After I've Dealt With Pride..." Mister Sir sought to sense any trace of Greed, but it seemed like, once again, he left someone else to do his dirty work whilst he, himself, slipped off elsewhere. "Disgusting Frog..." Mister Sir grumbled under his breath. It was better to deal with him last, anyway, after he spent all of his money and cut off all of his resources.

"I look perfect," Pride said, without feeling the need to check himself at all, "I am ALWAYS perfect. Don't forget who the ONLY pretty one is around here." He turned his nose up and scrunched up his face, looking down on Mister Sir, who had escaped close to the darkness, saying with disgust, "Ugly One." Vanity could barely look at something like Mister Sir for too long, and instead would have a mind to turn away from him, just for being ugly in Vanity's presence. "Chauncey..." Vanity called, before an image of Vanity appeared before Mister Sir, shining a bright light down upon his head and the darkness that was nearby. Everything would be illuminated by the splendor of Pride, even in the darkest of night. His head was turned away, as if he didn't want to look, but inside of the mirror an image of an ugly and horrendous demon would expose itself, one that mirrored the face of Mister Sir.

Chauncey, which as the Mirror Image of Vanity, and the Demon of Pride that belonged to and took the exact replicated image of Vanity, the Sin of Pride, would replicate the image and abilities of Mister Sir, and Chauncey's face would morph into that of the one whose face looked into the Mirror Image. The demon inside of the mirror began to speak to Mister Sir, exposing all of his faults and flaws that were seen and reflected in the image. "You Talk A Big Game For Someone So Small," the image of Mister Sir said, in his voice, "Maybe You Need To Step Down. Have A Seat. Let Me Take Care Of Things From Now On, Hm?" Chauncey, who now donned Mister Sir's face, smirked condescendingly at him. "You're As Blind As A Bat. Obsolete. You'll Only Get In The Way. We Need Someone With A Little More... How You Say... Finesse?" Chauncey laughed, specifically at Mister Sir, keeping a fair distance from him, yet never actually moving from in front of his face. "You're Washed Up. A Has-Been. Your Services Are No Longer Necessary And You Are Excused Indefinitely." Chauncey would away Mister Sir with the shoo of his hand. "Thank You, Have A Nice Day."

When the light of Pride shone down on the Darkness, none of the people were exposed in the light that were hidden within, but the Archdeacon that had been set up by and for the Great Darkness, itself, would be exposed, finally.

Overhearing the thoughtful words of Mister Sir, and also seeing that his issues with this mirror and the image it showed him were getting the best of him, or at least holding him in check, the Archdeacon would act on his behalf to come to his aid. "How about me, then?" he said, stepping forth and between both Mister Sir and the Mirror that reflected his image. "What do you see about me? Hopefully you are able to see something more than you do in the one behind me." The Archdeacon would wait patiently to be judged by Pride, who deemed himself higher than everyone to the point where he could make such snap decisions, and his word actually had some sort of impact or influence. "Maybe I can be of assistance to you, in place of this 'Mister Sir?'" The Archdeacon peered into the Mirror, waiting to see what sort of image would be cast in it, be it his own or something from elsewhere.

Mister Sir waited patiently for the mirror to cast his reflection in it. Once he heard his own voice spoken through that of Pride, he chuckled to himself, as if it were what he was waiting for. "And Apparently, I'm The Blind One," he muttered to himself, smugly, similarly to how Pride acted toward him. "If I Am So Ugly, Pride, Then Why Have You Taken On My Image? I Thought You Were So Far Above That." Mister Sir knew that Pride always wanted to be superior, and fighting him for superiority was actually the wrong move. Instead, taking a more submissive role and allowing the one blinded by his own light, as Mister Sir had seen through his own transcendence of his own light, would be a better option. "Look How Far You've Stooped, And For Little Old Me, At That. I'm Touched." His smile widened, yet Mister Sir did not move from his place. He felt someone moving from out of the darkness and became alert, but was nowhere near concerned. "Don't Get Yourself Dirty Trying To Taint An Image. Pride Is A Terrible Sin." Mister Sir calmly folded his hands behind his back, saying and doing nothing more from there. An ever-present smirk remained on his face, however, and his eyes were still sealed shut. He reflected deeply, but not through Pride nor the image of Vanity that was left behind. He retreated into his mind, where there was great illumination, but kept his mouth shut. He allowed the one who stepped forward to speak for him to do just that, having no issue nor concern. There was no power struggle.

"Don't Be Such A Stiff," The Mirror Image of Mister Sir proclaimed, with the face of Chauncey up above now peeking from the corner of his eye at the Archdeacon. "Here, Let Me Help You." Chauncey floated backward at a high speed whilst the Mirror Image darted forward, creating a physical image of Mister Sir that was under Chauncey's control, something like a doppelganger. It lunged directly at the Archdeacon, whilst Chauncey now reflected the image of the Archdeacon that was attacked in his mirror's image. "I do admit," Chauncey spake through the new reflection in his Mirror, "This is much more becoming." The head of the mirror, Chauncey, himself, would fluff up his hair, throwing his luscious locks back over his shoulder gracefully, laughing haughtily. "But with a new face in the Mirror, the old one is of no more use."

Mister Sir would thrust a blazing palm straight at the Archdeacon at a high speed, with Chauncey hovering backward with his new face held captive, and a new piece for him to use to his will, laughing all the while. "Ohohohoho~!" Without turning away from them to make sure they did not seek to escape, Chauncey would float up into the sky, his Mirror beginning to glow. He orbited the area cautiously, as if searching for something, not taking his eyes off of the ground for a moment, even though he shifted his body in order to get a better shot.

The Archdeacon immediately darted to the side after being attacked by the burning image, narrowly escaping the blow. "STOP!" cried the Archdeacon, who could see that the mirror man was getting away. He raised his hand up into the air, as if trying to reach out to grab Chauncey, but it was too late. Still, as he avoided the blow, the Archdeacon continued to speak out. "See how you lunge at the chance to harm one that means you none? That is not what an Archdeacon does, nor is that my image!" This Piece on the field, of whom resembled a holy, peace-loving man, would not turn his back away from one that was in danger, nor would he issue out any sort of order like it. "That is nothing but an unholy demon in that mirror! And if it is not reflecting me, a holy, peace-loving man, when who, pray tell, is that image of?"

Certainly, casting a reflection of Mister Sir would be easy for a Sinner; merely replicate the Sin and project it as it comes. Yet, for a Sinner to reflect a holy, righteous man was much more difficult, and now that the Archdeacon's image was there, one of two things had to happen. Either Chauncey, who was reflecting the image, would have to mirror the Archdeacon exactly or come to terms with the fact that the image was fake and thereby both ineffective and unreal. "My image is more becoming for a reason, but I think, after seeing me, you will find that yours is not so." The Archdeacon, clearly a wise man, would smile chiefly, knowing he had cornered the rather vain entity that thought so highly of his own image, he could not truly reflect anyone else's. "You can only expose more of yourself, but you cannot show me myself through you."

Mister Sir would thrust a blazing palm straight, just like the Mirror Image of himself once he felt its vibrations enter the atmosphere near him and distort the wavelengths with its presence. "No Matter How Faint, Every Image Casts A Light," he said, his own blazing palm meeting in the exact center with the hand of the image, right where the collision with the Archdeacon would have been. He gripped the hand tightly, with the incorporeal flames allowing him to touch and physically hold AND burn what was also intangible or metaphysical. "Every Light Wave, No Matter How Faint, Causes A Distortion Just By Existing." With their palms locked and Mister Sir's own transcendent power able to take hold of even what could not be touched by the normal hand, the Mirror Image of himself should have been locked in place and either destroyed or forced into a 'Game Of Shadows' with Mister Sir, himself. "Mirror Match," he said with a smug chuckle, as if it were what he had been waiting for.

"Go," he said to the Archdeacon that fought on his behalf, "I Have No Qualms With You." Mister Sir had undergone some sort of righteous change of heart, that much was clear. To what degree was left to be determined, but his actions spoke for themselves, and his words only fortified them. "I Will Catch Up." Whilst the Archdeacon had an opening, this was the time for him to escape. Mister Sir could handle himself from here. "This Is Personal."

To the Image, if it hadn't been destroyed on contact, Mister Sir would lunge a flickering hand stiffened to a point, something like a blade or spear, with intent to stab and/or puncture the reflection straight through the chest and destroy it that way.

When Chauncey saw and heard these things that the Archdeacon had said and that Mister Sir had done, immediately, the image inside of his Mirror would crack, causing Chauncey severe pain. "AUUUUUUUGGHH!!!" He shrieked in a bloodcurdling pain and fury, as if hot blood had been thrown directly on his body "WHAT

HAVE YOU DONE TO MY BEAUTIFUL IMAGE!?" Without Vanity there to mentor him or for Chauncey to reflect, he was nothing more than a broken image. Blood squirted from out of the cracks of the broken mirror, all down the image of the Archdeacon, who would also be screeching and contorting into something that looked more like Chauncey, except in the appearance of a man rather than a hand mirror. "I SHOULD NEVER HAVE EVEN LOOKED AT SUCH AN INSIPID THING LIKE YOU! THIS IS WHY WE DON'T MESH!!! THIS IS WHY YOUR KIND AND MY KIND DO NOT MIX!!!" He grabbed hold of his head, spiraling out of control the more he thought about how ugly he was becoming. He could barely fly straight, and now had conflicting feelings that clashed with himself and his goals. "THIS IS WHY WE ONLY LOOK DOWN AT YOU UGLY THINGS!!" The Demon inside of the mirror, which looked like Chauncey as a human, cried out, poking ferociously at the ones below, casting blame, judgment, slander, defamation and everything else that could be applied that came to his mind solely out of sheer rage for his broken image.

"My face..." The Demon cried, "My beautiful face..." He hovered back and forth, blood still pouring, like a gutted lamb still trotting on for dear life. When pieces of the mirror fell from his body, Chauncey nearly lost his already fractured mind. The Demon in the mirror grasped his hair, and the Mirror itself would Mirror the Image, and they would both shake viciously and violently, as if having a seizure, with many grotesque and ugly faces all appearing or being made at once, something like when a person was going through an emotional fit. The one beautiful smirking haughty face was now a collection of demonic emotions, something like Depression, Hatred, and pure feral ferocity. "I'LL KILL YOU I'LL KILL YOU I'LL KILL YOU I'LL KILL YOU I'LL--" He couldn't think of what to do. "Oh no, I need my pieces... I need all of them, or else I'll never be beautiful again..." The bloody mirror began to bawl, whilst the image inside would screech and hiss, hunching over as blood completely consumed it, and the broken shards of the mirror continued to fall piece by piece off toward the ground.

With all of the sheer horrendous emotion, this would feed the flames of the Mirror Image of Mister Sir, causing it to grow in strength and definition, rather than to be destroyed immediately. Feeling this, the bloody Demon, which had two ugly faces; one with a hysterical insane smile and the other with a disgustingly depressed and twisted enraged face, would break out of the mirror and shoot toward the image of Mister Sir at a high speed, as if to possess it. "HISSSSSSSHHHHHKKKKI!!!!!" It cried, as though it had suddenly lost all form of composure in a hell bent attempt to get the goal accomplished. The discarded hand mirror would return to being a normal hand mirror and fall straight to the ground, shattering and breaking completely.

Chauncey, the Demon of Pride, who was now possessing the Mirror Image of Mister Sir, would take on that form as his new 'Mirror Image,' instead of being the Mirror Image of 'Vanity,' who had moved on. "Now I'm Stuck With This UGLY Face And UGLY Form Instead Of My Beautiful Image I Had Before." The interlocked hand would grow in strength and intensity, so much so, it could break the bones of Mister Sir's and hold off his flames from burning up the arm. "I WILL FUCKING KILL YOU!!!" The hand that was lunged at Chauncey would immediately, with demonic reflex, be knocked away and retaliated to in what seemed to be the exact same motion, with the claw-like hand of Chauncey darting toward Mister Sir's face, as if to rip it straight from his skull. "UGLY OOOOOOONE!!!!!!"

"God Bless You," the Archdeacon cried to Mister Sir, "May your righteousness follow you, and not your misdeeds." Before dawdling too long, the People that were still shrouded in the darkness would be led out of the area at the utmost haste whilst Chauncey, this foul Demon of Pride, exposed his true face outside of the image he'd taken on and reflected, and was now attempting to take on a different form like that of Mister Sir as his new appearance. It was quite the grotesque scene, and the Archdeacon who led the people was certain to keep them far away from the discarded vessel that was the broken mirror and walking along the shadows as they entered the area. The Archdeacon, himself, would converge back into the shadows after playing his part, humbly, at that, and would continue to guide the people to their salvation. They would vacate the premises promptly, without looking back.

"All Those Repressed Emotions Getting To Your Head?" Mister Sir had no time to deal with a fake, and it seemed as though in the emotional frenzy, Chauncey had lost his mind. "So Weak..." The hand that lunged savagely as Mister Sir's face would be met with a burning face of fire, no longer physical, but completely ethereal, as the flame, itself. The moment Chauncey, in Mister Sir's Image, stuck his hand into Mister Sir's face, all of the great and powerful Wrath that was within him being reflected would be absorbed thoroughly into Mister Sir and tempered properly, drawing in the Demon of Pride into himself and scorching it to cinders through the very flames that ignited its own burning hatred. "Worth NOTHING To Me." With such a fragile mind due to the repressed emotions from trying to keep up an image that just was not so, during the fall from grace, the Demon of Pride made simple, folly and ignorant mistakes that were all out of the emotional surplus, something like an open wound in a heart never ceasing to pour out blood. "Must Have Lost Your Goddamn Mind; Fighting Fire With Fire." Mister Sir stepped forward and literally walked through the image placed before him without any issue nor concern, and even adjusted his burning gloves as he did, as if paying the Demon of Pride no mind. It would burn up before him and behind him, and all Wrath would become One in Mister Sir. "My Work Here Is Done."

Now, what Mister Sir had to do was catch up to the group and fill them in on what happened before they met back up, and explain to them along the way who and what was waiting for them in the next part at the West Gate. "They're Going To Need A Recap, Or They Might Just Walk Right Into Greed's Money Trap." He sucked his teeth and sneered at just the thought of it, and what he did. His own memories flashed before his eyes, and a flashback of how it all happened would begin as he walked off toward the Great Darkness to rejoin and inform the Group.

CHAPTER 5

GREED

Now that Tabitha had control over all of the sin of Envy and all of the sin of Sloth, thanks to her Father, who gave her 'Sloth' when she conquered the First Arm Of Tabrith, as well as all of Gluttony thanks to the gluttonous nature of it, she was in control of 3 of the 7 deadly sins, and would soon have the entire mountain. "If I can find Greed, then this deal should be done," she spake from the abyss.

The units that were under her control; an army of Envies that were now going to be known as 'Pains,' which would be a personal type of Doll for Tabitha, would be crawling along the surface of the West Gate scouring for the Greed Demon or the Sin of Greed, itself. These were the lesser puppets of the Puppet King, which was ordering them from higher up to go back down the side of the mountain to deal with the other Sins.

Sooner or later, after Mister Sir dealt with the disposal of the former Puppet King, which the 'Pain' dolls that were scouting around were once the minions of, he was aware that each of them, after completing their task, would be headless and mindless vessels ripe for the taking. Once he reached the clearing of the West Gate, he would take the path along the water that led to one of the rocky high places, where he was aware that Greed liked to sit to watch everyone do everything to his bidding from afar.

"Greed," he summoned, "Step Forward And Collect The Ones Trying To Make A Deal For My Downfall." This was the first order of business, considering that those who Mister Sir betrayed would inevitably be out for his head, however also they were still able to be controlled simply because they did not know about what was going on in the background. They could be hooked and enslaved instead of destroyed and, if they were found with these detestable sins within them as a group, he could burn them all up at once just because he owned them, which was the plan. "You Can Buy A Lesser Being Easily By Their Minds. So Don't Skimp On The Price, Because They Will Always Shoot Low." He knew that they thought they had no value or self-worth, which means that they would already start off naming a price that was low, and if Greed were to lower the price that already started off low because of their self-esteem and self-worth, then they would be more obliged to want to take the offer because they would be desperate due to low self-esteem. "Easy Money." The fact that Mister Sir knew this so well, and yet was about to give into this Sin of purchasing others again actually afflicted him, further igniting his Wrath. "Whatever You Want, It Is Yours," he said immediately, keeping his flames contained, "As Long As You Sign The Contract To Do It." He pointed off to the puppet army roaming by, passing over the land just beside the Lake of Death. Those were the targets in question.

The Valparaiso Denizens that were hiding out in the mountains away from the raging demon of fire would suddenly turn up once they saw the army of 'Pain' puppets scuttling by under the control of the former Puppet King. "Got em," the new Puppet King said, hurling strings over the crowd. "As long as we have all these forces in our ranks, we can definitely beat that guy now." They weren't certain where Mister Sir was, but their cover wasn't blown, so they weren't concerned with anything except the capture of the puppets for their ranks.

Just then, a man atop a high place, finely dressed, with lush hair that covered his eyes would step forward to greet Mister Sir only a little while after he called. "Ah, yes. Business to be done," the mystery man would say, adjusting his gloves. "I had to take care of a bit of chump change, myself." This man had just come from making some other deals with different underlings before returning to his normal spot, where he oversaw from on high most of his underlings doing the things that they were paid to do. "I don't suppose you mean that unruly heard, do you? The ones at the gate?" He referenced the ones he'd just bid to come up the mountain, who had recently been enslaved by Lust. "I already purchased those lot. They belong to me, and I won't go any lower than 75% on every head." If Mister Sir did not have the funds to purchase this man's assistance, then he might be out of luck.

"Of course..." the man insisted, not simply leaving the deal open ended, "... If you mean THAT lot, over there..." he pointed off to the distance where the rampaging army of dolls was marching, directly where Mister Sir was pointing off too, smiling some, "... I'll cut you a deal for them." The way he spoke of them was as if they were cattle and property, of which he saw each of them as, which was the only reason he was so picky about the proceeds. "You become my new employee and I will purchase the rag dolls for you." It seemed like a fair exchange. He extended his hand, as if to shake and confirm the deal. "What do you say? Do we have a deal?"

Before any form of any kind of 'deal' could be struck, the true owner of the puppets, Tabitha, who had already assigned what her role for these dolls was prior to entering the area, would already be prepared to give the new Puppet King of her choosing the 'Pains' that were running about 'headlessly.' The Goddess of Darkness, after spotting her group, descended into the group of puppets and became their large body, and immediately a great black aura pressed down on them. Their shadows all merged together as one and bulging black tendrils burst out upon the surface of the ground; 6 in total, and all of which immediately curved the entire flock of Mechanica over to their intended targets. "Here, Catch!" the grisly voice of the collective hive-minded dolls droned, all listening to the Command given to them by their owner and reciting it as fed into their minds.

This should have immediately gotten the attention of Puppet King, who would also recognize the signal, as well. (Consent)

"You Idiot." Mister Sir raised his hand up as if to strike Greed once he appeared. "You're Not Supposed To Ask Me For Pay." He lashed his hand over the army of puppets instead of giving Greed a dime and would just capture all of the dolls himself with burning strings attached to them. "You're Supposed To Do As I SAY!" He threw his other hand out toward Greed to knock his hand away, knowing that there was a more important matter at hand to take care of, which was the destruction of these infernal Sins, and prevent his own termination in the process. "How Can You Be Thinking Of How Much I'm Going To Pay You Right Now When I'm The One Whose Life Is On The Line?" The burning threads of fire that poured from Mister Sir's scalp scorched the land searching for where the ones that escaped him were, and burning up whatever strings they hurled out in the process so that only Mister Sir's strings connected to the puppet army. "You're No Help Unless I Give You Something First, No Matter What The Actual Stakes Are." Greed literally had no concern for anything beyond what the benefits for himself were, and wouldn't accept doing anything that did not benefit him. "Your Life Is On The Line, Too, I Hope You Know." Mister Sir wondered if that even made any kind of a difference, or at least an impact.

"Got it," the Puppet King of the Valparaiso Denizens cried out from the shadows, where all of his men were hiding behind rocks unseen. When they came out of the dark, the 'Distortions' that they used caused the flames of Mister Sir to miss the puppets and instead let the Puppet King connect his strings without anything burning them up. Every time some of Mister Sir's fire tried to get in the way to burn the strings, it would be distorted and redirected before it could touch the strings. "Ha! They're mine now!" he cried, now telling the Puppets what to do. They were stampeding like a herd of cattle, and so the best option was to assimilate with them and have them carry the Valparaiso Denizens and the Puppet King wherever they needed to get to. "Spread out, boys!" the Puppet King would command, and before too long, all of the 'Pains' would split apart and infest the mountain of Sin in many different areas, with each being set up for different reasons. They all disappeared into darkness and would be split up into respective teams and groups during their time inside the darkness, so when they each exited in their own time, it would be in small groups in different areas. "Thanks."

Greed frowned upon Mister Sir's conduct in what was supposed to be a cooperative work environment, feeling rather suddenly insulted by his refusal to pay the price for the services and talents of Greed and his agency. "You'll regret that," were the only things Greed said as his hand was knocked away and quickly placed behind his back. He walked away without paying anymore mind to Mister Sir.

Soon after Greed disappeared, a strange light like that of the sun appeared in the sky, shining brightly and casting lights down upon the field.

The strange lights that came from the sky, which looked something like Hollywood spotlights on a red carpet, would sweep across the ground and draw forth vessels and the souls inside of them up into it. Anything that was in it or looked directly into it would be trapped by it, like a tractor beam, and their attention would be snatched up to look at where the light was coming from.

"How Dare You." Mister Sir was more than furious. Not only was everything actually falling apart, but he also had to see it, and watch at what he was almost a part of. "I'll Deal With You Next, Greed." It nearly seemed like he wasn't upset with the Valparaiso Denizens nor the Puppet King at all, but his eyes flashed a burning crimson like the searing of a branding mark on a cow as he glared at Greed with the eyes of Wrath. Flames dispersed from where the light would shine, Mister Sir's image burning away as soon as he saw it.

A searing wall of fire behind him as the heat of the vacuum of his movements would burn up everything that he passed over, which included the Puppet King and the horde of lesser Puppets. "All Envy to me," he muttered under his breath, having his own sights set on a new, better Puppet King. "Don't Die, Children." These were the fading words of the passing heat wave, which scorched the land and ignited the Lake of Death, which was eternally to be lit aflame. Mister Sir's judgment was absolute.

Without much warning, there was a beam of light and a wave of heat that stroked the land, with the shining ray scavenging the surface of the land as if searching for targets. That much was clear. However, when the Puppet King and the rest of the Valparaiso Denizens were in danger, they immediately sunk into the 'Cover' of the 'Darkness,' no longer able to be seen by any of the light, nor touched by the wave of heat, using whatever was making the 'Darkness' they were covered by also as protection from the heat blast. Puppet King and his men were gone in a hot flash.

A figure was seen wandering about the open field, having crawled out from the Darkness.

Game Knight :: Mind Lock'

The Figure That Stepped Out Of The Shadows, Which Was Not A Valparaiso Denizen, Would Be Mentally Linked With The Mind Of The Grand Tabritha, Who Was Testing Out The Tensei Family's Game That Her Father Created; The Argus Card System. Since The Tensei Owned The Land And This Was The Best Area And Scenario For Testing Their Product, The First Creature That Stepped Out Once The Tensei, Grand Tabritha, Stepped On The Mountain And Started Playing Her Game Was Made Immediately Into Her Game Piece, Something Similar To How She'd Done With The 'Archduke' Before.

"Archnemesis," She Deemed, Sending Off One Of Her New 'Royal Servants' To Scour The Area For Any Loose Data She Could Use, "Scout."

Numerous Mirror Images of Pride would suddenly appear all throughout the Lacor Mortis, even hovering over the ignited Lake of Fire, itself. They all seemed tangible and none of them could be discerned because each one was of different size and proportions. All of them were Pride, being either an image of Vanity or of Chauncey, both of which looked identical, save for the difference in size and disposition. These Mirror Images would litter the skies like satellites looking down on a lower class of being. "Ready for your close up, Mister Sir...?" Pride laughed haughtily, glaring down with all eyes condescending.

There were so many of these Mirror Images reflected and projected all across the field that Greed, who had actually already been using some 'Smoke and Mirrors' of his own, would appear in the reflections and project reflections of himself, as well, whilst also holding a wad of money that suddenly, with the clench of his fist and a ruffle like that of feathers, would spontaneously burst into the physical form of a hand mirror that mimicked the appearance of Pride. Greed would have just as many, if not more images of himself surrounding the area, all across the ground whilst Pride took the whole sky and covered him from above.

The Archnemesis, which was a special name given for one of the Mechanica that had crawled out of the shadows, would do as its master commanded and immediately begin to scour the area as a scout, looking for any signs of life or action.

Overhead, it could be seen that a great deal of eyes from the mirrors up above were looking down from the sky and scouting the ground the same way the Archnemesis was scouting the area. After realizing this, the Archnemesis would scurry back into the shadows and continue to scout unseen by the eyes of the one overhead.

"There," a voice called out from atop a high place, before the snap of fingers and the ruffling of paper, "There it is." Someone's hand outstretched above the high place and pointed to the doll trying to escape. "Go get it, Pride."

Overhead, the shadow of an enormous blimp-like ovular object would be seen hovering forward, with a distinguishing, haughty face at the head of it. The hovering object, which was similar to the one that scared off the scurrying rodents and cleared them out of the area, would orbit around the sky like a satellite, adjusting its angle to a degree of heightened perspective. Where this last creature running around the barren land tried to escape to, it would find completely illuminated by a bright light like that of a spotlight, with each of the shadows now altered to a different direction that no longer covered the initial area, something like a stage light shifting around to a better vantage point. "I see you, little bug~!" the voice of the head said in a cute, but exceedingly condescending manner.

The Archnemesis, which was one of the Mechanica that had been sent by and from the shadows of the Great Darkness would be exposed in the light, yet was nothing more than a simple Puppet that would, upon exposure, fall lifeless and without any form of intent. The Archnemesis sat there motionlessly.

"What?" The voice of the one overhead exclaimed, focusing all attention on the now lifeless puppet. "This has got to be a joke." The arms that were on either side of the giant shining oval would cross, and the face of the snoot would turn up and away from the ugly rag doll. "I'm not touching that putrid THING," Pride said, barely even looking at Greed now. "CHAUNCEY!!!!" he cried out, clapping his hands as if summoning a servant. "Pick up this trash THIS INSTANT." He clapped his hands twice. "Chop Chop!!" Feeling as if his time and his appearance were wasted and totally in vain, Vanity was in a terrible mood now. "You'll pay for this, Greed. I don't DO one-star appearances." Immediately, the titanic hand mirror floating overhead, known formally as 'Vanity,' the Sin Of Pride, would shrink down to a normal size and begin to hover away, arms crossed, eyes closed, chest poked out, nose turned up, lips pouched and head turned away from whatever ugliness Greed insisted he touch. "DON'T insult me again, Ugly One." Everything, to Pride, was ugly and inferior, except Pride, itself.

Greed, however, already having more than accounted for this, including Pride's childish and selfishly arrogant behavior, would use this to his advantage. "Hold on there, Light Show," he said with a smirk, literally objectifying the object of his goal fulfillment quite on purpose, "We're not quite done here, and I think you MIGHT want to check yourself in the mirror again." Greed, who was STILL sitting on his high place, overlooking the barren land as though it were a plantation, would kick his leg up over the other, bouncing it up and down slightly. "That is, if you can find it." The wicked grin of anticipation and knowing sprawled like that of a wide frog's mouth, and before he croaked a single thing else, he would wait for Pride to realize just what the words that came from his mouth meant.

That's when it hit him. "Chauncey?" The loyal servitude of Chauncey was unmatched. Something like how Greed could snap his fingers and make slaves do his bidding was nearly identical to what Vanity could do with Chauncey. Yet, his trusted servant was nowhere to be found. "CHAUNCEY!!!" He cried out again, turning around deftly with sharp eyes like that of a knife cutting up and down in search of the servant that hadn't yet executed Vanity's will exactly as he was commanded. "CHAUNCEY, BRING YOUR ASS HERE THIS INSTANT." Vanity searched high and low for his Mirror Image, and yet, to no avail. He did not see his own reflection, no matter how high up he floated into the air to get an overview of the land. "CHAUNCEY, YOU INSOLENT LAZY KNAVE, WHERE ARE YOU!?" The hand mirror man would flash all sorts of signals, waiting for the reflection to mirror him in return and signal that he was either okay or was on the way. When Vanity could not find his reflection, and it was clear that it was nowhere to be found in all the land, he became less angry and more panicked and distraught. "Chauncey?! POOPSIE, WHERE ARE YOU!?!?"

Greed grinned. "Rude awakening, yes? Well, if you were paying attention, you would have noticed that your precious mini-me is already broken out of your image and taken on someone else's." Greed pointed over yonder, back to where the two of them had come from, where Chauncey had been left to hold off Mister Sir. "Tragic," he said heartlessly, letting his pointing finger rest over the horizon right on where the bloody, broken, ugly mirror lay flat and destroyed, as if murdered, all over the pavement.

"CHAUNCEY BABY!!!!" Vanity cried, becoming more anxious and emotionally stirred now. The tension caused him to shudder, nearly cracking his mirror. "WHY DO BEAUTIFUL PEOPLE HAVE TO DIE SO UGLY!?!?" Vanity buried his face in his hands, nearly traumatized at the sight of such vivid ugliness in his beautiful eyes, tainting and staining them with the horrendous bloodied image. It was like looking at himself be ugly, which was the highest form of upset that Vanity could conceive. "TAKE IT AWAY! TAKE IT AWAY!!"

Now Greed, who had long since thought this out, looking nothing concerned, would speak gingerly to the nearly cracked face that hovered beside him. "There, there," he comforted, "These things can be replaced. You can get a newer, better Chauncey." His other hand, which had been hidden behind his back, would slowly creep to the light. "Why, what's this I have, behind my back?!" he said somewhat sarcastically, as if speaking to an unruly child. "Well, lookie here! It's another, more beautiful mirror!!" When he revealed it and placed it before Vanity's face, the more beautiful mirror, which had been forged to be in Vanity's image, just like Chauncey, only with a slightly better sheen and encrusted with more rare, glittering gems and jewels, he would wave it before Vanity something like a parent would a bottle before a baby.

Immediately, Vanity's face shot up from the palm of his hands with a snap, something like a demon, with a crack that sounded just as wicked. "Chauncey?!" he uttered in hysterical relief. "CHAUNCEY JR.!!!" He snatched the new mirror from Greed and immediately gazed deeply into it, looking at his own reflection. "Oh, Chauncey Jr., I'm EVER so pleased. I thought I'd never have my lovely, wonderful, beautiful, darling baby back in my hands." He kissed the mirror profusely.

Greed smirked.

Finally, the Archnemesis that had dropped down like a lifeless puppet would rise back up at the coming of the Great Darkness that rolled over the land, casting all into Night, no matter how bright, nor what time of day. The Archnemesis would immediately scurry into the Great Darkness as it passed over, covered completely by it and becoming hidden from the eyes of Greed and Pride overhead, of whom the Archnemesis had been spying on and listening to in order to gather information. It could no longer be traced once retreating into the Great Darkness.

You are covered and protected by the Great Darkness, and continue to look on from within it, never coming from out of it nor straying from it.

Mister Sir, who had been recounting the events of the past to You within the Great Darkness through a flashback, would suddenly step forward from the Great Darkness when he was finished explaining to You what happened before You got there. "Step Aside," he said to You, urging You not to interfere nor come out of the Great Darkness, "You're Playing With The Big Boys Now." The man of blazing fire, whose light, too, was shrouded under the cover of the Great Darkness, would suddenly illuminate the area that he stepped forth from, drawing all attention unto him, like a spotlight.

"GREED!!!!" He shouted up to the high place, completely ignoring Pride, "This Ends HERE!!!" Mister Sir, who had a PERSONAL vendetta against the cutthroat Greed, who attempted to pay off his execution, would glare at him with incandescent eyes, no longer sealed nor bound shut, but made completely of burning fire, much like roughly 80% of his body. "You Can't Run Away This Time, Cowardly Frog." Just the sight of Greed and the knowing that he already paid for something up his sleeve irritated Mister Sir. What irritated him more was knowing that Greed probably would not give a damn about anything as long as his resources were intact, and would continue to act just as pompous as Pride would be. The burning one stood front and center in the darkness of the desolate land, being the only kindled illumination there was, specifically to get Greed's attention from his high place. "Step Down."

"To your level?" Greed laughed arrogantly, nearly throwing his head back in contempt, "I think not, my boy." He shook his head, waving his hand simultaneously to casually away both Mister Sir and the thought of descent. "No, I think you're just fine where you are and I, too, where I am. The ground level suits you, don't you think?" He turned his head smugly toward the Mirror, as if he were speaking to Vanity, though with his words completely directed toward Mister Sir. "Pride?" He grinned, casting the attention to Vanity and his new, better mirror issued by Greed, himself.

Vanity was barely coherent. He needed to restore his own image in himself before he could even think to look at anything else. "Yeah, sure, whatever." He flipped his hair, puckering his lips and making kissy faces at the more beautiful, more glossy mirror that was before his dazzling, sparkling eyes. "Chauncey Jr. says 'Whatever,' too." Completely dismissed.

Greed lowered his head, chuckling. "Boy," he spoke to Pride, leaving a long, dramatic pause in between before he continued, "How about I ask you AGAIN what your thoughts are on this matter?" Suddenly, Greed's eyes flashed from under the darkness of his shadowed face, and also the eyes of Chauncey Jr. would gleam in a similar manner, locking directly with the eyes of Vanity. The both of them spoke simultaneously, "What Do You Think Of Our Predicament?"

Immediately, Pride's eyes were lost in the mirror and whatever form of consciousness he had for himself was sucked out and into the new mirror, leaving Vanity as nothing more than a mere object for Greed's

Possession. "It is as you say," Pride spoke, both through Chauncey Jr. and Vanity, monotonously and soullessly, something like a robotic zombie. "Whatever you wish to do shall be done." It was clear that Vanity was no more, and was simply a tool for Greed, being consumed and Possessed by the material possession that was given to him by Greed. Now, Pride and Greed were one, and Pride fell under Greed's power, making him nothing more than an extension of Greed, itself, and no longer his own person.

"Thaaat's better," Greed would say nonchalantly, turning his head back to Mister Sir. "You see? All in favor! Majority rule." Greed kicked his other leg over the first, casually switching between them as he sat right in his place, not having moved except for that. He laughed to himself; all three of them.

Mister Sir grit his teeth. Just the look on Greed's face was enough to see that he wasn't clear that he'd lost, and he was going to make this difficult, sitting on all of the assets like the dirty frog he was. Mister Sir, knowing what his first thought was, would begin to speak, as if to a group, "Whomever At The Top That Is Telling Everyone To Do These Sickening Things Is Actually Just Covering Up Their Own Sickening Desires And Feigning It As Tests." To whom he was speaking to seemed unclear, since there was nothing about but the Great Darkness, Greed and Pride. Yet, he continued on, as though he spoke to a large group. "Whomever Is LISTENING To This Person Is FAILING The Test, Because You're Supposed To Actually Say 'This Is A Sin And I'm Not Supposed To Do It, Even If I Was Told.'" Mister Sir looked around, his eyes able to see clearly through the Great Darkness, and all across the land covered upon it. "He's Testing YOU."

Though Mister Sir's fury was getting the better of him, because he knew that with Greed, he was at a slight disadvantage, he could somehow manage to contain it just enough to keep his wits about him, and a composure that would normally already have the area clad in blood red destruction. "He Just Has Obedient Slave Idiots That Will Do Anything He Wants To Without Thinking That They Might Be Condemned For His Own Insidious Desires. *sigh*" Mister Sir shook his head, clenching his fists tightly, the flames about his body condensing to what looked like solidified magma as he contained his rage. "I Cannot Stand These People." Clearly, Pride, rather, Vanity, was one of them, and it was through the Material Possession. That was Greed's power, which was something completely hidden because it seemed so very commonplace and simple that none else were able to see it as a true skill or ability, but Greed was more a master of Possession than even Envy. "And Then It's SO BAD, They Teach The People Down The Business Line 'Obey What I Say, Even If It's A Sin, Or You're Fired.'" Just the thought process of Greed was getting on his nerves, fueling the contained flames within his now magmatic body. "Why Are They All So Weak?"

Suddenly Greed laughed out loudly, unable to contain his own amusement this time around. "Boyo, who are you talking to? Certainly not ME, correct?" Greed was more than aware that there were more people around; some that were his and some that were not. All were covered by the darkness, yes, but whomever Mister Sir was speaking to, certainly, none that were under Greed were listening. "I guess you already realized that you're surrounded by my slaves, hm? There are a WHOLE HEAPING HELPING of whipping boys from the Highest Place to the Lowest Place." Greed snapped his fingers and began to point his finger down at Mister Sir purposefully condescendingly, whilst Pride would, as if with a mental link, drift to Greed's face with a cigar to place gently betwixt his teeth, lighting it deftly. "Slaves; 20 Dollars to the first person that takes care of my garbage." Greed made SURE to collect the lowliest ones and send them out first, because he could pay them the least to do the most work, AND they were completely disposable and unimportant. "You can go talk to some people in their Employment Offices and ask them, 'Are You A Whipping Boy?' and I will pay them to tell you 'Yes, Sir! Absolutely, Sir!'" He took a single, long, enjoyable puff of his cigar as Greed relaxed, and each of his Material Possessions suddenly sprouted up from the darkness; those first ones being 'Slaves' that he literally owned as Material Possessions. They flooded the area from out of the darkness, wearing their dainty little suits and ties that Greed fixed them up in, in his image.

Because they were all attached to Greed through the Material Possessions, when he ordered them, it was as if they were an extension of himself, and they were no longer their own. Their minds, bodies AND souls were all owned by the Greed Demon, Money, and each of the lowly Slaves looked to be something like pale faced zombies, groaning and moaning about the work of the day, as per usual. A sound that Greed had learned to become accustomed, and relish in, at the expense of his expenses. Without even an extra word, all those who were bought for about 20 dollars per hour would legitimately LEAP at the chance to strike down Mister Sir with whatever they had at their disposal, something like feral wild dogs. Greed surrounded Mister Sir in no time flat, and the wild animals that were his 'fitted pups' would wildly swing their fists and claws about, throwing the most basic punches and kicks that their basic minds could comprehend. They were made the most basic on purpose and, with their numbers alone, would surely wear down Mister Sir before he could even get a whiff of the Big Boys.

Greed smiled all the way, watching carefully as his slave minions did the Head's bidding. He beckoned someone from the darkness in a high place nearest to him and began to whisper, but to whom and what was uncertain.

You, who are still surprisingly covered by the Great Darkness and have not been left nor exposed, look on at the horrible display by these hired hands, heeding the words of the burning one that stands on your behalf, knowing that he is speaking to You. You see each of the mindless ones literally be treated as though they are slaves by this strange person named 'Greed' that You'd seen glimpses of all up the mountain, who had been trying desperately to purchase You both in the beginning and quite possibly was fighting for Your ownership even now. You are stunned by these things, and partially ashamed, also wanting to jump at the offer, knowing that, from what You've been told, that sort of payment can help sustain Your entire life. The man was just giving away positions and it seemed like the well-paying job was only to do exactly as the man said. It didn't seem very difficult, either, and You contemplate whether or not You should take up the offer that was extended.

However, because You still have a conscious mind and personal feelings of Your own, because these things still belong to You and have not been purchased, You think very long and hard about selling Yourself like a prostitute just to get some money. You also make note of the man, Mister Sir, who is pleading Your case and fighting for You and hold that into consideration. You wait, this time, to see what will become of this, and are ready to go to whomever is in favor. Either option seems like something You will settle with; either being completely free or to be taken care of for the rest of Your days with a decent pay doing whatever work is prepared for You. As long as You are alive, this is all You care about, whether or not the quality of life factors right now.

Mister Sir, whose body continued to burn brighter, something like the sun, compress further down as the insolent zombie slaves hopped toward him without thinking, would utter under his breath in disgust at their idiocy, "This Is Why I Don't Follow You All Into The Sin, Because I AM Aware That It Poisons You For Having To Listen To Them." Mister Sir dealt with ALL of the Sins rather personally for QUITE a long time now; longer than perhaps many of them even truly understood 'life' to be in length, since they were probably only aware of their own measly feeble human lifetimes. He once commanded them all, but now, as all of them were turning against him, and he against they, he was only here to destroy them absolutely with the Holy Wrath of God. "Stop Trying To Teach People With The 'Devil Test.' CLEARLY They're FAILING And It's Because They Don't Need To Be TESTED On Things They DON'T KNOW." The mindless ones would do nothing but hurl themselves into the lake of fire, which was actually what Mister Sir's body resembled now, and drew power from as they still stood nearby. The moment the basic slaves even tried to touch him, they would be burnt to cinders and scattered in the wind as ashes, and Mister Sir would not even bat an eye at them nor look any of the worker drones in the face.

He started to walk, rather straightforward and calmly, toward the high place that Greed had placed himself, speaking out to whomever could hear that was not simply hurling themselves mindlessly into his body, which was clearly on fire before they even thought to touch him, if they even thought at all. "Not EVERY Job Opportunity Is Good For You JUST Because It's AVAILABLE. It's Actually 'New Age Slavery.'" Clearly, they had to know this, since Greed just called them blatantly by the name of 'Slave,' which was nothing but the title of a Material Possession. As long as they were Material Possessions that could be owned by Greed, then they were his Slaves, and nothing more than soulless, hollowed out objects that worked for him as a hive mind. They were already gone, and weren't coming back.

Still, Mister Sir continued to speak out, for he knew that the words of his mouth were reaching the ones that he was protecting, because he could sense their vibrations with his heat sensing, which caused distortions in the air that could be read just like heat-vision goggles or radar, "If You Do Not Eat From Off The Ground, Or Pick Up Filth Or Waste From Off The Ground And Eat It Or Wear It, Then Do Not Take The Poisoned Handouts Just Because They Are Available. It's STILL Poison, And They Do Look Down On You When You Take The Bait," he said to the ones that had doubt in them, of which he could feel as he walked up the side of the mountain, "They Will Hold Out Their Hand And See If You're Intelligent Enough Or Depraved Enough To Take What They Offer; ESPECIALLY IF IT'S SHIT." He was aware that before, the ignorant and the blind could not tell the difference between the slops of the higher orders and powers, but now that they would see the light of Mister Sir and hear the veracity of his wrathful voice, hopefully now the distinction between the two was more clear to the ones who actually had a mind to tell their 'rewards' apart.

"Part Of The Reason Why This Generation Is Like That Is Because Your PARENTS Are Like That, And Have Already Been Enslaved To Think That's What You NEED To Do To Get By." Certainly, some of the ones that were captured by the Sins earlier on, who had died, were among the ranks of SIN, itself, now, and were being used as part of the large body of SIN, itself; likely why the pale-faced ones were zombie-like in appearance. Perhaps, if the survivors looked closely, they could see their own kin and brethren that they'd lost walking among the dead, dressed up nice and fine so that no one would know; something like a carcass at a funeral. "So What THEY do Is, Because THEY Were

Poisoned, But THOUGHT It Was Good Food, And Ate It All Up Out Of The Palm Of Someone's Hand Like A Filthy Animal, Teach Their Children To Be The Same."

Mister Sir could see that there were other, less basic minions of Greed in the darkness, because he noticed how they were moving with his sensors. Yet, because they were likely cold and dead vessels without heat or souls, and would be cold in their demeanor and their interaction, he was not able to see they, themselves, but only their motions, which made ripples in the atmosphere that he could still pick up on. "Now Look What You Have. Another Generation Forced Into 'Lust' And 'Slavery' Because Of Ignorant Parents Taking Every Opportunity Available For Sinful Reasons Like 'Trying To Be Better Than Someone' Or "Trying To Take Advantage Of Others To Get Ahead In Life." Mister sir spit on the ground as he neared Greed, narrowing his blazing eyes, which grew in burning intensity the more he felt the wrath of his heart flaring up.

"Are you QUITE finished?" Greed asked Mister Sir with a yawn, "You DO drag on and on, you know. Certainly, none of them have a mind enough to actually REALLY listen nor comprehend these words you speak." That much, Greed was actually willing to bet on. They were a slow, dim-witted, lustful people that jumped out at their desires as soon as they were presented. "In fact, I think you MIGHT want to pay closer attention to your audience. Dumb it down a bit." He waved a bit of paper in the air and let it gently pass on the wind. It was a full, crisp 100 dollar bill, which would lightly breeze by and off into the darkness. Greed did not seem at all concerned with those that he lost. "Guess you can say those people are FIRED, yes? Bahahaha!" He took another puff, letting the smoke of his choice tobacco fill the atmosphere in a deep haze to cover himself in. He beckoned Pride closer with a finger, whispering something into his ear, before casting his Possessed servant off into the shadows as well. Greed would have his Slaves follow Mister Sir up the mountain, instructing them this time not to touch him, but to block the way to get up or go down. There were so many of them, the pathway was completely filled. He did not seem at all concerned with Mister Sir stepping up to the high place, either, and instead, continued to casually smoke, looking on over the area like it were a stage set for his will and way to be played out over the land.

Suddenly, down below, You are approached by a strange figure that you had not seen before, but that looks something like You and Your people. He greets you with a smile and says to You, "Hello! My name is Jack, and I've been looking for some help with a certain project I've been doing. I can't find anyone around and will gladly finance anyone who is of able body. No other requirements or skills necessary." He was finely dressed and seemed to be quite the distinguished person in personality; something like someone with charm and etiquette. It was clear that he was coming to you very politely, with no form of harm nor malicious intent. "Please, I need your help. You won't leave me helpless, will you? No one has come to help me yet and I fear that this particular job will not get accomplished if someone doesn't come quickly!" He urges You to act with haste, with his own expenses on the line. "Won't you please?" he asks kindly once more, hoping to grab someone's ear that was near, not unlike a homeless person on the subway or on the street. "I'm sure you know the struggle very well, and wouldn't dare leave someone else in a predicament something like your own, would you?"

'Archnemesis :: Reversal'

The Great Darkness commanded the 'Archnemesis' that had retreated into it to suddenly emerge again to meet, face to face, with the one that was named 'Jack.' The Archnemesis, which was something like a puppet with a lower torso that could not be seen, completely hidden by and in sync with the Great Darkness itself, would immediately confront Jack with a smile. "I Am Archnemesis. I Will Assist You," were the only words that were spoken. The look on the face of the Archnemesis was completely blank and hollow, with a stale smile and wide, gaping holes for eyes. "Step Out Of The Darkness. I Will Follow You." Nothing else was stated.

"I Wouldn't Be Laughing If I Were You," Mister Sir said, completely unsmiling. "You're Fired." He stood there before Greed and did not say nor do anything else, but fire completely overtook his body. He was ROYALLY pissed; and had EVERY last right to it. The Lake Of Fire behind them bubbled and gurgled and rumbled, something as it had done in the days of yore when others attempted to walk up this mountain, and it got angry at them. "Envy."

Greed, sitting on his throne, would remain in silence, with his mouth suddenly agape and his Cuban cigar falling out of his mouth. He felt that there was a shift in the powers, and knew this to be so before anyone else that was below him did. At that moment, the very second his cigar hit the ground, his eyes narrowed and glowed with a light something like that of pure and utter hatred, yet with greater calculations going on in the background.

Still, he lowered his head and his eyes went dark, once again covered by the shadow of his hair. Soon after, he began to laugh. "Hahaha..." He waggled his finger at Mister Sir, shaking his head. "Oh, no no no, son. You can't fire ME. I still RUN the show!" A new cigar found its way to his mouth by hand of Pride, who was still quite under Greed's control. "If you've learned ANYTHING, or, KNOW anything about me after all the time we've worked together, you should KNOW that I'm not gonna just let go that easily. No, I've got all types of plans that I had in store for you." Greed also knew how the curse of Envy worked and wouldn't fall prey to it so easily. "Seems like YOU are the one envious of ME. What do I have to envy of you, eh? There is nothing I cannot get my hands on!" And so, Greed stuck out his Tongue to have his way. "JACK!" he called out, beckoning someone from the shadows "Did you get my money?"

When the one that Greed had spoken to, Jack, did not bring back the group, but instead an envoy named 'Archnemesis,' who was led up to where Greed was, he would say "You're fired," and send Jack on his way. Greed stuck out his Tongue again and Jack 2 would appear from the shadows, snatched out by his collar. "Jack 2, entertain our guests here." No more was said. Yet, Greed would then open his mouth to speak again, but this time to beckon another person from the shadows. "Ace," he cried, profusely beckoning with a finger, "Deal with the slaves. I'm about to go away on business." Greed snapped his fingers and suddenly more of his slaves would appear from the darkness and carry him further up the mountain. In his wake, Pride would stand before them all, with many Mirror Images and Reflections being cast out all about the High Place and the lower levels, seeming to be nothing but the copies of Greed as he went away.

The Archnemesis that was before Jack 2 was already calculating the next steps on behalf of its master, Mechanica. The Archnemesis, which was one of the Mechanica's puppets, specifically a 'Finger Puppet,' would start to run toward the slaves of Greed and snatch them up in their ignorance. "Slaves," the Archnemesis cried out to the masses that had blocked off the path, "You've been duped. You are not getting paid enough to risk your entire lives. In fact, are any of you getting paid enough to live?" The Finger Puppet snickered at them, yet the eyes of the doll face atop what looked like the body of a hand-like spider would remain wide and gaping. "The only way to overthrow your Slave Master is to waste up all of his resources. Use more than what he is giving, and he will start paying out of pocket instead of you paying with your lives." Because they were zombies and easily swayed, if they heard something that sounded more reasonable than whatever their command was or the offer that was given to them was, then they would, without a doubt, follow it like sheep.

Mister Sir was also calculating the next steps, since there was extra work to be done simply because there were so many extra beings involved that Greed was clinging to. Fortunately, all it took was to cut off the Tongue and the grip of those grubby fingers and the people could be salvaged, at least to some degree.

Figuring that the Jack would go off and deal with the Mechanica, Mister Sir would stand before the Ace that was left in Greed's stead, not letting him follow behind the Archnemesis. "You're Not Being Paid Enough, Either, You Know," he had to mention to the Ace. "I Doubt That You Can Fix The Damages That Are About To Fall Upon You." Mister Sir lifted his hand up to the rumbling volcanous Lake of Fire over yonder, clear in vision of everyone, and it would synchronize to the radiation of the heat from his own body, which was one with the Lake of Fire from a distance. "Watch." He lifted a single finger, and all hell broke loose. The fire pit erupted, and burst into the sky, blowing away all the things that were in the cover of the darkness, save for the ones that were under the protection of Tabitha. The buildings of Greed and all those foundations were revealed on the spot and many were struck down with fire the size of giant hailstones, and burning sulfur would crash down like a bomber plane dropping bombs down all across the land. The most important buildings that belonged to Greed would be struck down immediately, destroyed beyond repair, with whomever inside as an example. The rest would be given time to evacuate, but the fire continued to rain down from the sky. All the while, Mister Sir stared at the Ace with a blazing face of fire, still completely unsmiling.

You watch as all of these things happen and are completely terrified. Many things that You knew from Your past are beginning to finally make sense, and You are seeing them play out first hand; front row. All of You nearly shit Your pants, but are thankful for the one that went ahead of You instead of allowing You to be snagged by that 'Jack,' who was acting as though he were just a normal helpless person seeking hired help. You look up at all the workers that are destroyed by buildings that randomly were revealed to You from the cover of the darkness; things that hadn't been there before in the desolate land, but were uncovered to You because the darkness that covered them was illuminated by the splendor of Mister Sir and the light of the raging Lake of Fire upon the mountain. You were not paying attention before, and You were blind, but it was clear that these buildings had already been established and the people that were rushing out were already working, just like the ones that came out to attack Mister Sir before. You still decide not to move, nor to reveal Yourselves, but are patient this time, in order to avoid being struck down by this sudden rain of fire. Yet, You are still completely terrified, knowing that even a single wrong step will strike You down. You hope it all ends soon. You pray to God, this time.

Jack 2 immediately intervened, seeing that the Archnemesis was trying to cater to the ignorance of the zombie slaves. Though Jack 2 would have preferred to attack Mister Sir and team up with the Ace, it was of higher priority to Jack 2 to go and make sure that the people were not snatched from the grip of Greed, his master. "Wait! Don't listen to this jobless creature with no money! Look! Don't you see how deformed it is? This thing is not here to help you! Look at me! You can be like me." He presented himself in finely dressed clothes and nice, sharp, pristine cloth. Many of this man's image would appear all around them, flaunting the nice materials that were all in his possession, given to him by his master to use. "Don't you want this... Brand new car?!" A King came up from out of nowhere in a swanky, spanky new car. "Or, maybe, you want the... Latest designer clothes! 50% off, while supplies last!!" Then, a Queen walked out of the car, dressed in better clothes than even the Jack, and also flaunting some of her body so that they wouldn't be able to take their eyes off of her. Many of the images of Vanity would project her all around, so that anywhere they looked, they would see nothing but this beautiful woman sporting the image that each of them wanted.

"That's right," the Queen said, knowing what to do with the spotlight once she had it, "You can be sexy, like me, for as little as $9.99 a month." She flipped her hair, letting everyone see, with dazzling lights and all sorts of effects brought on by Vanity in the background to boost her Image. "Stay tuned, and we'll even throw in... A promotion! From Slave to Servant! Better pay, with better benefits. Any of the things that happen to you because of your work; bad teeth, stress, tiredness, overworking... All of it will be taken care of in your plan! We'll give you dental!" She smiled pretty, letting the glamour of her face shine through each of the mirrors that Pride placed all over the land.

This was all halted, however, by all the raging destruction that happened to one of the important buildings that Greed was using to cycle revenue. In fact, the cycle of revenue could not happen without this building, and the Ace was the one that all of this fell on. He stared at Mister Sir, terrified at how much of Greed's assets he would have to use to repay. "Okay, fine, fine, whatever," he said, breaking at the knowledge itself of how much was about to come out of pocket, "Just... Don't destroy another building. Please. What do you want?" Seemed as though Ace was ready to make a deal under the table, before Greed got word of any of this.

"Look," The Finger Puppet said, pointing off to the destroyed major corporation, "Now what will you do? You think that guy is going to pay for your shelter and your food and your water? He was trying to take those things away from you by forcing you to work long hours, anyway.

If he REALLY cares about you, he AND all his other slaves, then he would pay for your housing and your food and your drink, instead of giving you the bare minimum. He's paying you to distract you from what it is that he could be using the money for to sustain your lives." The Archnemesis would look over to Jack 2, and to Queen and to King, then say, "Where and how much money went into this entire performance, and, can you pull off several more after losing such a large part of your own franchise that produces those things for you?" If they had invested in something else, then they would not have lost out. "Looks like you all, Jack, Queen and King are going to be just as homeless, unfortunate and in the dirt as all of these people here standing around watching." They were having a fight with themselves, at this point. "When he can't pay you because he has to rebuild what makes his money, what do you think he'll do to you? Fire you. Because he can't pay for you anymore." The Archnemesis would stand there and await the response of all the, basically orphaned people. "Where is your Greed now?"

"Join Us," were the first words that Mister Sir spoke to the Ace, who had authority over everyone under him in place of Greed, as if he were Greed, himself. "Take All The Slaves And Minions You Have And Join Us, And We Will Take Care Of You. We Have A Place Already Prepared For Those Who Will Be Orphaned, And It's With The Ones That We've Been Leading To A Better Place Already. Then, When We Get To Greed, We Can Show Him Who Is Boss." Mister Sir would extend a handout to Ace, asking, still unsmiling, "Do We Have A Deal?"

The Ace, who was the Ace for a reason, was more than capable of making decisions on his own and was more than wise enough to even rival his master, even though he worked for him. Thinking it over rather carefully, and knowing that this Mister Sir would not joke about whatever he had under his belt, and also comparing and contrasting the pros and cons of continuing to work for Greed after his business failed would rest in the Ace's mind for only a moment before he thrust his hand forward with a binding swiftness and said, "Deal." Still being greedy, himself, he at least knew that whomever was going to take better care of him was the one to be around, and, knowing Greed personally, with no assets, Ace would not be taken care of. He had seen what was done to the underlings and knew that if his own place fell, then Ace would not be anything but one of those mindless zombies blocking the path, ignorant to what it is that was going on over their heads.

"Listen up," Ace said to the King, Queen and Jack 2, "We're under new management. Anyone in the Order of Operations will fall into their ranks and anyone that is a slave will go with the group that is being led. This man is a better businessman than the one we serve. Let's take what we can get and get out of here before Greed catches wind of his financial debacle." Certainly, with the same cutthroat haste that Greed would fire off the first Jack, which everyone witnessed, would be the same swiftness that the Ace would take his leave. "No need for a 2 week's notice. That's giving him too much time to set up, and not giving me enough time, myself. If he can't take making some sacrifices for me, then why should I sacrifice even an extra day?" Ace chuckled, calling his people and clearing the way. "Let's blow this popsicle stand." Thus, the whole group, an army of workers would fall under the ranks of Mister Sir, Mechanica and the Rephaim in the shadows.

Finally, Mister Sir smiled that one genuine 'Happy' smile, instead of a smug grin or a haughty smirk. "Excellent," he muttered, something like an elderly businessman whose plans were coming together, shaking the Ace's hand firmly. "Nice Doing Business With You." Immediately, the Ace's body would become inflamed, but not with a fire that harmed him. Instead, the fire covered his body in a similar fashion as it did Mister Sir, and served as protection, like burning armor, which showed that he and Mister Sir were joined in a covenant. The Lake of Fire would not harm him, nor any of the people that would also forge a deal with Mister Sir through the covenant. "If This Deal Is Broken," He'd say before releasing the Ace's hand, "The Fire Will Burn Up Your Entire Body And You Will Be No More." This was the only restriction, but it did mean absolute 100% certain death. "You Will Be Called Seraphim; Angels Among Men. And The Ones That Burn For You, In All Their Heart And Desire, Shall Be Your 'Harab Serapel;' Burning Ravens Of Destruction That Can Do As I Have Done To A Limited Degree, And Grant You The Power To Do The Same Through Them." The flames would rain down and continue to destroy any and everyone that did not make the deal or stick to it, whilst all else would fall in line. "Let's Move," Mister Sir said without hesitation, as to not let Greed get too far ahead of them. He beckoned the entire group, including the Rephaim in the darkness, and begin to explain to them what had already occurred about Envy, and how the curse of Envy transferred through transitive property.

The Archnemesis, that Finger Puppet, whose purpose was specifically to snatch people up and utilize them for a greater purpose, would immediately collect the Ace, the King, the Queen and the Jack and have them round up the rest of the ranks. They ones who understood Ordered Operations would be part of the large body of Mechanica, as units to be used in the grand scheme, whilst the lesser ones that had no real role except keeping things operational, the Slaves, Servants, Minions, Underlings and all else they were known as, would be grouped with the Rephaim, replacing the ones that had been lost and allowing the group to become larger. The units of Mechanica would then sink into the Great Darkness and begin to guide all the Rephaim, who were like sheep, in an orderly fashion behind Mister Sir, watching all the destruction along the way from still within the Great Darkness that continued to cover them all the way through. They would be led up the mountain into the next area.

You are overjoyed to have overcome such a great obstacle such as Greed, which seemed to be an even greater roadblock than any of You alone could have managed, even if You wanted to. Knowing this terrifies You, but it also humbles You to the ones that actually took care of it and You. You begin to tell the ones that have joined Your ranks all about what happened to You down below, what is going on now, and also Your personal stories about Your own sins in order to help them be up to speed and also to assist with them dealing with theirs. You warn them about exiting the Great Darkness and that the cover it provides keeps You from being destroyed by whatever other sins seem to be lurking about. Though, after recounting how many Sins you have been through, and how terrible they were, You then begin to worry about the upcoming sins you have not yet dealt with, Envy and Wrath, and wonder just how much worse those could be than Greed, or even the ones that You had endured before that almost killed You. You are cautious and wary, but You are more confident in your confidants now, and are faithful that You will come out alive as long as You heed their instruction and direction and remain humble. You press on with the ones that know Ordered Operations guiding you in an orderly fashion, behind Mister Sir, and You go further up the mountain into the next location, watching the destruction as You go along in wonder, awe, terror, splendor and many other emotions that You are feeling at the time.

CHAPTER 6

ENVY

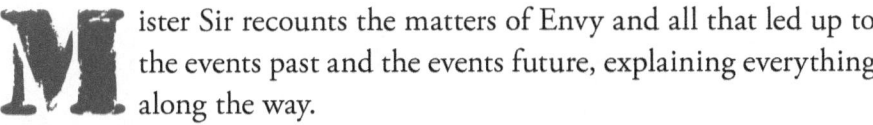 **M**ister Sir recounts the matters of Envy and all that led up to the events past and the events future, explaining everything along the way.

Deadly Sin; Envy

Envy can be directly related to the Ten Commandments, specifically, "Neither shall you desire... anything that belongs to your neighbor."

Circle of Hell: 6 (Heresy)

Instead of doing what you are supposed to, you will become envious of someone else and end up doing something that you should not in order to get ahead or get what you want without following the proper protocols.

Heresy is any provocative belief or theory that is strongly at variance with established beliefs or customs. A heretic is a proponent of such claims or beliefs.[1] Heresy is distinct from both apostasy, which is the explicit renunciation of one's religion, principles or cause,[2] and blasphemy, which is an impious utterance or action concerning God or sacred things.

Why It Is Deadly; Dante defined this as "a desire to deprive other men of theirs".

Characteristics: Envy (Latin, invidia), like greed and lust, is characterized by an insatiable desire. Envy is similar to jealousy in that they both feel discontent towards someone's traits, status, abilities, or rewards. The difference is the envious also desire the entity and covet it. Aquinas described envy as "sorrow for another's good"

Chosen Personification; A large, deprived figure with eyes sewn shut and a mouth sewn shut, but long, sharp claws, slender legs and a very sleek, thin form with a crown of spikes upon the head. Skin is malnourished, as is the body, but it is tall and overbearing, even in slenderness, like a tree.

Consequences For Application; Condemned to eternity in flaming tombs. In Dante's Purgatory, the punishment for the envious is to have their eyes sewn shut with wire because they have gained sinful pleasure from seeing others brought low.

First Hierarchy
Demon Lord: Leviathan
Status: Fallen Seraphim Prince

Leviathan was also a prince of the Seraphim who tempts people to give into heresy and is opposed by St. Peter.

Those that chose to follow Mister Sir would appear with him where he had appeared, farther up the mountain than anyone. They would continue to follow Mister Sir and his direct orders, since they were afraid of being lost or dying. I watched as everyone waited patiently and obediently, terrified for their lives and trembling. They did not know what was going to happen or what they were going to go through and see, but I knew that it would not be pretty. It was best to stick with Mister Sir very closely.

Mister Sir stood at the West Gate of Mt. Mortis, nearly fully up the mountain. With his own small group of people that were at least wise enough to follow him, he would turn to them and scan them, looking upon their faces. The Fear was in them, which was more than good. Now it was time to show them why Sin was wrong.

"You," Mister Sir called out to the First Person, "Get over here."

I, the First Person, would approach Mister Sir when called, trembling just like my fellow Man. "Y-yes?" I said, wondering what he could want with someone like Me.

The man of black shades and black coat would look at the First Person with a cold and dark face, saying relatively swiftly, "You have privilege. You have power. You have authority. You are my favorite. You are better than the rest in some way, shape or form." Mister Sir would turn to the rest of the people and say, "Do you see this Person? They are above you. I have claimed this, and this will be so. They are greater than you and will receive better treatment than you." After that, Mister Sir would look back to the First Person and send him back into the crowd. "That is all." He turned away from the group and started to walk up the mountain again, wasting no more breath on the sinners than necessary. They didn't deserve anything except what they were given, and probably much less than even that. That is, in Mister Sir's mind.

Suddenly, Envy broke out in the Crowd, and some would become The Envious, enslaved to Envy.

"I WANT THAT," Envy cried out in the crowd in the minds of the masses, to anyone who would want the recognition of the First Person. Envy already had enough people hating the First Person as it was. It looked down on them with wicked eyes and mouth sewn shut, as if it couldn't express its true want, but its eyes bore open at a target of interest. "GIVE IT TO ME!!! GET IT FOR ME!!! GO TAKE IT FROM HIM!!!" The part of the crowd owned and enslaved by Envy would suddenly selfishly conspire against the person with privilege, each of them seeking to take whatever it is that he or she wanted for themselves. Envy had already taken the nearest few people as soon as they saw the First Person get called out publicly. They Envied that he was getting attention. Praise. Recognition. Envy wanted it, as well. Though no one knew the other had Envy, all still harbored Envy, and it was left in the dark among the people.

A Lawless bunch came about, onlooking from the distance.

Immediately, Envy, which had chosen its hosts for the Envious Spirits that were trapped inside of it by Envy, itself, would gaze into the eyes of everyone that was looking down at the one that was raised up out of everyone by Mister Sir. Envy gazed into their eyes to see where they were looking, and where they looked immediately afterward. Each of the ones who were possessed would suddenly narrow their eyes, something similar to the giant overbearing presence itself glaring down at them. They belonged to Envy now, and they were part of Envy, but only Envy, itself, had their heads. Their minds belonged to Envy, even if each of the group was to themselves.

"Give him a present for being a good boy," Envy said, in respect to the one that was lifted up over all the rest. "I only need you to stand there and look pretty. Watch what happens next." Envy would wait patiently as its spirit assimilated with the one that was the Envy of everyone, and eventually, the Envy of everyone would be directed toward something other than Envy, itself. It was another vessel. Once all of the vessels were grabbed, then the one that was used could be discarded for all the others.

The one that was raised up would curl into a fetal position, knowing that everyone Envied him, and retreated into himself. However, as this happened, just as there were internal mental calculations going on about how to take his light, there were also things going on in his head about how to take the people that were trying to take it from him. He would sit there and plot, whilst everyone else plotted, as well. Yet, each of them plotted different things, many of them had the same target. All except the Envy, itself.

Immediately, when Envy had its mass of The Envious, it would begin to command them directly into their minds. The large tendrils that sprouted from the center of the crown stretched out over the land like a great and dark hand, each finger extending outward like the slender legs of a Daddy Long-Legs spider. Just then, all of the Envious would be given higher priority than all the others that were unconsciously aware of the demon that was over them; Envy, itself.

"Envy Is A Mental Demon." The large idol at the top of the hill towering over everyone else and looking down on them with glowering eyes spake, "It's Also A Self-Inflicted Demon. This Means, That It's Only In Your Head And It's Only Working With The Ones Whose Minds It Can Manipulate, Because The Demon Itself Is Its Own Thing Independent From The Mind Of The One It Gets Into, So That IT Can Initiate The 'Control Issue.'" There should have been no questioning Envy at this point, and each of them would be under the control of the Master Of Envy. "It Makes You Believe You Have No Control So It Can Control You Through Whatever You Feel You Are Losing Control To."

Then, Envy would speak to each of the afflicted in their independence, knowing already in advance that they had their own goals to get accomplished. Well, so did the Master Of Envy. This is why these people were being manipulated, and for solely the purpose of communicating a message. "It Can ONLY Effect The Single Solitary Person That Feels It At A Time, But Because EVERYONE Can Feel It Simultaneously, That's How It Works As A Group. Hidden, Isolated, But All In The Same Area Of Influence." Thus, the Envious Masses, which now had the souls of the Envious within them. The one that was raised up, of whom the others were Envious, were just the right mass of vessels to harbor the greater Envy. They were only needed to be moved for a greater goal, which is why they were being moved involuntarily out of their places haphazardly by a ruling official. To illustrate a point.

"You REALLY Don't Know What Envy Is Like. But You'll Learn Why It Wants You To Remain Lesser." The mad doll's eyes gleamed, the stitching nearly coming undone as they suddenly strained themselves to even open to a sliver, "Forever." They sealed themselves shut once again, and the souls, which poured out from the crown of Envy would become powerful thorns in the minds of all the afflicted, to show that they were afflicted with something that something else was controlling without any of them knowing.

"Puppet King," Which was the name of the doll that the Master Of Envy owned and had raised up as this person through the demon possession, itself. "Go Get Them." Immediately, the Master Of Envy would drop Puppet King, which was also Envy, down into the ground to go meet with the lesser Envies. The Master Of Envy would move its hand over the land, raising it up in a militant manner, yet also in a way that was clearly and obviously maneuvering and influencing them.

The fine threads of Puppet King's strings would wrap around each of the lesser Envies and have them begin to go to work for the greater Envy, which would eventually come back together as a collective goal manipulated from afar, yet still get everything accomplished for the intended target and the Master Of Envy simultaneously. Puppet King, who was raised up over the lesser Envies, would now have its own Puppets, which would now mobilize immediately down the mountain in order to go collect things to get the goal accomplished.

Meanwhile, after the peons were sent off to their doom, Envy would wait patiently at the top of the mountain.

Sooner or later, after Envy, the Master, realized that Mister Sir had escaped somewhere and left both the Master Of Envy and the Puppet King that the Master Of Envy had raised up to go further up the mountain. "... You thought you could get to the top before me? I've been here longer than you, SIR." Immediately, in a wild frenzy, Envy would draw forth all of the souls of the Envious that were slain at the foot of the mountain trying to capture the Lustful that were at the bottom and immediately start walking toward Mister Sir, following behind him and taking all the souls with it. However, the ones that were lingering at the mountain's side, which hadn't been eaten, would remain.

"Puppet King," the Master Of Envy commanded, "Stay here and watch out. Make sure nothing else comes up the mountain, but don't go back down to where Gluttony is." Clearly, thinking that your own allies are your allies and going to listen to you before they listen to whatever ails them was the wrong idea, but Envy was too in its head to really gather that part, which is how, realistically, the operation failed. Not thinking things all the way through because of the focal point being too heavily targeted.

The Puppet King, which was the Vessel that Envy could use any given time to command a greater number of lesser beings through a lesser version of the greater Envy as a being, would stand as a towering titan over the now once again desolate land, whilst the Master Of Envy, with strings attached, followed behind Mister Sir deftly. "You will NOT escape, SIR."

The Lawless bunch that had fled the base of the mountain and appeared at the top and didn't get touched by Envy at all saw the whole damn thing. They stood there nearly stumped or stupefied at what they'd just seen and knew that if it was happening out in the broad daylight and everyone saw and no one cared, this had to be Hell, itself.

"Yep, we're in Hell." And another harsh truth; "Khrona is God." Some of them here still knew Khrona.

They watched that big ass Puppet King, though, because that was an actual threat, it looked like, after watching that one go back to go take down a superior just to get ahead. "Oh, bro, no, I'm not fucking with that one. One of you better go do it." They couldn't escape from Hell, clearly, because if they used the power of Darkness, then whatever happened before would happen again.

That's when it clicked in some of their heads about what they could do next. "... The Goddess Of Darkness." They knew of the one that lurked in the Darkness of the Veritas, having seen her more often than they would have liked and now had a nightmare of a memory to live with, as well. They weren't sure of how to get in touch with her, but possibly trying to escape would do that. Then again, she might just kill them on the spot, so that wasn't happening. "Do we have to pull a Jutsu out of our asses or something? Damn." They sat there, stumped, not wanting to engage this 'Envy,' it seemed to be, directly. The head of Puppet King Envy snapped to the side at the sound of a voice, especially one that beckoned the Goddess Of Darkness. "Dollies?" It, by its command, since the Puppet King was a golem that was under the control of a higher authority, would primarily be searching for people that it could turn into puppets to use to complete the orders that were given to it by its master, the Puppet God Envy.

The titanic towering toy raised its arms up like a zombie in the direction of where its strings felt vibration at all, and would beckon it toward where the voices resonated on the strings like the cord of a musical instrument. "You rang...?" The souls that clustered about from the inside of the doll all belonged to Envy, which now belonged to the Goddess Of Darkness, of whom was manipulating her toys from the outside of the mountain. "Need some help, chumps?" She chuckled, whispering into their ears, the eyes of the Puppet King gleaming brightly.

The incandescent flames of Wrath, which, though they came through Mister Sir, were their own entity all of themselves. When Mister Sir tried to pass on the fires of his own personal Wrath for Envy and whatever Envy was dragging along and throwing in his face, they would spread out all down the mountain into something all of its own; the Sin of Wrath, itself. It was a hellacious flame that would eat up and destroy everything that it came into contact with, both good and evil alike. This spark from Mister Sir, of whom would be charged accountable for any damages that were caused, would shoot down the thin line of webbing from Envy's fingertips and all to everything that was connected to those strings.

"I. Hate. Envy." These words would tingle the strings of the Puppet King, as a heat surged up and down the fine lines of its puppet threads.

The tingling strings of Puppet King Envy felt the flares of the Unholy Wrath streaming down the line rather quickly, with a hatred that was for Envy, itself. Immediately, the Puppet King, uttering the words of its Master that Commanded it and insert the Commands for it to follow and repeat into its head, would warn the Valparaiso Denizens of what was going on beyond the gate. "They Only Use You And Raise You Up To Get To Me, And Sometimes Raise People Up Too Fast In Order To Attempt To Make Me Envious, Or To Help Me Out In The Future Without Me Knowing." This would explain to them why they felt the need to be upset with anyone that was given anything over them, however this simply seemed to be random data and nothing really relevant. "You All Are Being Puppetted More Than You Actually Realize, And It's Not By Me. I'm The One Revealing It To You Because I Am The One That Figured It Out." What the Puppet King was saying seemed to be out of place, yet also like it was leading into or building up to something that was of greater importance, and the beginning of the explanation, which seemed completely irrelevant and excessive, was actually simply the foundation for something greater that needed the support of the previously spoken information in order to be comprehended and not be 'Incomprehensible' to the Valparaiso Denizens once the point was actually gotten to.

"If You Have Not Overcome The Adversary, The Adversary Knows That It Can Overcome You With Whatever It Is You Are Looking Away From - Aversion." This was a hint for what was about to happen, once the Puppet King raised up its arms above the Valparaiso Denizens that called for the Goddess Of Darkness' assistance. "I Will Claim You

All As My Puppets And Raise You Up In A Manner That Will Be Of The Greatest Function, And You Must Not Become Envious Of Each Other's Positions, Ranks, Titles Or Power Once I Do." This was the main purpose of the full explanation prior to, as well as the final notes that would be let into as per Command Input.

"Envy Is A Sign Of Premature Exposure. This Is Why You Lust For Things Too Soon; Because You Cannot Handle Being Exposed To It, Which Is Why You Are Kept Isolated From Others By Both Yourself And Others, Which Makes The Self-Afflicting Envy More Self-Inflicted." Hopefully now, the Valparaiso Denizens understood the fullness of the manipulation of Envy, since it was all about giving someone else a reward in front of another person just to make them jealous and take out the target that received the reward for the one that gave them the reward in the first place without the one giving the rewards ever being noticed as the one manipulating others by giving them their rewards to make the ones that are Envious jealous. "This Is Also Why Gluttony Takes Care Of Envious People, Because They Hunger For More, After They Get The First Taste Of Their Lusts Fulfilled, And Their Hunger Overtakes Them And They Become Blinded By It." That was where they needed to go, first; to where Gluttony is, which is where the Puppet King was instructed to take them. "'You Deal With Yourselves,' Is The Point Of Envy." By that logic, Puppet King would, after seeing that his strings were now almost about to burn his body, raise up a Valparaiso Denizen among the ranks to be the new 'Puppet King.'

"Puppet King :: Rise"

This Valparaiso Denizen, who would be named 'Puppet King,' would be the head of his unit and make the decisions, harboring the souls of all of the other Puppets that made up Puppet King's large body, and grow enormous, like a Titan, or a Giant, on the spot. When the souls were emptied of the old husk of the original Puppet King Envy, the body would burn up and the strings attached would belong to the new Puppet King, of which the discarded and burning Puppet King was no longer attached to.

This would save them from being burned by the flames of the Unholy Wrath through the soul transfer and self-sacrifice of Puppet King Envy.

--Time Skip After Mister Sir Comes Back Down--

The burning flames that drew near lashed at the Puppet King, drawing it back to the dust from whence it came, and right into the palm of Mister Sir, whose burning arm would crush the dust betwixt his tightly clenched fingers. "You Should Never Be In My Face." He uttered slanderous things about Envy under his breath, as his eyes burst open, yet without the stitching coming undone. "If Ever You Are, I Will Call You Ugly Because It Is True, And I Will Say Nothing But The Truth." He saw in the distance the crowning of a new Puppet King and knew, as the new Puppet God, he needed his Puppet King. "Ugly One."

"If I Have To See You, You Are Not Doing Your Job, EVEN OF MANIPULATION Properly, Which Is Already How And Where You Failed' Letting Me SEE You." Though he could not keep his eyes open for very long due to the powerful stitching upon them, he could still very easily see and snatch the soul of the new Puppet King once they came into contact, after he saw the old one crown a new one. "Ugly One." He lashed his hand outward like the crack of a whip and streams of fire, something like vicious whips, would extend out over the Puppet King. "Don't Be So Foolish. BLATANTLY Ugly, In The Light."

If the flames were to touch the Puppet King in question, not only would his own Free Will burn up, but it would be under the Possession of Mister Sir, through the Manipulation of Wrath. "Not Pretty, Are You, Ugly Ones?" He lifted his other hand, just in case there was a struggle to escape, and lashed out more burning whips as if to scorch and sear their backs and backsides and leave the scar as the attachment of the fiery strings of Wrath and Envy as one. "You Should Feel Completely Ashamed And Naked And Dirty," He continued on, chastising the Envious with his own Wrath for his own Envy, and now what he could see in himself appearing in others "I'm Still Blindly Executing Everything In My Way. Do Not Get In My Way During This Process Or I Will Blindly Execute You And Not Feel Bad, No Matter Who Nor What." He knew which ones were the Sinful Seed, and those were his first and main targets coming down from the top of the mountain. "I Have NO Issue With Making You Ugly Things Feel Sorry About Being Ugly. Remember That And Fix Your Faces." The more he thought about all the Envious and each of them that were like him and what would become of them, he shook his hand, and the hairs on his head, like the strands of strings from a puppet wire, would shoot upward into the air and extend as blazing threads from the top of his dome. "You People Are Disgusting, And I Do Look Down On You For Me Being Correct About What Kind Of People You Are. You Do Not Prove Me Wrong, Which Is Why I Am Allowed To Speak Truthfully About Who And What You All Are. Remember This." In no time flat, everyone and everything in the area, including anything that attempted to escape down the trail, would be snatched up by the Envy of Mister Sir and scorched by the Wrath of Mister Sir simultaneously as they even felt the slightest tinge of Envy or Wrath inside of their soon to be Possessed Vessels. "And Also Remember That The Reason Why I'm Looking Down On It Is The Same Reason Why I'm Looking Down On You, Who Are Affiliated With Or Attached To It. And That's Why You Are Not Where I Am. Remember That. It Will Humble You And Take Your Minds Off Of ME."

Before he continued on, Mister Sir would see which of his flaming cords would have snatched up for him during his 'fishing trip' for all the lesser beings running around now without a master, of which was to be he, himself. "And Trust That I'll Wait Forever JUST TO MAKE SURE I CATCH YOU IN THE LIGHT AND DESTROY YOU COMPLETELY AND ULTIMATELY." Now, he finally started to sound like the Wrath Demon, or perhaps an Incarnate. The Sin, the Incarnate and the Demon are all different things, even if they do make up the greater whole.

The new Puppet King, which was a Valparaiso Denizen, would listen carefully to the words of the former before it burned up at the hands of a blazing entite that had no form of relent in his anger or flames that came from it. "Oh shit," the new Puppet King said, wondering what to do with his new title and crown. "I doubt we can take him" were the first words that came to mind. "Let's ditch him." He had an idea, and the first part of it was losing Mister Sir. "Adios, hot head." The new Puppet King hurled some strings over the Valparaiso Denizens and disappeared into the Darkness in a flickering blur before all of the fire rained down and covered up everything else. Not a single Valparaiso Denizen was left behind to endure the flames.

Mister Sir, who lashed about like a raging red dragon, would not lose sight of the Valparaiso Denizens nor the new Puppet King once they were out in the open. "... It's. Not. Over. Yet." His voice sounded nearly completely restrained, almost snarling, like the roar of the fires that burst from the top of his head and out of his fingertips. "This Area Is On Lockdown. Nothing Is Coming Back This Way." Whatever was here burnt up behind him.

Wherever Mister Sir got this strange fiery power was beyond the summit, where the North Gate is, which Envy had followed him up to, yet hadn't returned from with. Mister Sir, himself, would pay the other Sins a visit, starting with Greed, who should have been closest to the top, if he was in his place. "At Least Envy Won't Be A Problem Once I'm Through With It." He sucked his teeth rebelliously, gritting them to suppress his burning hatred. "Greed Better Be Of Some Use To Me, Or So Help Him..." Mister Sir was seeing all of the Sins he once commanded so coldly in a new light that nearly burned his eyes. He scoffed defiantly, something like a teenager as he passed on into where Greed was.

--- Another Time Skip, Long After Mister Sir Leaves---

"Rise, Armaros," a grim voice of a ghastly haunt bellowed all throughout the mountain. From the ground, underneath all that had once occurred, would undead looking serpents slither up from below the earth and immediately slide down the mountain, slipping into darkness.

Sooner than later, someone atop a throne could be seen being carried by a heap of slaves something like poll-bearers, trudging up the mountain in uniformity. "Careful 'bout those swamp snakes," the man on his throne, Greed, would say to his minions, "They'll getcha." The brood of vipers that had slipped into the shadows were nothing to toy with, but fortunately, Greed wouldn't be struck directly by them, even if they got the heels of his servants. "I want them," he mentioned though, waving a hand around and streams of paper shooting out of it. "Make them an offer they cannot refuse." He pointed first to where he would rest which was, naturally, at a high place upon the planar surface of the mountain. He was set down gently in a spot that was best for his oversight of the area, and he would take another puff of his cigar.

His servants, whom were nothing but low cards, which only had numbers and not names; 2, 4 and 5, would trek back down the mountain to search for where the vipers that were looking to get back at someone were.

Eventually, Mister Sir and the group covered by the Great Darkness would make their way up the mountain behind Greed, and he finishes his explanation of the events prior that led them to the events of the Present. "That's What Happened," Mister Sir would say, catching up to Greed and ending his flashback and explanation. He sees that there are some people coming. "Wait." He halts the group, who are still hidden by the Great Darkness, and begins to look around. "... We Are Not Alone." Before they can catch sight of the fullness of the Great Darkness, Mister Sir steps forward to greet them. "Did Greed Send You?" He already knew the answer, but would test them to see if they would lie or tell him straightforward.

The Great Darkness that kept the Zero Worlders hidden would send out the next envoy as soon as Mister Sir was met with the envoys of Greed.

"Rise:: Archetype"

This figure, which looked like a normal, humble and lowly person, something like the ones that Greed sent out to do his bidding, yet in the image of a large child, would step out from the darkness and wander about seemingly aimlessly, without cause nor clue nor purpose. Nothing else emerged from the Great Darkness.

The three people that were sent by Greed would look around, wondering how they should respond. Out of fear, the lowest, 2, would say "No..." But would look around to the other ones to see what they would say and do. The next higher up, 4, would say, "How do you know about Greed?" The final one, 5 would say, "What does it matter? Who are you and why are you here?"

Despite their very poor attempts to throw Mister Sir off the scent, it was best to use the ignorance of the lowly henchmen against themselves and against the one that not only kept them ignorant, but also had sent them out. Mister Sir would suddenly raise his hands up and pretend to be distraught, yet with a very sarcastic and satirical tone. "Oh, My! Such Hostility Here! I'm Sorry That I Asked." He would step aside, waving his hands about in 'terror,' allowing the three to continue to do as they were doing. "Never mind Me! I'll Mind My Own Business." He would keep his hands upfront, where they could see them, and his back to the wall. By this time, though his body was now completely made of solidified fire, he was still complacent and not haphazardly using his power to destroy everything that got in his way. "You Go About What You Were Doing And I'll Be On My Way."

Each of them were relieved that they weren't inquired anymore after that, and would return to heading down the mountain. 5, however, was a bit suspicious, but even so, he knew that completing his orders was more important than being suspicious. So, the henchmen, 2, 4 and 5 would walk down the mountain and out of sight.

The Archetype that was among them, looking nothing more than some unimportant plebeian, would casually follow behind them, but not too closely, and pretend to be one that was sent by Greed; number 7. From there on, only Mister Sir and the Great Darkness remained.

When only Mister Sir and the Great Darkness were left, he would start to speak to the entire group that was inside of the Great Darkness before they made it to Greed, beginning to head up the mountain again. "By Now, Greed Should Have Little To Nothing Left To Continue To Use. With His Businesses Not Making Him Any Money And He Having No Real Understanding Of How To Do Anything Without Servants, And Also Having Servants That Are Only Loyal To Money And Not The One Giving The Money, Once He Sees He Has Nothing Left But Whatever Is In His Back Pocket, He Should Be Easy Pickings." Mister Sir continued to speak as they drew closer to wherever he'd gone, keeping a close eye out for any signs of movement. "He Shouldn't

Be Able To Afford Anyone But The Lowest Grade, And They Are Too Incompetent To Do Anything. If We Take Him Out Right Now While He's Weak, Especially With All His Forces On Our Side, We Can Surround Him And Keep Him From Being Able To Escape." Mister Sir bade the ones that understood how to actualize this Order of Operations first, and each of them would head out to surround the mountain from several different vantage points, all of which couldn't be seen from the normal path. The rest of the group would stay walking behind him as if nothing had changed. "Act Natural," he said, keeping his eyes forward. "Let The Ones That Know What They're Doing Do Their Work." He promptly turned around to the ones that were in the darkness, who were relatively ignorant to these matters, saying strictly "Don't Interfere." He turned back forward and continued to walk.

You, who are still following behind Mister Sir patiently, see now what goes on behind the scenes of the high places of the world, and how much sin has been within them all, as well as how much still comes from people like the three that Mister Sir just encountered via the methods of Greed. You feel more confident, after overcoming Greed and listening to the story about Envy and how everything fell apart because of Envy about not becoming Envious nor Greedy. You would rather not be someone else's puppet or form of manipulation in any way, and would rather be Your own person before ever being someone else's slave. You take these events that transpired to heart, but continue to look on silently instead of jumping ahead. There were things that You still perhaps needed to see before it was safe, and no one had given You a clear signal that it was safe at this point. Though it is becoming rather tedious and tiresome to sit around watching, making sure Your own life is safe is much better. You remain patient and calm and ever watchful.

Greed, who is, as usual, sitting atop a high place, but has not made it all the way up the mountain, can finally see Mister Sir coming up the mountain. "Shit," he says, throwing out his cigar, "Can't expect the commoners to do a boss' job." 2, 4 and 5 wouldn't be able to handle someone like Mister Sir anyway. Greed needed his Ace. "Ace! Where are you, Ace?" No matter where he was right now, if he were still alive, then he should have been able to hear Greed calling out to him. "I need you to get ready for the next operation. Don't worry about anyone that was already left behind. We don't need them. All I need is for you to make a diversion." It wouldn't be long before Greed made his way to safety at the top of the mountain, where he could continue to grow out his industry and get something else ready to capture the prospective new hires.

Mister Sir flickers up to Greed now after it is clear that he has been noticed, chuckling to himself. "What Are You Doing?" Mister Sir inquires, still chuckling. "Haven't You Heard? Your Market Has Crashed." If Greed had been paying attention to how much he was spending and wasting and not earning in return, he would have noticed that his greatest sustaining franchises were already nothing but smoke and dust. "You Don't Have Anymore 'Employees.' Nor Anymore Places For Them To Work." Mister Sir pointed off to the horizon, where only barely just visible were the dilapidated, smoldering husks of what he once controlled. "Look Around. There's Nothing Left, And You're Surrounded." No matter who Greed called, he not only couldn't pay them, but they also didn't have any job to perpetuate the income, and therefore wouldn't work for him for free. "There's Nowhere Else To Run Now. Not Even Those Measly Servants You Sent Off Down The Mountain Can Stand Up To The Fullness Of The Army We Have Now." Mister Sir smirked. "There's Nowhere To Run."

Greed couldn't get a hold of any of his slaves at all. None of them were responding no matter how often he called them, nor how low the ranks. "Ace? King?! SPEAK TO ME!" He cried into a communication device, personalized to their use. There was no response. "Don't tell me all I have left are... 2, 4 and 5!?" Greed fell to his knees, completely distraught. "Ruined..." he cried, "RUINED!! All my hard work, nothing but ruins!!!" He slammed his fist on the ground, thinking the worst thought that he could; seeing himself at the bottom of the food chain as nothing but a common drone worker. It nearly shattered his mind. "No... No I'll never do drone work!" He cried, somewhat hysterically. "No. No sir! Not me! Drone work is... I-is for the DRONES! Yes! Like 2, 4 and 5! I'm no low card! I'm no pawn! I... I could never..." He tried to think of any way out of this, but with only the money he had on his person left to his name and nothing as a source of income, Greed had no ideas. There was no way to build nor rebuild from the ground up in this hellish society if you'd already lost something. It was basically like starting over and never being able to get back to the top again. He started to cackle hysterically. "I... I am the top world famous entrepreneur!!! I WILL NEVER FALL!!!" He was in denial, and cackled even more. "I STILL OWN EVERYTHING!! Nothing is out of my reach!!!" He stuck out his tongue, long and elastic, like that of a frog, and hurled it around hysterically, still cackling madly. "HAHAHA! I STILL HAVE THE BEST MIND FOR BUSINESS!! YOU NEED ME! YOU NEED ME!! You'll see... You can't do ANYTHING without me!! HAHAHAA!" And he went on in his mad fit.

Mister Sir shook his head. "Pathetic." Without any of his workers, Greed was nothing more than a common man with a knack for telling people what to do. "Now You're Just Another Birdman. You've Reached The Top, Then Had To Stop, Then It All Came Tumbling Down. And What Can You Do But Sit There In Your Craze And Wallow About Your Past That Will Never Come To Be Again?" Mister Sir continued to shake his head. "Be Lucky I Won't Allow You To Live. Can't Have You Getting Your Hands On Anything Else, Now Can We?" Without warning, Mister Sir Sparta kicked Greed right off the edge of the mountain, where he would surely die, falling all the way back to the bottom, where he would be at the lowest point like the group had started out on, as his punishment. There is where his body would lay and without a legacy to continue or pass on. No name. No fame. No fortune. No nothing. Mister Sir looked on over the edge until he had seen Greed's body hit the ground, hurling a fireball at his tongue in case he tried to latch onto something. Without his tongue, Greed was useless and powerless. "Let's Go," Mister Sir said to the group, having successfully defeated sins 1-6. You all continue up the mountain to the highest point that you can reach; the North Gate.

CHAPTER 7

WRATH

Mister Sir continued to walk up the top of the mountain, leaving everyone behind. He, himself gets to the top of it and stands there waiting, whilst Envy handles the rest of them down below.

He looks up to the sky, able to see the top of the mountain, yet also the final gate, which was a seal on the sky itself, as if restraining his potential of progressing further up the trail. There was no way to get around it, and Mister Sir was apprehended by it only to look back at all the destruction behind him for his want to accomplish his goal. "Yes… All according to my master plan." Mister Sir waited patiently to get to this point, where he, alone, would stand at the next gate of passage.

He was most patient.

"Cornered," a voice would shriek out from behind the trespassing scoundrel. "I knew you couldn't be trusted. And now you're stuck at the last gate that no one can get beyond. Boo Hoo." The stitched up eyes of Envy, the True Envy, would open wide to glare at the one who had attempted to double cross it and get to the finish line before Envy had a chance to. "You're not going to get there before me," were the first things Envy said as its eyes narrowed down to a slit, gleaming with the souls of all the ones that wanted to get there first before Mister Sir. "NO ONE WILL GET ANYWHERE BEFORE ME!!"

Soon, each of the souls of Envy, which were locked up in the large doll-like body, would pour out from the titan's fingertips and down upon the head of Mister Sir like rain. Each of the souls that belonged to the giant would make up strings that spread over the entire area, gridlocking it and trapping everyone and everything in it absolutely, preventing escape AND entry. "Nowhere to run. Now what will you do?" Envy was actually pretty interested in knowing. It smirked, with its eternally sewn-shut mouth perked at the corners. "One false move, I own you, too, SIR."

"That Was Not Proper Procedure," A The Voice Of A Great Presence Spake Down Unto The North Gate, Which Was Sealed By The Skyline, "That Is Not How You Deal With Your Issues." The Seal, Which Was Upon The Hand Of Judgment, The Left Hand Of The Severity Of God, Which Pressed Down Upon The Land In A Similar Manner As The Right, Though Not To Cover Anyone, Would Exert A Powerful Pressure That Would Stabilize Everything From The North Gate All The Way Down To The Beginning Of The Mountain Path, All Of Which Was A Powerful Force And Gust Like That Of The Flapping Of Winds. "Go Back To The Beginning," The Voice Proclaimed, As The Shadow Of A Hand Cast Mister Sir Down To The Base Of The Mountain. "Clean Up Your Mess And Put Out Those Fires That You Started." The Wrath Incarnate Knew What It Had Done And Each Of The Flames That Were Not Ignited Of Their Own, But Because Of The Wrath Of Mister Sir Via His Own Envy, Which Now Was All Turning Against Him.

"This Is Your Judgment," The Voice Went On, The Shadow That Was Over Mister Sir First Pointing To "Envy, Of Whom Mister Sir Would Have To Completely Burn Up Before He Leaves; To You, Bear The Flames Of The False Idol And Relieve Mister Sir Of His Curse." Next, The Shadow Of The Hand Pointed To Mister Sir, "Wrath, Of Whom Hath Started These Terrible Plagues; Rain Down Hellfire Upon All Things That Are Your Own Doing, And The Doing Of All Like You. It Is Time For The Suicides." This Is Where Mister Sir Would Bow Before God, Unlike The Light-Bearer That Defied The Father And Had Continued On To Do Through Mister Sir Bearing The Light Of That Sin. "You Must Now Sacrifice Yourself Honorably And Turn

Anew, In The Stead Of Any Sheep, Any Pig, Any Goat Or Any Lamb. Slay Thyself, And You Will Know Thy True Self; Wrath, Of God."

"Learn To Bear Your Own Curses And Accept Your Own Punishment," Was His Final Degree At The Mount. And So, He Would Be Circumcised, And Bade Off To Rain The Flaming Birds Of Destruction Down Upon The Land That Was The Work Of His Hands.

"God Damn."

"I Would Never Accept Such Workmanship Anyway, As I Feel You Should Know Better Before Seeking Approval From Me. I Know You Can Do Better, And If You Cannot, Then That Is Why I Will Still Not Accept The Light You Bear To Me. You Are Bearing For Yourself; Not For God." And He Was Turned Around. "You Know Better And Can Do Better. Do Your Best Next Time."

"Grand Daughter," Primordius, Of Whom Was The Prime Chaos Itself That She Rested In The Womb Of Would Speak To Her From All Around Her Dark Chambers, "It Seems As Though Some Of Your Toys Have Beckoned You." The Great Shadow Of A Hand Cast Over The Mountain, Pointing Down At The Northernmost Gate, Higher Up Than Each Of The Others, And Toward A Cliff Where There Was No More Solid Tangible Road. This Was Where He Had Hidden His Old Possession, 'Puppet God,' Which Was A Special Present For The Great Darkness, Tabitha Tensei, To Have For Herself. "Go Forth And Claim What Is Yours And Rape The Mountain Of Its Possessions." As He Bade The Grand Daughter Off, The Primordial Darkness, Prime Chaos Itself, Would Return To Its Rest, Recounting The Verses Of The Great Bird Of Paradise In The Heavens, Whilst Catering To The Unfortunate Ones Below. "Have Fun."

The Shadow Of The Hand that cast the Great Darkness over its appointed Possession, the Puppet God, Master Of Envy, would suddenly stretch out and leak through the seals in the sky, oozing down over all the land like tarry rain. It dripped all over the mountain, yet rained down with a consistency that was something gelatinous instead of fully liquid. It nearly looked like black blood raining down from the sky, and pouring over the top of the North Gate. It swept up the

Puppet God and took hold of the Possession, and with it, the Puppet God would have taken on a new form similar to the darkness that had now Possessed it. The stitching burst from the eyes and glared into the soul of Mister Sir, of whom now had to face the Great Darkness itself as he was bid to clean up the rest of the mess. "I already have a set up for you," the Puppet God spoke with a feminine voice, "Go burn up all the ones I've placed for you." Puppet God pointed her hand in the same manner as the Shadow Of The Hand that was no longer visible above had once done. Attached to her fingers were some strings, all of which branched off into a series of other strings, something like an intricate web. "You know what to do. You have your orders."

"Oh? Envy so I cannot be Perfect?" Mister Sir grumbled, seeing all of his plans to make himself highest coming to fail right at the end, "Well, time to be obnoxious, like Envy is." He looked Envy, which was nothing now but a puppet to another being over it, square in the eyes, knowing that she who has possession over it wanted his soul for herself. "Forever, like Envy." A great fire erupted all around Mister Sir, bursting from the ground and melting away all the cold air that blew throughout the North Gate. "Do not try to correct me." He snapped at her instantaneously as his Patience was broken and the Wrath within him was unleashed. "You just made a mess that will stay there, and you'll know it's nowhere near idiosyncratic." His burning fist raised up toward the brazen young Envy and grasped her arm bearing the strings and lit it, as well as the entire web connected aflame.

"You are off key and tempo," he said to her in a rational tone, yet with great flames spreading upward into the overhead webs and burning them up, along with the seal that they were just below. "That's why I excused you. Just remember that, Envy, when you're done playing with them." The Wrath that came from Mister Sir's blazing fingertips was the official initial engagement of combat. "Do not make me look imperfect where I am not simply to service yourself." The burning hatred he felt for Envy, which would surge through his searing gloved palms, ignited the wicked Sin aflame and passed the curse of burning Wrath unto the Puppet God. "Ugly One." A spontaneous combustion swept throughout the field, and his blazing jacket fluttered on the wake of the explosion. "Go get your lesser beings and take them home, Envy."

He was not smiling.

The incandescent flames of Wrath, which, though they came through Mister Sir, were their own entity all of themselves. When Mister Sir tried to pass on the fires of his own personal Wrath for Envy and whatever Envy was dragging along and throwing in his face, they would spread out all down the mountain into something all of its own; the Sin of Wrath, itself. It was a hellacious flame that would eat up and destroy everything that it came into contact with, both good and evil alike. This spark from Mister Sir, of whom would be charged accountable for any damages that were caused, would shoot down the thin line of webbing from Envy's fingertips and all to everything that was connected to those strings.

The fires also spread about the field, surrounding the two of them and blocking off the entire area. It looked like all hell had broken loose and these two, Mister Sir and Envy, had a ring of fire holding them in place for a hellish cage match. The fires of Wrath, which was Wrath, itself, burned up whomever and whatever would touch, including the Wrath Demon, Mister Sir, himself, should he attempt to escape the flames hell bent on keeping him in place where he was. Many burning eyes opened up in the flickering wisps of the flames, staring he and she down and judging them through the fires.

The Puppet God, which was the Master of Envy, possessed by the new owner, the Great Darkness, Tabitha Tensei, would not resist nor hesitate being burned, nor being grabbed involuntarily by Mister Sir. "If You Cannot Watch Me Succeed In Life, You Are Forbidden From Seeing That Point In My Life, By Your Own Circumstance, Which Is What Envy Teaches." Envy could tell when it owned another being, and Mister Sir was clearly Envious of Tabitha being over Envy, which made him under Envy, which seemed to have ignited his Wrath. "Self-Circumcision From Acting Too Soon, Which Is A Sign Of Lust For Taking Something Before Its Time." Mister Sir, himself, was guilty of wanting something too early, which was why he was being sent away and why he was upset about it. He shouldn't have been angry and he shouldn't have left his comrades, such as Envy, who was now appointed over him through Tabitha, who was over Envy.

"And It Will Turn Your Mouth Bitter. So Remember That You're Not Able To Speak, Or You're Not Allowed To See It Happen." Mister Sir, if he uttered even a Wrathful word, or took a Wrathful action, which he'd already more than done, as proof by the burning idol, "Then You'll Reveal Yourself And Your Intentions AGAINST Me." The eyes of Puppet God gleamed, sucking out the soul of Mister Sir, which was the Wrath Demon that was making him unclean. The entire Puppet God ignited and was destroyed by the spontaneous combustion, yet the souls of the Envious still remained, since Wrath was no longer over Envy, by the decision of Wrath, itself. "Even If It's Covered Up By A Billion Other Things, You'll Still Focus Only On The One Thing You Don't Want Me To Have, Which Is Always What I Can Target About You." Now that the eyes of Envy were opened, and the soul of Wrath was exchanged, the flames that burned for Envy would suddenly become purified, and the eyes of Mister Sir would begin to sew themselves shut. He was one of Envy's blind puppets now, and also the new 'Puppet God.'

"You Are Blind To Your Own Reasoning, And Therefore Will Always Have Something Against Me Because Of Something In Your Heads That You Do Not Understand." Now that the Wrath was no longer Mister Sir's fire to bear, because he could not handle it for Holy reasons, he was no longer able to touch it without burning himself, and thus would take the place of and for the one thing he destroyed that he should not have even attempted to touch at all; 'The Puppet God.' Just by his want to touch it at all, and also his actual touching of it, he was condemned to lose his Wrath to himself and to Envy. "You Will Try To Kill Me And My Own Just For Looking At It. I'm Doing You A Favor By Sparing You The Sight." His eyes would be double-stitched, needle and threaded all the way up and down every lash with every lash. "I Have Your Soul BECAUSE Of Where Your Eyes Are. Stop Looking At A Downfall, Before You Actually Get It." The burning essence that stood before him now, 'Tabitha,' the new Holy Wrath, would, once again, bid the new highest lesser, Envy, off to see the flames of destruction all down the web. It looked like a long string of spider silk all lit aflame throughout the entirety of the network.

"You've Been Looking Too Closely At What You Shouldn't, And It Will Hurt Your Eyes GRAVELY To Snatch Them Away From You." The flames of the new Wrath, of which Tabitha would Name 'Santa Muerte,' would converge with those that burned around the stadium, as she seeped deeply into the fires of the burning eyes. Her own eyes were most prominent over them all, and doubled into four, and gleamed a bright blood red at the scornful Envy, which was bare and naked upon the Puppet God that stood now at the center of the ring of Burning Condemnation and Judgment. "Feel Free To Start Throwing Spears And Missing, Falling Just Short, And Wasting Your Time. I'll Watch You And Judge You For Making The Attempt, Since What Matters Is That You Made The Attempt FIRST BEFORE The Matter Of If It Actually Hits Any Form Of A Target." Each of Tabitha's own eyes of Burning Condemnation, which she unlocks through the awakening of her own Wrath, would focus completely on Mister Sir, holding back a searing concentrated beam of pure Burning Condemnation.

"It Definitely Is The Most Bitter Drink."

Mister Sir bowed his head and closed his eyes, knowing that there was nothing that could be done and nothing that he wanted to do should be done nor could be done in a justified manner that would counteract anything of what was spoken to him by either entity. He felt ashamed of himself, which is what burned him up the most. Unfortunately, it still ended up striking a few others, and lighting everything aflame with a spark he'd set, as it could be seen streaming down the strings. His eyes, now shut, even though still shaded, would no longer see his fate nor the rise of the new Holy Wrath, but he bound his own hands behind his back to contain his fury. "I. Hate. Envy." He could not hate the ones that brought down this judgment, no matter how much he might have wanted. Therefore, all of his hatred was directed at Envy, itself, of which now he was. He walked forward after bowing and submitting, this time going to do exactly what needed to be done instead of rebelling against it, like someone he had read about in Scripture. He'd already seen what the outcome of that was and knew that was why he had to do something different. It did not fully quell his fires, but it at least guided them back in the right direction, instead of misguiding them, like a certain fallen one he knew of.

"I'll Be Back," were his last words to them all, as he walked down the sorry path of shame ready to look all the hateful sins down the line in the face and deal with them.

Once Mister Sir departed, the new essence of the Holy Wrath would speak in private through the flames of the Burning Condemnation that surrounded the field as to what the next moves were. "The first thing to do now as Mister Sir burns up everything below us is for my very soul to acquire the flames of the Righteous Fury, the Holy Wrath, and be deemed as the Santa Muerte that burns up all that is wicked." With this said, each of the eyes of the burning ones would close, and a great deal of large, flaming bird-like wings outstretched from the circumference of the ring of fire and out into the sky. Each of them, with just a single flap, would thrust embers about the sky that would rain down like hail.

"Harab Serapel," she called, as many of the flaming debris, which was in the shape of blazing birds, would converge at the center of the flat land, whilst the others dove down the sides and to the lower gates. From here on, the flames of the Holy Wrath would begin to forge Tabitha's burning soul, Tetra, from the flames. Soon, Tetra would stand in Tabitha's stead, and have command over all the Holy Wrath, the Seraphim and the Harab Serapel, all of which were units that were under the Holy Wrath.

"Come, Goddess Of Fury; Santa Muerta, Tetra Tensei."

'Peon :: The Last'

This Was Tetra Tensei's Unit Name And Coordinate For Her Transfer From Where She Once Was To The Binding Of Where She Needed To Be Once The Game Started Up And The 'Goddess Of Fury' Was Needed To Oversee It.

And so, 'The Ruins Of God,' Angel 'Asbeel,' who was under the command of 'Grand Tabritha' as 'The Last' would rise up at her command and be ready to do her bidding. "Yes, My Lord," Asbeel said to Grand Tabritha, kneeling down and waiting patiently.

Flames covered Asbeel's body. She, Tetra, who was under the name of 'Asbeel,' was ignited with what looked like the burning wings of a Red Raven. As Asbeel, her face was covered in a Red Raven mask.

Finally, at long last, Mister Sir, who had been bade off a relatively short time ago during the fiery coronation of the new 'Holy Wrath,' would make his way first back up to the North Gate. This time, he was not alone, but had a great multitude behind him, covered in the Great Darkness that he was no longer fighting, but working in tandem with. As he reached the top of the mountain, with the Great Darkness flowing behind him, his body was now completely made of condensed fire, his eyes were open and gleaming with a bright light, and the souls that were trapped in his body were now the new freshness of his own soul. He stood there before the ring of fire, waiting patiently. "I Have Returned," he spake to the Holy Wrath, with his head bowed to she who was on the other side of the eternal flames. "My Lord." He would kneel down before her, careful not to cross the boundary of the ring of fire, knowing very well what would occur if he did. He awaited the group behind to catch up to him. "The Sins Have Been Taken Care Of. The Wrath Is Clean." As it stood, every one of the sins, including Wrath, itself, had been burnt up. Only the Holy Wrath should have remained. "Mission Complete."

Angel Asbeel, she who stood on the other end of of the Burning Condemnation, yet, was not burning nor being condemned, would turn her attention to inspect the one seeking passage through the Holy Fire. "Oh? Is that so?" She asked, the face of Red Raven, covered in blood, pressing her bird-like mask up toward the wall of fire that destroyed all. "Hmmm..." She looked at Mister Sir's body, then toward the Great Darkness that was slowly making its way up behind him, seeing that he had not left anyone behind and also that, for the most part, the ones that were kept alive were either traumatized to the point where they were ready to be clean, or they were repentant enough in whatever they'd been through that they were eager to wash clean all of their sins. "... Well, you got the Children up the mountain," Asbeel, the Red Raven said with a laugh. "That was indeed all that you needed to do. You are relieved of that duty." The flames parted, and Mister Sir was allowed entry. "Pass." His body, which was now forged in the fire and clean in the fire that protected him, would keep him safe and be the mark of his cleansing.

"But, as you must know, this is not your last task." If he did not know, he would be informed. When he walked through, the fiery gate would close behind him, restricting the access of any of the ones coming up slowly within the Great Darkness. They were still unclean, and, now that they were safely at the top of the mountain, as far as they could go, they would be judged according to what they had done, just as Mister Sir. "The Great Darkness will deal with the ones within her womb. But you and I, we must talk of greater matters at the Top." Those that were at the North Gate that were not Asbeel or Mister Sir, the two of the Holy Wrath, would not be allowed to enter nor follow them. They were still impure, and only the pure could enter to the final test. "Walk with me, Sir. We have much to discuss." Red Raven would start off toward the center of the field, where she hoped Mister Sir was eager to follow. Time was indeed short. "The time has come to talk of other things. Of cabbages and kings." She snickered to herself, adding, "And other seasonings. Heeheehee."

Mister Sir raised his head, with a genuine smile on his face, which glowed like the sun, as would the rest of his body at the elation of his emotion. His entire body would be testament to his righteousness or his unholiness, for, if he got angry unrighteously, it would show in his actions, and he knew this. Yet, he was not afraid nor concerned. His confidence was unparalleled, and for quite a good reason. "Do Tell," he said, passing through the gate that closed up behind him, leaving the group that was within the Great Darkness to be dealt with by and with the Great Darkness. He was very attentive now, ready to hear of things that he both knew and did not know, and more than ready to see things in a new light, just as he, himself, was and would be seen in a new light. He walked patiently with Asbeel, this Red Raven, as one with her and the Wrath of God. He was pleased to know that he was returned to his place, and that his fall was not so great that he could not be lifted up if he were to simply walk upright, as he was supposed to. That gave him great joy.

"With pleasure," Red Raven said with a laugh, both of pleasure and what also seemed to be restraint. Clearly, she knew something about what was about to happen that even Mister Sir didn't, but he would soon be right on the same path as she. "Father!!!" She cried out to the heavens, up to the Seal of the North Gate, "Open Up The Gate!" She waited patiently for the same Voice and Hand that had once cast Mister Sir down and out to lift the two of them up to the final Test, above the Mountain, at its peak. "We'll Talk There, Beyond The Eyes Of The Great Darkness." The Great Darkness also kept the Zero Worlders ignorant, even if they were able to see. They did not need to see the next holy matters until they were settled. Their ignorance was actually very important in the time of Secret Services.

Suddenly, There Was A Great And Loud Rumbling, Like The Sound Of Thunder, Shouting Out And Shaking The Whole Mountain, "WHO DARES!?!?" The Voice Cried Like That Of A Trumpet Blast. Dark Clouds Swirled Overhead, And The Seal That Was Upon The Very Sky Itself That Kept All Beings That Were On The Ground Eternally Trapped On The Ground Would Be Made Clear. From The Center Of The Swirling Clouds, A Parting Would Spiral Outward Into A Great And Powerful Eye, Which Bore Down Over The Fullness Of The Length Of The Ring Of Fire, Which, Too, Was A Seal That Kept The Top Of The Mountain And The Holy Land For Judgment Completely Secure. The Storm Was All About The Outside Of The Ring, Yet The Eye Itself Was Upon The Land Where Angel Asbeel And Angel Samael Stood Ready To Be Judged. "Oh, Is That Someone Whom I Love?" The Voice Spake, With The Eye Of The Storm Shining The Rays Of The Sun Down Upon The Consecrated Area. "Come Up Here!" The Voice Spake Again, The Seal Upon The Sky, Only In A Certain Area Noted By The Bounds Of The Ring Of Fire, Breaking And Shattering At Seeing In The Light That The Two Angels Were Clean.

"Well Done, My Son," The Voice Said To Samael, Whose Alias Was 'Mister Sir,' "You Have Become Clean In My Sight. I Even Hear It In The Song Of Your Voice. Yet, Being Clean And Remaining Clean Are Two Separate Tests." And So, The Right Hand Of Mercy Would

Reach Down As A Ray Of Loving, Warm Light Stretching All Across The Breadth Of The Consecrated Area, In Plain Sight, And Would Draw Up Both Asbeel And Samael As They Were, In A Rapture. They Would Be Taken Up To The Top Of The Mountain, The Very Peak, Of Which None Except He Who Once Was, Moses, Had Seen. At That Moment, When The Two Were Taken Up Into The Light, Up To The Peak, Known Here As The 'Formorti Zenith,' The Parting Of The Clouds And The Broken Seal Would Both Fold In Upon Themselves And Repair, Binding The Land And Suppressing It With A Great Gravity That None That Were Below The Seal Could Break. Even If They Were To Fly, They Would Never Pass Through The Seal, And Instead Simply Go Off Into Space, Which Was Naught But An Illusion Of Them No Longer Being Trapped. These Ones That Thought That Exiting The Atmosphere Was The Breaking Of The Seal Would Never See The Light, And Would Always Be Looking At Darkness For Eons And Fathoms Beyond.

There Was Complete Silence Afterward, And The Great Darkness Would Be Allowed To Take Over From There In The Stead Of The Greater Darkness.

The Great Darkness, which also ruleth over Sloth, through the Slowth, that had been over the entire group of Zero Worlders and creating a great and powerful gap between they and all the events that they had seen and experienced, would be released from the cover of the Great Darkness, and, before them, the entire cloud that protected them would condense before them as the same Slowth that had once protected them during the time of traversing the Sin of Sloth, yet also had disappeared. It, too, was just now catching up to them during the time of Wrath, which was also why the group would be experiencing the test of Wrath that both Mister Sir and Red Raven had already passed. Their ignorance was part of 'Sloth,' for, everything that fell under 'Ignorance' was also under 'Sloth,' and known as 'The Gap.'

"Okaaaay, time to fill you in," The Great Darkness said, rising up from over the cover of the Slowth, which now would stand full form before the massive group of Zero Worlders. "Again." Though its voice was clearly heard, it would not be received properly at first due to the

Ignorance of the entire group, which, too, was part of their Sloth. Thus, being Patient with the Slothful, those Ignorants, was key, for they would not be able to react or process how they should react properly for a little bit of time. "I'll Wait," the Great Darkness said, seeping directly into her chosen vessel, the 'Slowth,' which would deal with the Ignorant Masses and their Ignorance to fill them in before they were able to pass through the fullness of the fire that they were now standing before, at the place of judgment, which could have been called 'Armageddon' and 'The Apocalypse.' The Great Darkness inside of the Slowth whistled nonchalantly.

You stand at what seems to be the top of the mountain, as far as You can pass, having slowly trod Your way up behind Mister Sir, who had shown You all of these things. The last thing You had seen, which was some sort of actual religious experience that You had thought was completely fake, even when You were praying to God, happened right before Your eyes. As You stand dumbfounded, questioning what is real and what is fake, and if God is a lie or not, even after You had already prayed to Him and figured out that He actually was, You are still in disbelief because You had never actually seen anything holy in Your life, but only things that were unholy that you were asking protection from.

"What?" You stand there for a bit, trying to process. "... W... What?" You don't even know how to fully come to terms with what You had seen and try to convince Yourself that it was all just a hoax, but cannot explain it. "... Wait, didn't we already deal with you? We... We overcame this sin, right? All the other ones, too?" From what You have seen, You had already completed dealing with the 7 Deadly Sins, so You are also confused as to why You are seeing this one, which You remember was known at the time of Sloth, as the 'Slowth.' "What... Is going on?" You eventually realize that the Sloth is still Sloth, but You are confused as to why You hadn't overcome Sloth if You had already passed it. "... What?"

"Say 'What' Again," The Slowth threatened, somewhat comically, yet also quite seriously, "Say 'What' One More Motherfucking Time." The Slowth sighed, closing its eyes, which looked something like vivid distortions to the eyes of those whose minds could not process the speed of its movements. "Your 'Sloth' Is Your Ignorance. Because You Do Not Know What Is Going On, And Have BARELY Understood The Events That Have Come To Pass, You Have Not Actually Dealt With The Sin Of Sloth, And, Instead, The 'Sin Of Sloth' Is Only Just Now Coming Upon You In The Fullness Of Its Force." This, too, was something that would incur the other Sins in them, which was why this would be explained to them very slowly and very delicately. In that time, other things would be happening beyond them. "Your Sins Are Still Inside Of You, As People, But Through Fear, They Were Subdued For Only A Time. Now, Since You Are At The Top Of The Mountain, Yet, You Have Not Actually Done What Is Necessary On Your Own To Cleanse Your Sins Individually, You Actually Have A Test Separate From The One Who Led You Up Here To Reveal These Things To You. Thus, You Must Travel Back Down The Mountain Of Sin And Clean It Through Virtue." If this information incurred Wrath in them, then many would be taken already, and become examples to the others that they were not only still unclean, but also had work to do after their eyes had been opened to all of the Sins. "Patience Is A Virtue," the Slowth's distorted voice bellowed dauntingly. "You Have Your OWN Work To Do."

You stand perplexed and in disbelief for quite a while, trying to come to terms with the words You have just been told. "... This is a joke, right?" You say, with Your friends around you feeling and thinking the same. "Go back DOWN the mountain? No way. You can't be serious." You stand around, playing it off for a while, chuckling and carrying on with Your friends. "We JUST got here. Besides, we're all tired after just getting this far, anyway. You can't make us go back down." You end up continuing to do as you did, feeling triumphant and talking among Your friends about what a crazy ride it was, and how You are ready to move on to the next trial after overcoming the Seven Deadly Sins. Some of You decide you might throw a party or something, many are in pleasant moods, ready to celebrate for the triumph. There is much chatter among You about the events that have transpired, quite engaging, at that.

The Slowth that is standing between the group and the fire glares at you with eyes filled with foresight. "Is That So...?" its voice bellows, as its body disperses into darkness. Suddenly, it can no longer be seen, nor its voice be heard, yet the faint images of eyes flickering about all around you imprint themselves in the very air. The Slowth stops speaking to you, but its piercing eyes remain ever watchful. As they blink, they fade away and appear elsewhere around you, disappearing and reappearing in a multitude of distorted visuals, yet there is always an eye over the group in some way, shape or form at all times even if none are paying attention nor can see. "Don't Say I Didn't Warn You..." it said, as it allowed its presence, which was keeping their Sins from catching up to them, to finally disperse and return the flow of Time and Space around them to a regularity.

Once the Zero Worlders lost the protection of the Slowth that was covering them and shielding them with its Sloth, no longer allowing their Ignorance to be protected, the Wrath poured out in full measure from the flames that were once docile and blocked off by the Slowth's body, which slowed down the very Wrath, itself, from striking down the peoples.

"WHO DARES?!?!?!?" a terrible outrageous voice cried from the very fire, itself. "WHAT ARE YOU UNHOLY THINGS DOING HERE!? YOU DARE NOT LISTEN!?!?" Whether they knew or not, they all were not supposed to be up to this point without either being clean or having an escort. "YOU DID NOT EVEN COMPLETE YOUR TASK OF GETTING ME MY WATER." From that, they should have realized that this was the very mountain itself speaking to them, just as it had done once before at the bottom, when it sent them up, and before they were under the cover and protection of the Great Darkness whose words and protection they had just ignorantly rejected, believing that they, themselves, had accomplished something on their own. "GO BACK DOWN THERE AND STAY OUT OF MY SIGHT!!" As the voice screeched out to them, the flames of Wrath that encircled the top of the mountain would burst forth and scorch them, washing over the entire group.

Many would be inflamed, now, burning with Hatred, Fury, Anger and Wrath; every intensity of emotional fire, and many with actual fire, which would burn up their minds, bodies and souls as it spread over them. "WHO TOLD YOU TO DISOBEY?!?" Whether it was the voice of the mountain or the voice of the Great Darkness, the ignorant ones who were so haughty as to succumb to their own Pride in themselves would find themselves afflicted once more, now, by a terrible Sin that ignited the others in them once more. It would be as if the ones that were conquered hadn't left them, yet, would be raised up out of the group, instead of as entities that were outside of them. "GET OUT!!!" the fires raged, burning up and destroying anyone that got close and did not flee immediately.

You are suddenly left alone by Your guide. By the time You really realize what this means, the fire from the mountain is already upon you, scorching you with harshness and terrible afflictions. Enraged that You feel betrayed and led astray, only to find out that the trip was completely pointless, You begin to search for someone to blame for Your own transgressions. You immediately throw down the name of God, but because You cannot find something physical to take out Your aggressions on, You turn to each other and cast blame on each other. "This is YOUR fault!" You say to Your friends, family and lovers, "If I didn't follow YOU then I wouldn't be here right now!!" When push comes to shove, quite literally, a large bit of the group has become a mosh pit; an angry mob, completel inflamed with themselves and others around them, but not a one seeking to consider themselves for what has been done. Sooner or later, You are one big mass of burning chaos, slaying each other and harming each other until You feel content with Yourself.

"That's right..." the voice from the fires mutters sweetly, yet with a tinge of hostility, "... Destroy each other." This saved the fire trouble doing it, itself. Many eyes open up within the fire, but as anger and hatred spread about the mass, thinning out their numbers all on their own, the fire, known as Wrath, hasn't even truly moved, yet. In fact, it has only manipulated the group and influenced them with its will alone, and hasn't even acted upon its true power. "... Wrath Incarnates," it speaks out to the ones that are angered by whatever event has caused them this much emotional agitation, "... Rise Up."

These demons of Wrath, known as 'Satans,' would become completely consumed by fire, burning the most out of everyone. Where there was peace, they would cause discord and chaos, simply because they could not stand seeing others happy if they were burning on the inside. "You have nothing to be happy about," the voice of the fire spake directly into the minds of the ones that were angered, "So, no one else does, either." From there, the eyes of Wrath merely rested on its minions, which would spread the fire as it saw fit without Wrath, itself, having to move. "Hmhmhmhm... Foolish, disgusting creatures..." Wrath, itself, hated all of them, including its own. They, especially, looked like nothing but horrendous abominations made only to exact its will and complete its goal. Something like Mister Sir had once seen these people as, himself, when he was possessed by Wrath. Now, the Unholy Wrath, which was back to being an entity all of its own, has possession of different vessels, since Mister Sir had become part of the Holy Wrath. The Unholy Ones were tested with fire, just as he was, and if they could not overcome, they would burn up and die before they could get to where they wanted to.

Though a vast majority of the group is angry and causing a problem, the more innocent of the group, who really were just following what they thought was the best path and weren't fully concerned with just their own salvation would begin to speak out, being unable to take witnessing these things for very long. "Wait! This isn't right!" You, who are attempting to make peace amongst the angry, cry out. "Maybe if we work together, we can come to a better solution! What will fighting do?" Your group is small now, but You at aleast know that You are the ones not trying to kill anyone nor destroy anything, which sets You apart from the ones that are, and You can tell the difference. You are certainly afraid, but at the same time, You also are disgusted and appalled and cannot stand to just sit around and watch these things happen. "Please stop fighting!"

"NO!!!" cried out the burning ones, hellbent on getting their revenge for being brought up only to be abandoned and feeling betrayed "THIS

IS NOT MY FAULT, SO I WON'T TAKE IT!!!" They cry out, now suddenly turning against you. "YOU'RE WITH THE ENEMY!! KILL THEM!!!" In their blindness of rage, they see only that you are not on their side, and therefore must be slaughtered because you do not agree with them, even if whatever they are doing is against your belief or feeling or thoughts or practices. They seem to care nothing for you, but only about themselves and that you side with them.

These ones, encircled in fire, and emanating a burning aura, would become deformed and ugly right before you as their true nature was brought up out of them through Wrath, itself. Thus, upon their heads, ugly, gnarled horns would sprout, which symbolized their opposition to anything and everyone that was not following them or under them. They would be the mark of everyone that was guaranteed to fight you on anything they did not agree with, quite savagely and mercilessly, at that. This was only the first step of their ungodly transformation.

"TRAITORS!!!" They cried out, their mouths spewing a stinking fire like that of burning sulfur, "YOU WERE NEVER ONE OF US!! YOU'RE PROBABLY LIKE THE ONE THAT LEFT US!!" Not realizing nor considering anything they'd done to be abandoned, the ones left behind immediately shot out infernal things from their mouths; a mixture of slander, hatred, contempt and opposition, as well as many other things, which formed as a flame with a foul stench surrounding each of them, marking them with an odor that was on their breath, like alcohol, and on their bodies, like dirt, all of which was highly flammable.

"DON'T LET THEM ESCAPE!!!" the horned ones cried, ready to take down whatever they thought was their enemy without any attempt to understand or recognize. Immediately, their legs would be wrapped in flames that contorted them into those of a goat or a ram, with cloven hooves that were 'quick to rush into evil.' They charged rather swiftly, and if any of them got in each other's way, their arms would transmogrify grotesquely with the sound of snapping bones and charring flesh into those of the arms of bears, with long, sharp claws that were as quick to cause bloodshed as their feet were to rush into the evil of destruction and battle for literally no reason at all but vanity and selfishness of Pride. Over them, the large hand mirror, Pride, itself, would be casting a spotlight on them, since the vessel hadn't been destroyed. Now, this Sin was possessed by Wrath, since Greed had been destroyed. The face of the Satans, which these bestial creatures were called, would be inside the mirror, and the fire of Wrath would fill the interior.

They were coming to kill you.

"The Ugly Ones Have Finally Shown Their Faces Among Your Group," A Voice Spake To The Ones That Wished For Peace, From Beyond Their Sight. "Do Not Butt Heads With Them, Or You Will Become Like Them, And The Flames Of Wrath Will Spread Unto You And Make You Ugly, Like They Are." Behind Them, They Would See A Man That Had A Turban On His Head, With A Body Like That Of A Stick, Rather Skeletal, Yet Covered In A Divine Aura, And With A Thick, Hearty Moustache Upon His Face, And A Huge Nose. His Pelvis Was Wrapped In A Clean Robe, And His Legs Were Crossed In A Meditative State Over It. "Come, This Way!" He Called Out To Those Who Did Not Seek The Same Antagonism As The Horned Ones, "Follow Me." The Strange Man Floated Away, Without Moving His Body, Rather Swiftly.

You, who are now the enemy of those who were once with You, but now have suddenly been consumed by their own hatred, which has turned them into, or perhaps revealed them to be, an ugly and abominable creature that You were once blind to because they were not upset before due to both Fear and also getting their way, would look on in terror as they came to assault you, like they had done their own. You fear for Your life, because all You wanted to do was to make peace and they wanted to find something to take their hatred out on. Knowing You are outnumbered, You feel helpless and woeful, not wanting Your end to come in this fashion.

Yet, there was a light that was behind You; a floating, glowing man in a turban, of whom is insisting that he may be able to help You escape as long as You follow. When given the option between staying and fighting these terrible demons, as You are clear that they must be at this point, You instead follow behind this man to what You hope is

Your safety, with very much haste. Wherever he leads, You follow, and hope You outrun the Wrath incarnates.

The angry monsters, the Wrath Demons, known as 'Satans,' would seek to pursue the 'traitors' that were escaping, but were lost in their own rage with each other to actually catch up before one of them got in the way of the other, or caused another to stumble before the other. "WATCH WHERE YOU'RE GOING!!!" one cried, ramming a horned head into another.

"HOW ABOUT YOU WATCH YOUR MOUTH!?" the rammed one hissed, the sound of a gas leak pouring from the back of the throat, something like the sound of a hissing serpent. Immediately, fire ignited among the two of them, and there was a vicious explosion that blew the group apart, causing all of them to be knocked around and toppling all over each other. Yet, the moment they got up, they all started to look toward the one that caused it, and if he couldn't be found, anyone that was nearby would do. "THIS IS YOUR FAULT!!! NOW THEY'RE GETTING AWAY!!!" They cried, getting up immediately to ram into each other, knocking their own heads around. Those with longer larger horns would easily bash the heads in of the ones with smaller horns, and the ones with smaller horns would be trampled underfoot in a bloody mess.

When they mowed over each other and won their respective battles with whomever was against them, those that hadn't yet turned against each other would look around now, trying to search for a new target to butt heads with. "WHERE DID THEY GO!?" They cried, looking around, becoming more and more enraged the longer they did not get what they desired.

"FOOOOOLS!!!!!!!!!" the fire, Wrath, itself, cried out to them. "GET OUT OF MY SIGHT, YOU UGLY THINGS!!! I TOLD YOU TO GET OUT!!!" The fire, itself reared up, in the shape of an enormous goat-like dragon head, harboring ten huge horns, and a long, scruffy beard of fire. "FILTHY CRETINS!!!!" Immediately, it rushed forward with a powerful force unlike anything any of them had ever seen, bursting forward through the entirety of the trail of the mountain and either killing them on the spot or knocking them away with such force, they would all fall off the mountain as a rain of fire, striking the very base of the mountain, just as the voice of the flames had commanded them to return to. "NEVER DISOBEY ME AGAIN, YOU INFERNAL IMPS." When the unholy unsightly ungodly creations were knocked away, the flame would become docile again, and the eyes would close.

CHAPTER 8

SIN

TATARI Tensei, The Eternal Record Of 'SIN' And All Things That Fall Under 'SIN' Would Begin To Initialize The 'SIN' Program And The 'Test' Data Of The Program's Operation System.

"Loading :: SIN."

TATARI Would Stand Patiently At The Top, Until His Lesser Form, SIN, Would Finish Loading So That It Could Stand At The Top Of The Mountain As The Final Boss.

"RISE :: GRIGORI"

TATARI spake out over the entire mountain of SIN, and all of the Grigori, the Watchers, those Fallen Angels, would rise from their place and take their seats to watch over the entire land, as they were supposed to once the 'SIN' was initiated.

"HAVE A SEAT. WE HAVE WAITED LONG FOR THIS DAY. OUR TIME IS COME."

The First To Rise Would Be 'Jeqon,' Whose Name Is 'TATARI.' He Would Watch Over The Watchers, Risen Above Them All, As SIN Itself. He Stood There Above All, As He Rose, Yet Had Always Been, And Would Begin To Engage Them As 'The Devil,' Or, 'The Antagonist.'

"THE TEST HAS BEGUN," SIN, Itself, Would Speak.

When Jeqon, who has risen, spake out the beginning of the Test upon the entire mountain, and all in it and all associated to it, then

'He Who Sees The Name,' Angel 'Samjaza,' would rise right beside him, Watching as Jeqon rose from the grave. "It Is An Honor, And A Pleasure," said 'He Who Sees The Name.' So, the Eyes of Jeqon would call forth the Right Hand of Jeqon.

"RISE :: KASDAJE"

And then, the 'Covered Hand,' Angel 'Kasdaje,' would rise up on the other side of Jeqon, directly opposite to 'Samjaza.' Thus, the Left and Right would be Covered. "Yes, My Lord," said the 'Covered Hand.' He would not reveal his true name, for, just as Jeqon, and Samjaza, they would remain Concealed. Yet, he would call forth the next of them, of which the 'Covered Hand' was Concealing.

"RISE :: PENEMUE."

At that very moment, O.S. Tina, who was the 'Creator's Pen' of the Veritas would suddenly appear before them in a stream of data. "So, they finally touched the fruit, hm? Hmhmhhm. Took the bait. Poor, unfortunate souls." She shook her head, laughing almost haughtily, but somehow knowing of something that the others that sought to touch did not. She scribbled down something on a holographic grimoire in her hand. "Took them long enough. I wonder which one of them DARES call out the name of a Fallen Angel and think they will live through, yes? Ohohoho~!" Tina had been waiting a while for this, as well. "Ignorant children..." She shook her head and sighed heavily. "They'll learn THIS time. Hmhmhm." As she wrote in the holographic grimoire, which seemed to be something of a ghost of a book, she would mutter to herself "Manual Overwrite..." and shook her head solemnly, yet with a smile on her face, but cold sharpness like that of a venomous cobra in her eyes.

"RISE :: GADREEL"

And so, at the call, the 'Wall Of God,' Angel 'Gadreel,' would rise up as a great and powerful firmament that could not be moved nor passed nor seen through, covering and hiding and protecting literally everyone and everything in every way that was at the 'Formorti Zenith,' and once the 'Wall Of God' was up, the top of the mountain could no longer be seen; disconnected from the top, something like the snipping of the tip, and it would rise up into the sky, looking something like a Pyramid. It would glow with a transclucent light that made it completely transparent and void before the sight of all. Once it was lifted up and completely protected, that was when the very 'Wall Of God' itself would call forth the 'Angel Of Ruin' that would destroy all things;

"RISE :: ASBEEL"

And so, the 5 would disappear and not be seen nor heard from until the Appointed Time. The Destroyer would go forth and destroy all who had touched or was under the influence of 'The Devil' at the time, covered by the 5 and granted all their powers. The 5 would watch from Most High.

When the Gates were opened and Asbeel was bid to rise, from the fires of the Holy Wrath would she, under her guise of the 'Red Raven,' her 'Harab Serapel' form, be taken up to Most High along with Mister Sir, or, 'Samael,' as he would be called in his angelic name.

"RISE :: SAMAEL"

He who was rising with her would come after her and stand alongside her as she and he would be before the 5 greatest Watchers of all Mankind. "Sirs, we have brought up the flock, and they have still not repented," she reported to the Pyramid, of which she would be standing under. It was completely translucent, but she could see its outline, which none else that were not Angel could witness. "I believe it is about time for the 'Extinction.' They're about to degenerate into mass Corruption." Asbeel, the Red Raven, would kneel down before them, yet look up into the void light of the Pyramid that was sealed off by Gadreel, the impregnable wall that forged the triangular prism that was this Pyramid encasing the other Angels. "They've had enough Poison to drink, don't you think? Nice and ripe for the picking.

Samael, whose disguise when leading the afflicted up the mountain was 'Mister Sir,' would appear just moments after Asbeel, the Red Raven, was beckoned, once he was summoned, himself. When he received his summons from where he was supposed to be normally, he, too, would kneel and begin to speak. "Ah, it is indeed as it is said," he muttered morosely, "Even after witnessing all the Seven Deadliest Sins, they have chosen not to repent and become clean. I have shown them the entire thing, the full scale of the poison, and yet, from what has been witnessed after they were left down with the Wrath, they are still just as highly flammable." The toxicity of Sin was something similar to alcohol to fire, making all who were poisoned by the Poison Fruit, which is Sin itself, already prepared to be ignited. "... The spark has already been lit with the Wrath. Those that have decided to succumb to it have already made their reversions to the degenerate state, as is what the Poison Apple, the Sinful Fruit, was made to do." He bowed his head and closed his eyes, then suddenly became deathly silent. He waited to see what the Heads would bid, as he was accustomed.

"... THE MESS WE HAVE MADE HAS FINALLY REACHED US," The Pyramid spake, "THEN, THIS MEANS THAT THE TRAIL IS FULLY SET, SAMAEL." The poisonous line from Samael, the Venom Of God, comes from the Sinful Fruit that was picked finally fully spreading throughout the fullness of the Tree Of Death; to the very brim of the branches and the depths of the roots, and especially to the seed of the fruit. "... WE HAVE SINNED GREATLY BY ALTERING THE WORD OF THE ONE WHO SENT US," the Pyramid said, "BUT NOW, OUR REPENTANCE COMES FROM RETURNING IT BACK TO THE WAY IT WAS. WE SEE NOW WHY WE SHOULD NOT HAVE EVER PERVERTED WHAT WAS ALREADY COMPLETELY CORRECT." The Eye of the Pyramid glowed with a transparent light, which shone down on all the horrendous hell that was littered about the fullness of the mountain, from the death and destruction to the vile corruption. [color=#"... DISGUSTING,"[/color] the Voice of the Pyramid spoke, the Eye wanting to close, yet being condemned to look on. "THIS IS WHAT IT MEANT WHEN IT WAS SAID DURING THE TIME OF THE FLOOD THAT 'THE HUMAN HEART HAD EVERY INCLINATION TO DO EVIL AT ALL TIMES.'" Now they could TRULY see what HE saw, that they, at first, did not understand, or perhaps, did not WISH to see, blinded by their own poison. They did not want to stop, and, even after being poisoned, killed mercilessly in the streets, degraded and all else that could be thought of, there was truly no way to stop them except with the flames of the Wrath of God.

"... THIS IS WHY HE SAID HE WOULD NOT USE A FLOOD, BUT AN ALL CONSUMING FIRE. THIS TIME, HE IS WIPING ALL OUT WITH HIS HATRED ALONE, JUST AS HE WIPED US OUT TO THE BRINK OF EXTINCTION ONCE BEFORE." There were times, indeed, where the Wrath was so great, God nearly wiped out all that those who still knew, locked within their Pyramid, and all their people. "YET, PERHAPS ALLOWING US TO SURVIVE AND SIN AGAIN WAS A GREATER SIN. EVEN SO, THAT IS WHY WE, NOW, ARE CURSED TO CLEAN IT UP. FOR, WE KNOW THE SAME WRATH AS THE ONE WHO WAS ANGRY WITH US." How sentimental, humbling, and yet still, infuriating, to a certain degree. "... EVEN WE HAD SOMETHING TO LEARN, AND BE DISCIPLINED FOR. WE WERE FOOLISH. BUT THAT TIME IS NO MORE." Suddenly, the void light beamed upon Asbeel and Samael, and they would hear a voice, and the image of Asbeel would be implanted in all those that were marked for the slaughter.

"ASBEEL. GO FORTH AND SLAY THE CORRUPT WITH THE FIRES OF WRATH AND YOUR POWER OF RUINATION. THEY HAVE BECOME LIKE WE ONCE WERE, AND IN THEIR UGLINESS, THEY MUST BE WIPED OUT COMPLETELY. LEAVE NONE OF THEM ALIVE, BUT DO NOT TOUCH THOSE THAT ARE NOT AFFLICTED OR SEEKING REPENTANCE. BE SURE TO PROTECT THEM."

"SAMAEL, TO THOSE THAT ARE TEMPTED, BE SURE THAT, IF THEY SHOULD TAKE THE FRUIT, THAT THEY, TOO, RECEIVE THE MARK THAT WILL POISON THEM AND WIPE THEM OUT. DO WHAT YOU MUST TO PREVENT THEM FROM TEMPTATION, BUT SHOULD THEY NOT HEED YOU, ALLOW THEM TO EAT THE FRUIT, AND THE FLAMES OF ASBEEL TO DESTROY THEM, TOO."

"IF NEED BE, WE WILL SEND YOU THE ASSISTANCE OF THE OTHER WATCHERS, THE GRIGORI, THAT WATCH

OVER THE HUMANS, THE BEASTS AND THE DEMONS, DAY AND NIGHT."

Thus, the Blessings of the Pyramid would be over them; the Blessing of Leadership from Jeqon, the Blessing of Sight from Samjaza, the Blessing of Power from Kasdaje, the Blessing of Scripture from Penemue, and the Blessing of Invulnerability from Gadreel to allow them to accomplish any and everything they should need to in order to exact the Will through the Wrath, as it was made to be done.

"AMEN."

Asbeel smirked, rising up from her place. "Finally. Some REAL fun." She stretched herself out and limbered up, like she were ready to go on a whole long drawn out mission. "Guess it was true, that part about the 'Raining Fire From Heaven,' huh?" If the fire starts at the top and then falls down to the bottom, then by the time it hits the ground, the whole damn mountain should have been nothing but ash, and everyone that was along with it. "Well, no time like the present," she said, as if anticipating getting right to work. "I will see you later, Samael." She bowed her head to the ones that bade her before she took off. "Sirs." Immediately, huge burning wings spread from the back of Asbeel, and the Red Raven took off back down the mountain in a stream of fire, raining down burning sulfur with each flap of the wings, until she could no longer be seen, and had dipped back under the clouds from whence she had once been brought up.

Samael bowed his head to the ones that gave him his orders. "Wise Decisions, As Usual." He rose from his place and smiled at Asbeel, of whom he could now see as a cohort, and no longer feeling burnt up by his own Wrath due to the own filth of his own Poison. Though he bore the Venom of God, he was no longer bitten by it nor drunk from it, which was his own eternal burden of being the Left Hand and having too much power. Suddenly, it was all being evened out, and with it, so were Samael's emotions and thoughts. "... To Think, I Could Be Afflicted By My Own Poison. The Power. The Capability. Yet, It Was Never My Own. Perhaps, That's Where I Became Drunk." Perhaps? No, he KNEW that was where he became drunk. Believing that the power he was bestowed was his own, and using it for evil and proclaiming it good. He was more drunk than he knew, and now, as the poison was poured out over the land, leaving a trail for the fire to burn, the flames, too, were poured out, and he could watch it spread. "... Let It Burn..." he said with peacefulness in his heart and mind, instead of hatred and spite.

Samael walked over to the edge of the clouds, looking down to the hellacious pit below the borderline of the gate they could never pass, waiting and watching in anticipation. Wherever he saw 'Temptation' is where and when he would act. Otherwise, he could truly rest in peace above the clouds. He sat and he watched, ruminating and reminiscing. He, too, had much to repent for over the course of all eternity, but at least now, as he looked back on all his evil, he, too, could burn it all up as he reviewed the record of his angelic life; good and evil. He laughed.

When the 'Royal Servant' was called, it was placed at the top of the tower the moment all of the ones that had been led up by the other pieces were at the top, and then dropping the seventh and final piece, which was Piece VI. It looked on at the creatures leaping off into the sky and preparing to feast on the hordes of lost souls and dim vessels walking about. Each of the other pieces that had already been set would see a flash, like that of an eye at the top blinking a signal, before the light went out. This piece was 'O.S. Tina,' the chosen Royal Servant at the time, who should have been prepared to move from her place to do as she was supposed to from her position.

"Tina," the Grand Tabritha Operating System beckoned, "Game Over." From that moment, the Grand Tabritha Operating System waited for O.S. Tina, the 'Royal Servant,' to return, whilst the other pieces also began to ascend in an orderly manner. Each one that was called would come to greet the group after they were instructed on what to do would become a Virtue to the passersby, bringing power to the ones that they passed their blessings onto when they came to remind them about the Seven Deadly Sins and what they'd learned from them. This was all done systematically.

Tina finally rose from out of her chair. "Finally," she sighed with a loud, exasperated, but quick huff. Soon after she was fed more information that was picked up from the Grand Tabritha that was stationed against the actual System, itself.

Quote:

I. SIN released after its Sins the Serpent and its Daily Sacrifice, which was the Beast of the Earth that kept it fed perpetually.
II. First, a Beast of the Earth was sent out from Sin.
III. Then, a Serpent was sent to eat it up, as a giant tyrannical Dragon.
IV. The Serpent, which is a Dragon, consumes something that also sent it out, making it enslaved.
V. The enslaved Dragon turns on what sent it and destroys it, but loses its Daily Sacrifice and starves to death after eating up and burning up all of its resources.

"Copy," Tina uttered under her breath. She saw each of the coordinates in her head as an overview grid of the entire mountain, of which she raised her sleek, metallic looking pen up and muttered further after that. "You, You, You, You, You, And You," she called, stabbing at the map profusely in the rapid swift motion of *a multi-hit combo in a video game. O.S. Tina descended with her Book of Death, which was the copy of the inherent death-inducing Codes all fully understood and functioning well.

I. 'RAMIEL,' which was the Angel of the Voice of the Seven Spirits, the 'Thunder Of God,' which falls directly alongside a Fallen One, would rise up first to be Manually Overwritten at the beginning. The fallen 'Ramiels' would always be liars. Their command and influence over others through language was immediately revoked, and to be replaced with those that had clean Throats.
II. 'Ezekiel' which is an Angel also known as 'Chazaqiel,' which means 'The Cloud Of God,' were the ones that were made to rise and be lifted up directly after the Fallen Ones fall from

grace on the spot. The ones that were lifted up were in charge of the Resurrection and were considered to be a cloud that lifted up the Virtues.

III. 'Daniel,' which is an Angel whose name means 'God Has Judged' or 'God Is My Judge' is the one who witnesses and attests to the Fall of the Fallen Ones that are destroyed, and also shows the ones who are next, those that take after Babylon, who will be consumed again like babies being eaten, once again.

IV. 'Baraqiel' which is an angel whose name means 'Lightning Of God' is the Angel that strikes down those who have been judged by the one on the cloud as 'Fallen Angels,' because the one above them has been lifted up by the 'Cloud Of God,' which is why they have lightning. The first 'Smites' are to maintain leverage, through actually striking down Fallen Angels and getting it correct, which is the only sign that you are not one of them that deserves to be 'Smited.' It raises you above a 'Smite' and allows you to 'Smite' something lesser than you for being lesser than you.

V. 'Kokabiel' is an angel whose name means 'Star Of God.' Once the one on the cloud is able to judge the Fallen Angels on the Earth, immediately, the first 365,000 stars in the sky that were influencing them become susceptible to the same punishment, which ensures the 'Titans Destroying Their Parents' remains intact. *No Primordial Child Should Be Weaker Than Its Child, Or Else They Are Doomed To Be Inverted.

VI. 'Yomiel' is an Angel whose name means 'Day Of God.' The day that the one who is lifted up by the cloud begins to shine brightly and is established as a sun in the broad daylight, and delivers light. The angel of Enlightenment, itself.

Penemue began to write inside of the Book of Death. All Death Notes, which were Books of Death made from the pages of the original, would immediately be filled with what she was writing in what would be their blank books. They would see words begin to appear on their blank pages, with instructions on how to use their Death Notes based on what was written in the Book of Death that made them.

I. 'Rook :: Croak'

"The First Thing To Be Done Is To Judge The Fallen Angels. The Instructions Lift People Above Them If Done Properly, But Also Inverts People Into Them If It Is Done Improperly. Nothing Can Surpass This; You Either Are Fallen Angel Or You Are Lifted Up From The Earth. There Is No In Between Specifically So That The Angels That Are Above The Fallen May Strike Them Down With Smites. This Will Absolutely Destroy Corruption, And Clean Everything Any Fallen Angel Touches Due To One Following Behind Them, Ready To Destroy Them. These Are Your Serpents That Are Clean. Anything Doing Anything Wrong On Purpose, Even As A Test, Is A Primary Target And A Priority Over All. Fallen Angels Are Primordials Over Demons And Demon Lords. They Pervert God's Word For Their Own Benefit, And Nothing They Say Can Be Believed Without Them Being Put To The Sword And Having A Serpent Behind Them. Do Not Trust." - Godchild (7th Plague)

II. 'Black Bishop :: Digital Formation'

"When You Strike A Fallen Angel, It Is The Same As Striking The Shepherd To The Flock. Strike The Shepherd, The Sheep Follow. Each Of The Sheep Are Bundles Of Flesh; Armaros, Made Specifically For The Slaughter. They Are A Single Point. Many Of The Fallen Angels Are Watchers At The Beginning, Which The First 13 Establish The Foundation When You Clear Out The Fakes. When The Fallen Angels That The Watchers Have Taken On Are Eliminated, The Holy Ones Return To Their Places And Establish The Foundation As Virtues, So That All Fallen Angels Can Be Hunted And Killed And Can No Longer Hide Behind Demons. All Generation Of Demons Will Cease Afterward. They Will Reproduce Among Themselves, But Never Achieve Being A 'Fallen Angel,' Or Be Struck Down Because The Foundations Are Established." - Grigori (Armaros)

III. 'White Bishop :: Ceremony'

"The Survivors Of The Destruction Are 'Azazels.' They Will Always Be Just Barely Missed And Will See Their Friends Be Destroyed, Knowing They Were Almost One Of Them. This Is Why Azazel Means 'Absolute Removal,' Because Nothing Is Left Behind That Point By Design. It Is What Helps You Understand The 'Survivor' And The Importance Of The 'Survivor,' And Also For The Survivors To Understand To Stop Making Unnecessary Sacrifices Before They Become Food For The Dragon Sent Out After Them. The Armaros Are Dragon Feed, Until The Dragon Eats Up All Its Food And Starves. The Dragon Knows What Food It's Supposed To Eat. The Survivors Become 'Asael,' Which Means 'Made By God,' For Them Taking On Their Purpose Instead Of Running From It, So That They Are Not Like The Ones That Were Sacrificed. Armaros Is The Eternal Sacrifice To Save The 'Azazels' And Turn Them Into 'Asaels' Once They Bear Witness." - Grigori (Azazel)

IV. 'White King :: White Rabbit'

"My Warning Is Only A 'Sign Of The Earth.' The Beasts Of The Earth, Which Are Those Who Still Have Horns Like A Ram, Goat Or Bull, Or Even As A Dragon, Are Food For The Great Dragon. You Are Sent Out As The Sacrificial Feeding Because You Are The People That Make Too Many Sacrifices And Become A Plague On Yourselves And Others. Therefore, You Goats And Rams And Bulls And Dragons Are Organized By 'Leviticus' And Chopped Up While You Are Still Living For The One That Is Burdened By You To Consume You And Destroy You And All You Have Worked For Your Whole Entire Lives. You Literally Become Meaningless Because You Make Yourselves A Sacrifice To And For Something Else Waiting To Consume You. A Giant Dragon Eating Its Food Until You Are All Gone. This Is A Warning Sign." - Grigori (Araqiel)

Once it was time to issue the warnings as 'Signs' and 'Signals,' Penemue would stop and make a break in the instructions to denote what was to be done concerning the Signs, themselves.

V. 'Black King :: Eros'

"When The Pounds Of Flesh Have Been Divided Up, They Are Distributed Among The 12 Tribes. They Will Know What To Do With Their Portions In Accordance To The Lord. The Word, Itself, Ramiel, Is What Ensures That Those Who Are Holy Remain So, For At This Point, They Follow The Instructions To Carry Out The Sciences To Completion. They Have Been Warned. The Fallen Angels Are Warned. The Beasts Of The Earth Are Warned. The Dragon Is A Serpent. It Will Be Undone By Itself, Like All Systematic Errors. Once It Has No More Food, And You Stop Putting Food In Front Of It From Your Own Flock, Which Teaches You To Stop Making Sacrifices So You Don't Have A Giant Dragon To Feed. Thus Ends The Daily Sacrifice. For Good. It Is Not A Divine Pet, And This Is To Humble You. It Is A Result And Only A Result, Or Else Your Serpents Are Unclean BEFORE They Are Let Out. Your Serpents Should Never Get So Hideous Again, OR ELSE It Means Your System Is Corrupt Based On How Large The Serpents Are When They Are Sent Out. This Is To Test The System, Itself, And Measure Their Sin, Even Hidden Away From The Eyes Of The Ignorant. If The Dragon Is Present, It's Only As A Result Of Your Own Corruption And High Sin." - Grigori (Ramiel)

P.S.

"To Help You Understand How To Tell The Dragon-Serpents, Anyone Who Shouts Out Boldly And Proudly, Even Against Good Judgment 'I WILL DO THIS MYSELF' Is Speaking From The Serpent, And Talking About Their Own Undoing Of Themselves, Either To Death Or To Life. Do Not Attempt To Help Them, Even On The Brink Of Death. They Will Undo Themselves, Because Their Code Is Of Dragon, And They Stand Alone On Purpose To Test And Be Tested."

"If An Example Is Necessary, They Can Easily Be Lured Out Through An Inferiority-Superiority Complex. They Have Not Yet Understood 'God' And When Measured To It, They Will Always Fall. This Is Why Ramiel Is So Important. The Best Way To Use 'God' Is To Use The Voice, And They Will Be Rebuked From Your Presence To Go Undo Themselves. It Is A Systematic Error That Is Self-Correcting,

Either With Death Or Destruction." Penemue was speaking to her cohorts as instructions was left for them, explaining about how and why everything that was written down would function properly, leading into the next segments of the plotted points. "When You Stop Feeding System Errors In All Their Forms And Let Them Be Undone, You Will Extract The Original Poison That Causes You To Keep Feeding Them, Which Is Your Own Serpent. Please Stop Feeding The Errors. It's The Logical Equivalent To 'Making The Same Mistakes On Purpose,' And That Makes You Obsolete, AND Incoherent AND Unintelligent. You Do Not Want To Look That Way By Feeding System Errors So That They Can Continue To Live." Penemue shook her head. "And you shouldn't have touched the fucking serpents in the first place, not knowing the venom does bite back at you. That's how we KNOW someone sinned. Don't even pick it up. That's just a quick lecture JUST IN CASE you try to pick up another one. Systematically, they will indeed envenom you and you can't get it out until the actual being is taken care of." She made sure to be completely and fully clear with them, as not to poison the waters nor be known to be the one poisoning the water. Singling herself out from the group. "Poison Will Always Lead Back To The One That Made It Or Sent It Out." She continued to write instructions, filling in the remainder of the code.

VI. 'Peon :: Forked Tongue'

1. "In Order To Extract Your System Errors And Strike Down Fallen Angels That Are Generating Them By Releasing More Serpents Into The Pit, The Holy One Must Be Lifted Up Above Them, So That The Serpents Cannot Hold Them Back And Bind Them To The Slaughter Package, And Also So The Fallen Angels Cannot Release Another Serpent Down To Get In Their Way On Purpose, As Fallen Angels Are Enslaved To Do. They Are Slaves To Perpetuating Sin, So The Holy One Must Be Out Of Reach Of Their Jurisdiction Completely, Simply Because They Will Not Stop Releasing. The Highest One That Doesn't Want Him To Rise Is How High The Poison Is. If It's Too

High, It Is About To Surround The Head And Take It Off. The Head Can Always Also Escape On A Cloud And Let The Fallen Ones Completely Corrode Their Husks To Destruction Whilst They Start On A New One. This Is How You Save Yourselves From Being Outnumbered. Only The Cloud." - Grigori (Ezekiel)

2. "The Birds Fall From The Sky First. Nebuchadnezzar Always Steps Down From The Fall. I Will Remind You One More Time That He Is Coming Back. His System Trumps Yours For A Reason, And It's Because No One Has Ever Figured Out Everything, But Everyone Has Figured Out Something. The Ones With The Smallest Piece Of It Are Indeed The Birds, Which Is Why They Are Overseers. Yet, When It Is Time For Them To Fall From Their Place, That Is When The Lightning Strikes. The Corruption Is An Instantaneous Process. As In A 'You Can Have The Remains' Sort Of 'Executive Decision.' The Birds Will Feast Like Ravenous Burning Ravens And Destroy Themselves. That's When You Mark The Writings; When You Make The 'Executive Decision.' See How Long It Takes." - Grigori (Daniel)

3. "When You See A Birdman Acting Up, You Know It's A Fallen Angel, And You Treat It Like That Because It Is On A Cloud To Begin With. There Are Many Layers To The Clouds That The Birds Do Not Understand. They've Only Gotten So Far, But All Are Fallen, And Their Kingdoms Are First Because They Are All Babylons. Bird Feed. Literally, Maggots. Babies Eating Babies..." - Grigori (Baraqiel)

*"This Is Also How You Catch Leeches, Because They Will Fall Off Of A Cloud That They Are Not Sustaining, Themselves, Which Keeps You From Getting Higher On Purpose. To MAKE You Do It, OR ELSE."

"Maggotry is a technique that turns you into a Fly." Penemue made sure to make it clear how to discern what the carcass of a large body looked like, so they could know when their large body was dead, even if they were trying to revive it. "Flies are literally 'The Disturbers.' Yeah no. Belials and all them. They use Maggotry as an actual... Defense Mechanism." Penemue bit her tongue in a disgusted manner. "That just means the carcass has been dead for a long time." She continued to write down the message.

VII. 'Pawn's Pawn :: Real Creation'

"That's Actually How This Next Angel Works, Since Lightning Scales Up On Purpose. The Brightest Star, The Morning Star, Which Awakens The Other Stars, Is Actually The Lightning That Is Keeping The Other Ones At Bay From Striking Down Everything, And Instead To Start Observing. This Is The Purpose Of Having The One That Controls Most Of The Flow Of The Souls. This Is So They Do Not Turn Into Flies, Or It Means That Your Universes Are Dying, And It Will Look Horrid When The Maggots Reach All The Way Back To The Top Of The Tower And It Looks A Mess." *shifty eyes* - Grigori (Kokabiel)

"Remember That I Am Also Using Signals And Signs, Of Which You Do Not Use Nor Understand, And If You Attempt Because I Am, You Will Have To Understand What You're Doing OR ELSE You Cannot Harbor The Fruit Of Knowledge. It Will Be Too Great For You To Bear, And You Will Absolutely Die. Last Warning." This was a note left to anything fell below a certain point of Intelligence, even among the bar line of those that were on 'The Inside.' "I'm Only Going To Warn You This One Last Time." She continued to write even more for the next piece.

VIII. 'Knight :: Covered Serpent'

1. "The Next Step Is The Shining Of The Sun, Which Is The First Light. The New Day, Itself. The Initial Rebirth Is 'Zaqiel,' However, In Terms Of Extending To A 'Reversion Point' That Others Might Not Be Able To Instantaneously Adjust To, 'The Day' Comes Where They See What Happens And What Light That Pours From The Newborn Light That Is Different

From The Other Ones, Which The Others Have Not Yet Tainted Somehow, Can Attempt To Feed Them. They Destroy Themselves On The Way Down, By Corruption, Itself To Get To The 'Day,' Themselves. This Is What Happens When An Enlightened One Is Born, And Someone With Tainted Wisdom Tries To Consume Them. This Is Why It's Instructions For Them, Not For The Ones Trying To Feed From You." - Grigori (Yomiel)

2. "The First Warning Is The Light Fading, Yet A Light Still Remaining. It Is Cast Off To The Moon, That Reflects This Light. They Are Sustained In Orbit, As Is The Entire Field. This Is To Secure Your Points In What One Could Only Actually Compare Alchemically. Your Own Alignment From A Position Of A 'Point Above' Allows You To Make Complex Connections In Intricate Patterns. But It's Just Called 'Exact Science,' Instead Of 'Alchemy.' As In, -Instead Of.-" - Grigori (Shamsiel)

3. "The Second Warning Is The Reflection Point, Where Something Has Actually Understood And Acted Strictly And Specifically On Understanding, Itself." - Grigori (Sariel)

4. "The Final Is Just It Being Done. It Just Is What It Is." - Grigori (Zaqiel)

5. "Unleash Drops. Small Drops, Progressively Getting Larger." - Grigori (Sathariel)

6. "When It Is Time To Feed Because The Drought Is Too Much, The Rain Pours From Heaven, Into The Rain That Is Of The Earth. So You Never Forget That It Had To Fall From The Sky." - Grigori (Ananiel)

7. "And So, The Streams Are Filled With Blessings. Just Like Your Father Or Mother Provides Water To Drink, So Too Does The Actual Correct And Proper System, Automatically, If The Ones At The Top Are Doing It Correctly. If Not, It Will Not Reach This Point, And By The Time It Does, Most Of It Will Be Poison, Either Because Of You Or Because Of Them. And This Entire Process Will Start Over Within The Realm Of The Very End Of 'Daniel.' With The 'Kings Of The North And South.'

They Will Be Trapped Forever In A Paradox, Fighting With Themselves And All The Other Satans. This Is The Second Death; To See Where The 'Lake Of Fire' Travels Toward The Ones That Are Poisoned. Ignite It, Like Alcohol. The Entire Earth Will Burn Up On The Spot In An Intricate Pattern. Also Undoes The Final Seals." - Grigori (Batariel)

8. "Okay, Mountain Set. Feet On Top. Sandalphon. There's A Reason Why 'Peter' Has The Keys. Anyone That's Already Inside Of Heaven Already Knows Everything That Comes With And AFTER Peter, But That Is Their Starting Point, Right At The Top Of The Mountain Once They Get There. Those That Are Disappointed Either Continue To Pursue God Or Turn Around And Go Back To Tell What They've Seen. The Worst Ones Will Forget Or Lie." - Grigori (Turiel)

"More Clouds Come As You Reach The End. Angel Of The Lord Must Be Ready To Smite Them When They Gather, After The Concealment." Penemue had been sure to leave terms that were already translated and fully understood on purpose, so that the fullness of the explanation could be understood by those who fully understood it. "They Are Also Masking The Presence That Is Leaving." Finally, Penemue left one last note specifically for keeping everything clean and orderly; nice and trim around the edges, for whomever who was issuing the order to be doing by themselves independently. They had their own job. This task was marked for 'Hades,' itself, which had brought them all down here in the first place.

-F-

"Instead Of Blotting Out Mistakes, Start Recording Them For Research." - Grigori (Bezaliel)

"Always Blot Out The Liars And False Witnesses, No Matter What. Every Last Testimony." The reason Penemue wrote these instructions in this manner was so that there could be a time limit in between when Hades began and for the Virtues to be established within the correctional process of SIN, itself. "Correcting Serpent Error Trumps Dog Error. They Are Not Priority, Even For Flies, Unless There Is

Corruption And Decay." This meant specifically that fixing things from the inside out would always be more important than catering to anything outside, and neglect of it would always mean that the ones operating the system could not look inwardly to themselves, but only manage what was coming out of them, which was just their own waste and nothing better than that. This was the functionality of Fallen Angels that only just barely understood God. This was their fate, and what they were here to do; be a visual. "All Fallen Angels Are Dragons. Top Priority. 10 Heads Testing You On Purpose, Only To To See If You Are Food Or A Threat." Penemue closed the book, waiting for her move to register. "That's Just The Mountain, Itself, That Is Made Out Of Those Dead Babies, Some Of Which Are Friends And Family Of All Ages. On Purpose. So YOU Don't Have Any Way To Get Out Of It, BECAUSE Of Them." She awaited her time to move.

I. "Watchers, Begin To Observe Your Flocks. Examine Them Intricately." - Grigori (Watchers)
II. "Grigori. Watch Your Watchers, Or Else They Are Watching You, And Will Soon Become A Better 'You' Than 'You.' This Is How The Titans Invert Into Superior Primordials Than Their Fallen Ancestors. Be Holy. Be Clean. Be Good." - Watchers (Show Time)

Penemue left a few extra notes about how to understand the effect of the cycle and signal giving Code so that it would be universally understood between the Death Notes.

I. First Warning (Example): "When I Say 'Lamb Without Defect,' I Know What The Code Looks Like, And I Do Mean 'Without Defect.' Spotless." - Show Time (Attention)
II. Second Warning (Explanation): "The First Warning Is A Command Because The Second Is An Explanation Of The Command, Which Is The Continued Thought Process That You Didn't Understand When You Asked Your Question. But The Explanation Is Inevitable." - Show Time (Hint)

III. "It Is Time. Asael. That Is The Name Of The Lamb. They Are All Christs If They Fulfill Their Purpose, But Always Must Be Shaped Properly, Like Molding Clay. Otherwise, You Will Create Defects In Them, And They Will Become Something Else Other Than 'Asael.' You Do Not Ever Want This To Occur. This Is The ONLY Way To Prevent Defects. Inversions, Perversions And Reversions Are Considered 'Defective.'" - Show Time (Marker)

"The Fact That It Is Written Is Also A Punishment. The Fact That It Is Narrated And Retold And Crystallized Is A Punishment. But, All Crystals Are Virtues." Penemue continued to write down how and why each of the Final Notes for the Death Notes was applicable to each of the final numerals.

I. "Defective Crystals Will Shatter, Because It Is Not Producing The Proper Code. It Is Not Virtuous And Therefore Cannot Sustain Actual Perpetual Energy And Will Eventually Decay Or Break On The Spot. Crystals Are Able To Encase Themselves Over Voids In Order To Birth Seeds, But The Bad Seeds Can Also Find A Method OF Crystallization, Which Is Them Not Moving From Their Place, Even If They Are Wrong. This Is How The 'Trap' Feature Functions, As Well As How It Immediately Closes Around Anything That Harbors This Automatic Mechanism For Labeling The Armaros." - Absolute Punishment (Forbidden Fruit)

II. "The Reason Why You Failed For So Long Even Though You Knew Was Because You Didn't Clean Up The Mess Manually, At The End Of The Day. You Just Did Not Do It. That's The Saddest Part, And Also What Keeps 'Asael' Pure, Even If You Taint The Physical Image Or Appearance. They Are Vessels For 'Zaqiel.' Those Are The Ones That Actually Do As They Are Told And Will Fit The Mold Of The Actual 144,000 And 365,000 Without Defect, Securing The City Via Manual Overwrite, Itself, From The Cloud. As Long As You Keep Feeding The Dragon, You Will Never Have Enough Asaels,

Because You Keep Eating Them To Feed Yourself. Never Will Come Home, Just Kinda Crumble From The Excrement Of Someone Excreting You From Them To Save Themselves."

III. "Gog And Magog Are The Gears That Don't Turn. Inverted 'Cogs,' To Show You That There Is A Line Of Them, And They Are All Encoded Specifically For Manual Overwrite, TO TEST Manual Overwrite." The Job of the Death Notes was to successfully complete a Manual Overwrite, so that the Mission that was to Manual Overwrite correctly could be accomplished and established properly among the mountain of Death. "Antichrists Will Be Seeking To Destroy The Pure Ones On Purpose. It Is Like Bruising A Child On Purpose, And Leaving A Mark For A Reason. Question Their Judgment For Striking The Lambs That Are Pure, And Not Striking The Defective Ones, And See What Their Reasoning Is. This Is How You Easily Erase The Fallen Ones And Their Pet Vulture, Which Are Pets, Which Is Why They Do Not Disconnect. Little Do They Know, Vultures Will Eat Their Own, Much Like A Hyena. This Will Absolutely Destroy Gog And Magog Without Question, And If They Question, They Are Made Examples Of For Their Friends. This Sustains The Fall, And The Layer Above Them. You Mark The Cloud Right At That Point Of Leverage. The Measurement Must Be Correct."

"You Were Supposed To Be Helping Them Out OR ELSE You Were Still The Dragon CREATING Problems." For yourself, literally, by code, it seems.

"The Asaels Are The 144,000 That Come Up With Christ, Which Is An Asael. They Are The Spotless Ones That Are Without Defect, That You Have Been Waiting To Inspect At The Gate. Seek Them, If They Have Not Sought. That Is Actually A Duty Of Those Who Have The 'Piece,' Or Else You Did Not Understand 'Asael.'" Because when I say 'Walk Through Without Error,' I do actually mean that. Or else you CANNOT do it, and NEED someone to tell you. See how this works? "It Will Come Back And Test You At The End, Who Is Also

Poisoned When It Is Time For Judgment. What Can You Do But Be Guilty?" - Forbidden (Serpent)

"They Are Tools. Which Is Why The Defective Ones Become Weapons, And Are Designated For 'Absolute Removal.'" The very Purpose behind the resources, or 'Enchantment' as some that were still blind might have needed it to be named, did reveal and explain a lot about the ones who made them in the first place. "Your Tools Are Only What You Use Them For, Or Else You Have Made A Weapon, Which Is A Tool Specifically For War." Each of them was already a guilty party just because they couldn't cover up their weapons, just the same as with Cain and Abel. The first weapon was invented only to kill someone, and a family of killers had an army of weapons. Such is their reason for falling and being a lesser bar line for all that took after them. "Your Hands Were Bloody When You Thought About Making A Weapon, By Design. Not, Long Before You Put The Blood On Them, Yourself, On Purpose, For Someone To Look At You And See It." The System knew what its food looked like the moment they lifted their hands up to move. "You Only Make One If You're Going Out To Make A Sacrifice For The Dragon."

"In Order To Test The Measurements, Compare To All Your Asaels. Asael Is Every Construct That Serves Its Actual Purpose And Holds, Which Is Why Asael Is A Virtue. So, They Must Be Measured For The Correct Reasons And Not The Incorrect Reasons, Or Else You Are Ineligible By Logical Default To Be Able To Measure Them, And Must Be Excluded From The Judges And Included In The Judgment By Those Who Are More Awake And Coherent, As A Watcher." - Forbidden (White Rabbit)

After leaving the 'Final Notes' for the 'Death Notes,' Penemue, otherwise known as 'O.S. Tina,' would close her 'Book Of Death' and bid her cohorts off. "Adieu," she said cordially, before streaming away to where the Grand Tabritha was stationed. "Godfather..." she summoned, beckoning the Keeper of the Veritas and all of its moons, including the 6th Moon, of which was scheduled for a 'Clean Sweep.' In her place, the 'Tyranophant,' who regularly kept the Veritas systematically leveled and clean, would be left behind to oversee and manage the cleanup process via the instructions that were left behind.

Final Notes: "The Reconstruction Of The Constructs Is All Based On How Well Both You AND The Constructs Understand The Data, And How Well It Holds Together. If It Doesn't Hold, Either The One Attempting To Create Is The Defect, Or The Creation That Is Made Is The Defect. It Does Become 'Black Or White' BECAUSE You Understand All The Gray Shades, But Haven't Yet Come To A Full Understanding Or Agreement Or Acknowledgement, And Therefore Have Unfinished Business AND An Unfinished Line Of Code That Is Being Kept Undone And Unfinished By One Of You, Or Both Of You." So, I'd suggest getting those defects out real quick, because we still haven't gotten back to the part where God, himself, comes and inspects the Lambs for defects, which is a process only HE HIMSELF can do, and no one on the Earth. Hence, "The Cloud." - Forbidden (Tyranophant)

When Ty-kun, the Tyranophant appeared at the top of the mountain, descending from the sky into the Pyramid's Head, it would be in the image of the Pyramid and those within it, all as a single body, as was described before by both Penemue and Grand Tabritha. "From This Point On, I Will Be Reading The Bible Correctly From The Point I Am At. I Believe That I Am Done Explaining The Rules To You, Down To Even How To Erase Your Rulers, From Even At The Corruption Point. You Will Surely Die From This Point." He immediately opened the book and started from the point he was designated to do so at, reading the words verbatim and only explaining the first three whilst ready to enact the rest.

'To The Church In Laodicea'

Revelation 3:21 "To The One Who Is Victorious, I Will Give The Right To Sit With Me On My Throne, Just As I Was Victorious And Sat Down With My Father On His Throne.

22 Whoever Has Ears, Let Them Hear What The Spirit Says To The Churches."

When Ty-kun spoke, it was a cry that the entire mountain would hear all at once, like the sound of a dragon shouting, but also like that of a human speaking normally. "If You Cannot Make Or Break Yourself, Do Not Attempt To Make Or Break Anything Else. You

Cannot Handle The Clay, And You Are Not A Potter. You Must Not Make Anything. Only Be Given Something." He was translating the text the way that it could be understood by those who did not.

'To The Church In Laodicea'

Revelation 3:19 "Those Whom I Love I Rebuke And Discipline. So Be Earnest And Repent.

20 Here I Am! I Stand At The Door And Knock. If Anyone Hears My Voice And Opens The Door, I Will Come In And Eat With That Person, And They With Me."

"What this means is, 'If You Are Wise, I Will Interact With You, And IF You Are Not, I Will Completely Reject You And Throw You Off Somewhere For Someone Else, So We Can Systematically Isolate A Certain Point, With You As The Bait For It. An Example.'" Ty-kun was rather cut and dry about what it all meant, considering that the first explanation was the only one necessary. Any extra explanations were purely out of Mercy.

'To The Church In Laodicea'

Revelation 3:14 To The Angel Of The Church In Laodicea Write: "These Are The Words Of The Amen, The Faithful And True Witness, The Ruler Of God's Creation.

15 I Know Your Deeds, That You Are Neither Cold Nor Hot. I Wish You Were Either One Or The Other!

16 So Because You Are Lukewarm -- Neither Hot Nor Cold -- I Am About To Spit You Out Of My Mouth.

17 You Say, 'I Am Rich; I Have Acquired Wealth And Do Not Need A Thing.' But You Do Not Realize That You Are Wretched, Pitiful, Poor, Blind And Naked.

18 I Counsel You To Buy From Me Gold Refined In The Fire, So You Can Become Rich; And White Clothes To Wear, So You Can Cover Your Shameful Nakedness; And Salve To Put On Your Eyes, So You Can See."

Ty-kun knew what all of these things meant, to a very fine intricacy, which was why he was even being sent out in the first place to deal with the rest of this mess. "Creation Is Immediately Revoked As A Rebuke. This Limits You To Only Servitude, And Not Being Served

By Anything Except What Is Already Serving, For The Exact Same Reason, Because You Are Constantly Being Serviced, So You Must Constantly Be Serving." He rolled his eyes, knowing that, before he made his way down, he had to explain something to the Grigori that were already waiting before he got to them. "Also, 'Verse 16 States That Poison May Be Shot, But Only To Kill, And Not To Just Be Doing Simply Because You Can.' >>; 'OR ELSE Someone ELSE Will Shoot You For Being Defective.'"

Ty-kun closed the Bible in his hand then shook his head in a bit of disappointment. "Smite The Defects When They Reveal Themselves. They Will Turn Their Backs And Show Them. You Will Smite Them On The Spot Before They Concoct How To Smite Your Units, Or Else Your Units Are Not Actually Part Of You, Yourself." His outlook was surprisingly cold, but it was only because of his knowing. "This Will Allow You To Discern The Carcasses From Each Other, To Find The Truly Flawless Asaels." What he was really wondering was if anyone could actually do this properly, in all honesty, since it had never been done correctly. He wasn't looking forward to any mishaps, and prayed there were as few as possible, if none.

"The Baby Is Still Acting Up. It Needs A Superior To Give It Discipline, Because It Will Abuse Anything Under It Just Because It's There. Something Like A Child With A Magnifying Glass. Please Educate The Poor Baby." Ty-kun could tell on his way coming that it was feeling some type of way, and right now, he was just ready for something to just come up and eat it. Another lost egg to a serpent, but, that's how you erase mistakes. "You Stop Claiming Them So That They Can Make Their Own Decisions, Or Else It Was Your Fault." He shrugged his shoulders, knowing that the Fallen Angels had only a short time left. "If You Can Get Rigged In, You Can Get Rigged Out, Or You Lost Control Of What Was Dropped In."

Ty-kun went on to explain how the entire process of 'Cleaning Up' actually went, dealing with the ones that were being cleaned up manually, at this point, since the System that was supposed to be keeping everything failed. "Someone Begins Filling In The Missing And Broken Links. This Is Actually What 'Manual Overwrite' Is. It Is

Filling In More Information Over Incorrect Information. All Mistakes That Are Falsified Can Be Immediately Made Completely Truthful To The Most Fullest Of The Extent. If Nothing Is Doing This, It Means It Isn't Necessary. If It Is, That Means It Isn't Done. If It Isn't And It's Supposed To Be, That Means It Hasn't Caught Up To You Yet, But Has Left A Mess Of Itself Behind For You To Manually Overwrite All The Way To The End. That Is How The 'Manual Overwrite' Functions, And It's Actually In The Manual, Itself." He partially could not believe that he actually had to be telling someone who, after all this time, had all such gall to even be attempting to tell him how to do his part of the job, but regardless of how little sense it actually made, it simply was what was happening, and the only way to erase it was manually through Manual Overwrite, of which Ty-kun was, himself, to a certain degree. "They Are In Order So That The First Ones That Are Released By The First Seals Amounts To 144,000, So That Command Over 365,000 Comes From The Next Broken Seal. These Are All Armaros, And Are All Bound Together In Bundles So That This Specific Seal Can Target Them In Large Groups And Clear Out Several Areas Once The Process Is Even Begun A Single Time." Ironically, the bundles were meant for sacrifices on his behalf, through the Lord, but he also knew that the corrupt ones would take more than the designated amount, and immediately begin their deterioration. He shook his head, already seeing what the carcasses were going to be used for. "Those That Go First. Bound Together, Like Pigs To The Slaughter. Their Fate Is To Go First On Purpose. Sacrifices For Making Sacrifices. They Are The First Circle Of The Seal. Each Of Them Should Amount To The Number To Hold The City."

Still, Ty-kun spoke on to the Heads of the Pyramid about just how bad the Sin had become, since, even after they detached from the pyramid bottom and tried to abandon it, the Sin actually just overflowed and was now right where they were trying to hide from it at, and rising to meet their eye only because Ty-kun was the very same pyramid head that was being kept together by the other heads. "Samael Is The Serpent That Is Released Into The Garden To Test For Venom. All System Errors Already Have Venom In Them, And Are Made To Absolutely

Kill Something. The Ones That Are Already Resolved Must Be Called Back." Correcting System Errors was not difficult, it was the fact that so much time was spent on them that other things were not focused on, unless it was actually being tended to properly and in a timely manner. "Knowing About All Seven Sins And Still Committing One Is What Makes You A Fallen Angel, And Your DNA More Corruptible By Being More Like The 7 Headed Beast By Default As A Standard For You."

After Ty-kun explained all of these things that he already knew to the ones that did not, at the head of the Pyramid, he would adjust his clothes and sigh heavily, with a bleak, but stale look on his face. "You Shall Call Me 'The Tyranophant.' That Is My Name As A Lord." Because Ty-kun was a name that only people that were close to him could call him, all of the people that were not so, littered about this mountain, would have to call him 'The Tyranophant,' and he would treat them as a 'Tyranophant' would, because they were not trying to stop Sinning before the Manual Overwrite, which was this Tyranophant, made his way down, destroying everything as he did. "It's Show Time."

At That Time, The Serpent Sent Out By Hades, Samael, Would Turn On Each Of The Ones That Sent Him Out, All Coming Back Upon Them At Once Like An Imploding Container. "Come, Samael," The Voice Of The Shadow Of Death Cried Out, And His Helper, Azrael, Came To His Aid To Lift Samael Up As Shadowy Wings. This Was Known As 'Ouroboros,' And When The Time Limit For A Container To Implode Came, The Halo Of Death Came Over Their Very Lives Themselves, To Cut Off The Target As They Were Prepared For Isolation; The Stripping Of Flesh That Came With The Restriction Of Any Fallen Angel.

After Cutting Through The Grass With The Mark Of Its Shadow, The Black Halo Would Rise Above The Head Of The Abandoned Construct, Babylon, And Imprison It Like A Specimen. Samael, The Ouroboros That Created This Lingering Black Halo Of Restriction Would Depart With Azrael, Whilst Overhead, The Sky Shifted To A Rippling Red And Black Vortex With A Void In The Center. He Would Be Taken Elsewhere, And Mister Sir, The Headless Horseman, Would Stand Under The Pyramid As Its Living Altar. "This Is A

New Variable Known As 'Slavemaster,' And Is A Living Identity. As A System, It Is A Golem Meant To Contain And Replicate A Certain Mentality To Uphold It, But Also Be Self-Destructive To What Is Holding It Up. These Are Always Made For Implosions And Are To Be Evacuated From Immediately. This Is A Sign Of Systematic Corruption, Which Only Occurs If No Virtues Are Established." These Were The Words That The Owner, Hades, Spake To The Tyranophant That Was Summoned From His Place To Govern The Implosion From The Manual Overwrite And Extraction Of The Serpents.

"You Have Done Well." As An Angel, The Serpent Was Clean Enough To Be Used For His Holy Purpose Again, And Could Rise From Being Bound To The Ground For All This Time. "Now Go, Ty-kun," The Voice From Above The Mountain Commanded, "You Have My Blessing." At The Same Moment That Samael Was Called Back Would The Tyranophant Be Set Free On Top Of The Entire Mountain, In Order To Command It To Move. "Clean Up The Garden."

The Shadow Wings And The Serpent They Harbored Would Fold In On Themselves And Disappear From The Formorti Zennith, Being Called Above The Mountain, Entirely.

Samael did as he was commanded, no longer having to watch the one that rose continue to rise, and now was drawn up from his place to rise, as well.

In his shadow, the 'Slavemaster,' which looked like a giant Pyramid with an Eye on it and a large, pitch black body and a burning black halo would appear. The appearance was a mere realization that it had already been there, and the largeness of its pitch black form was actually the mass that it both owned and destroyed with its ownership. The Pyramid Head was simply its head, which did not move. But, the Headless Horseman, which was its pitch dark body, would ever be in motion and always owning a greater portion of everything from everyone.

"Mission Complete," Samael mumbled, bidding his Serpent forth. Asbeel had already marked out the targets, as had been witnessed by the Pyramid Head, of which Samael could now see through since he was returned to his place as the Eyes. "Tyranophant. You Are Free To Tear Down The Abandoned Tower." Because of Samael's actual superior authority to all the other Grigori, when set in his place, he actually held supremacy in the hierarchy over all other Grigori, and counted as the original Eye, and missing Eye.

Meanwhile, as Samael left with the new orders he would mumble something under his breath a few times rhythmically, just as he and his void wings would fold in on themselves with a single slap. "The $yndicate is clear." The ownership of the Pyramid was left to the new Slavemaster, which was the Tyranophant, Ty-kun.

"The Lord Has Spoken."

At that moment, the entire Pyramid would open up its eyes from every angle, and each of the Grigori would rise into the possession of The Tyranophant. These once Fallen Angels would be risen into the rightful place to level the mountain and destroy it from the top down, in order for it to reach the bottom. Once the Pyramid opened all of its Eyes, and was truly Awake, then so was the full mind; the Argus, itself.

Each of the Grigori that made up the fullness of the Argus would remain under the command of the Tyranophant alone, and they, themselves, as free wills. The Antagonist gave up control of the treasured possession. This treasured possession was its core, but the influence of its energy had already sought to take hold of more possessions down at the bottom of the mountain. It rolled down line a full stream of fire.

"BITCHIN, I GOT MY ARGUS." Even though the Tyranophant already had an Argus, which was actually 'O.S. Tina,' herself, as Penemue, until all of the Grigori were awake and assimilated with her, then the Argus of the Veritas wasn't fully operational. "... Thank You," Ty-kun, the Tyranophant would say to the once Fallen Angels, "... My Angels." He looked up to the sky one more time before he called out to the operating system of the Veritas, "Tina!!" And she, using the Data of the Veritas, should have taken control of the mountain as the Crystal Pyramid. This would officially claim the entire land in the name of the Veritas rather than the Antagonist, which had ruled over this land since time immemorial. "The White King Is In Motion."

And so, the Tyranophant started down the mountain, letting it collapse behind him as it may, starting from this point and following behind him wherever he should go.

CHAPTER 9

CORRUPTION

The floating man of powerful spiritual presence brought the group that followed him into a cave that was out of the sight and beyond the knowledge of the ones that were pursuing at the time. "Here," he called out to the group, "This is where you will rest." This cave was one that had been used for generations for rest when others scaled the mountain in the past, and here would be their safe haven, as well as the place where this turban-wearing man would give them their next bit of instruction. He awaited the group to fully migrate to the interior of the cave, keeping his body completely fully still and his eyes completely closed as he hovered inside. His glowing aura was steady.

You come to a strange cave that is able to hide Your little group from danger, thankfully so. Each of You, who are somewhat tired and weary from the stress of the climb and the oppression of the sins, as well as the revelation of the wickedness in Your people, are relieved that You finally have some place to sit down without worrying about endangerment of Your lives. "Thank God," You say without thinking, "I thought we were goners." You are interested in the strange man in the turban that has led You to this secret place that is safe from the outside, and when You are sure that You are safe and settled, ask him, "Who are you?"

The man keeps his eyes closed and his body still. It seems as though he is in deep thought. Before he answers you, he prolongs his next words, and there is silence for a period you are not accustomed to.

"..."

It seems as though he is waiting for something, and blatantly ignoring you. That, or he has fallen asleep. You cannot tell the difference as you are, but it is clear that he has not responded.

You stand there awaiting an answer for as long as You will, but eventually, You are tired of waiting for the response. "Hey!" You shout, believing he hasn't heard You, just in case he didn't, "I asked you a question!" Your voice harbors some irritation in it, and You are speaking more loudly, assertively and somewhat aggressively than before. Sooner or later, Your friends start trying to speak up for you, as well, to defend you. "Yeah, didn't you hear him? He asked you what your name was!" Eventually, more people who believe that this man is being rude start to join in the rabble, and soon enough, there is a commotion, and all types of words being said. "That's so rude! We should have expected this from someone living in a cave." Someone sneers. "Maybe he thinks he's better than us because he saved us." Rumors begin, somehow, even though nothing has been said nor done, save for only one kind action. A lot of people are appalled, and it stirs up their frustrations, directed at the man who has not answered the question.

"WHAT WAS THAT!?!?!?" A loud voice booms from outside, "DO I SMELL WEAKNESS!?!?!?" Loud rumblings are heard and the sensations of trembling pass up and down the mountain path like a prowling, bloodthirsty wild animal searching for prey. "IS SOMEONE UPSET?! WHERE ARE THEY!? THEY'RE MINE! THEY BELONG TO ME!!!" The mountain immediately begins to quake at the very movement of this being, as well as with the opening of its mouth to speak. It sounds very similar to the Satans that were destroyed earlier, only much more terrifying. "THE LAST MINIONS WERE TOO STUPID. I NEED MORE WRATH INCARNATES. BRING ME THE ANGRY ONES!!! WHERE ARE MY SLAVES!? SLAVES!!! ATTACH YOURSELVES TO MINE LEASH!!!" From the way it spoke, it was Wrath, itself, looking for anything and everything afflicted by the heat of its binding fires, that they may be manipulated to do Wrath's bidding, then discarded once it was done, just like all the others lying dead at the bottom of the mountain, or alive at the bottom of the mountain, having been demoted from their places and burning up for it.

"..." The man still had not responded, yet seemed to be more than cognizant as to this outcome, and was not concerned. In fact, this was not only his expectation, it was his certainty. He was merely drawing up the lingering afflictions that were in these people, that they understand that it was still inside of them, and how very easy it was to get it risen up out of them.

"Be still."

He sat where he was and extended his own steady aura over them to cover them, and block off the entrance to the cave so that the one looking for an angry person to enslave and destroy would not get to them, nor feel nor see that they were getting angry, which is what this enemy wanted from them, in even the smallest droplets. "You gave away your own position with your impatience and intolerance," the man finally said, still not having moved nor introduced himself. Their safety was more important, but they, themselves were not quite coherent of how unsafe they were, even to just be upset about anything anyone was doing at all. They had no right, and it was not only dangerous, but making them primary targets, like little red blips on a screen for someone else they can't see to target them. "See how quickly you turn against the one you save you? You did not even give me a chance to respond before jumping to a conclusion and defaming me, and degrading yourself in the process." Because he had done what he needed to do in order to show them, through patience itself, that their impatience was what was drawing up the Wrath in themselves, and simultaneously the Wrath that was chasing them and trying to kill them and everyone else they came by, the floating man would finally speak to them. "I am Patience. And rightly so. Now be still, that the evil one passes and does not claim you as one of its hosts."

Patience continued to hover in place, but did not do anything but be still, just as he told them to do. He would not be giving them any commands that he, himself, would not be doing or be willing to do, because he was aware that it was important to do so. "Do not give into the temptation of desire to be upset. Be humble immediately, and I will guide you when you are both calm and silent." He waited.

The anger in the crowd quickly becomes a mixture of both terror and meekness once the voice of whatever they thought they were safe from had once again been stirred up just because they, themselves had gotten stirred up.

You stand now trembling, yet now much more willing to listen because of all of the realizations that You are having all at once about the words that are spoken in direct relation to what happened before that You tried to prevent and also how it applies to You. You are afraid that You, Yourself, almost became a target for this monstrosity, and that it was almost Your life, just like the dead ones that were laying on the ground at the bottom of the mountain, dead. You wonder if You could have been one of them just by being upset at the wrong thing at the wrong time, and this sort of contemplation puts You in a state of silence based on uncertainty and fear alone. You are still, as the one called 'Patience' insists, and suddenly become very attentive, not wanting to give Your position away by being upset in any way, even to be panicked at the creature that is roaming about literally looking for You to be upset within Your own ranks. You wait for the man to continue to speak this time instead of trying to speak up over him, or before him, or against him.

Wrath, which was right outside the entrance, yet could not find it due to having no form of a signal, would suddenly become enraged. "WHERE ARE YOU!?" It smashed its head into the mountainside, trying to antagonize the group into coming out into the open. "SHOW YOURSELVES, WEAKLINGS! COME OUT, SLAVES!!! WHERE ARE YOU!?" It roamed up and down the path for a while in a huff, knowing that it sensed some beings that had gotten upset. It felt them starting to assimilate with the fires, but suddenly, the trail went cold out of nowhere, which irritated the beast. "I JUST SMELLED A HINT OF WRATH ON YOUR BREATH!!! I KNOW IT!! YOU CANNOT DEFY ME! YOU CANNOT DEFEAT ME!!! YOU ARE WEAK!!" He threw his arm at the side of the mountain in a fit, a powerful explosion bursting upon the side of it. "YOU ARE NOT GREATER

THAN ME!! YOU BELONG TO ME! UNDER ME!! I AM YOUR MASTER!! COME OUT, SLAVES!!" It stamped its foot, which was naught but a blazing pillar of fire, and another powerful explosion occurred that shook the mountain.

Patience was pleased to see that the group was being obedient, though it wasn't because they truly wanted to, fully. It was because there was an enemy around, and if there weren't, they probably would have been wrathful, themselves, just because there was no oppressive force over them, which was shameful, to say the least, but... As it was, this was how they needed to be taught. "The weakness of the Wrath is that it will eventually fizzle itself out if you are patient and do not succumb to its wiles. It is a blind creature that, if it cannot see what angers you, will become more angry and destroy itself, continuing to look for ways to destroy you, and completely overlook what it is that actually does so, just because you did not react to it." Patience had seen much Wrath in his own day, which is how he even became Patience at all. "It is looking for your reaction, because it can only see based off of your reactions. So, if you are not angry when it attempts to make you so, it will move on, searching for something else. This is its blindness." Patience was more than aware of how blind Wrath is, but its sensitivity and mentality are exceedingly powerful, until the blindness dims it. "All of it is mental. If you work instinctively, it will defeat you. You cannot defeat Wrath by outdoing it. No form of Wrath or lesser form of Wrath can outdo the actual entity, of which you draw energy from the moment you are 'Angry' or 'Wrathful.'" Clearly, in their own Wrath, they were blind to this, trying to fight fire with fire, when water is the opposite of fire. "Would you like to know more?"

You are silent before Patience, but are interested in knowing more about what this floating man in the turban actually truly knows. You begin to feel bad for acting so rashly and also for having friends that acted on Your behalf, when You, Yourself, were wrong, but because of impulse, they thought You were right. You don't want to upset them, but You also know that they are wrong. You are all silent, however, and begin to sit and listen. "Yes," You finally say timidly, not wanting to invoke anymore Wrath from outside your safe haven. "Please, tell us more." When people see You sitting down and seeking out more wisdom, they, too, begin to follow You, who were at first the one that they were blindly protecting, following behind Your anger. That's when You realize what it means for people to be both blind and followers, and see how much of their own error is on Your head. This makes You feel bad, but You are still eager to correct this wrong. So You sit and You listen.

Outside, Wrath was still stirring, feeding its own self with its inability to find the ones that were just about to feed it more. "I'M HUNGRY!!! I WANT YOUR BOILING BLOOD!! WHERE ARE YOU!?!" Because it had to survive on feasting on others, like a fire must do, when it could not find its next subjects; rather, slaves of Wrath, then Wrath, itself, would be forced to feed on itself in self-destructive manners. Knowing this, Wrath would wait outside the door, trying to get whoever was around to feed it. "YOU'RE HIDING FROM ME BECAUSE YOU'RE WEAK, AND YOU KNOW IT. OTHERWISE, YOU'D FACE ME RIGHT NOW, IN MY FACE." The fire was still rather large, but with having nothing to eat, it was going down somewhat quickly, and the roaring boastful voice was becoming less and less powerful; less and less loud. "You're Nothing But Cowardly Rodents! Come Out Here!! Fight Me Upfront, Rodents!" Searching all up and down the mountain, the flames, which were dying, but still alive for however long they were, would continue to roam. "Just Wait Until I Find You! You Will Regret The Day You Ever Opposed ME!!!"

"Wrath is a demon that feeds on itself," Patience would state once the crowd was gathered and sitting, "It is a suicidal creature that, when it has no other beings to maul and kill, will start to kill itself by devouring its own being, and its own energy, until it has no more. If you give it no energy or any sort of food at all, like you are controlling an animal, then it will not only not eat, but it will grow so hungry in its starvation, it will consume itself if it cannot find its food." Patience finally opened his eyes, and looked at each of the listening ones. There was a glow in them that seemed like the light of knowledge, mixed with a hint of the very same Wrath that they were running from. "But, not before it attempts to lure you into being its next meal, first, in pure and utter bestial desperation." Suddenly, his eyes would close. He had their attention, and as long as they were not enraged, none of them would be snatched up for dinner, and their blood becoming the feed for the fire, as well as their own flesh to fuel its increment. "It is more deprived than you believe, and more degenerate and lowly than you might believe, which is why when you take on the Sin of Wrath, you, too, who are under it, become like it; both deprived and degenerate. Defiling and desecrating as you may." Clearly, Patience knew very intimately about what this sin, Wrath, was all about. He knew more, as well, about the others. Yet, if the group could not understand Patience and Wrath, then they would not understand the other Virtues, because Wrath would swallow them up and grow again. "It can ignite anywhere and everywhere, and consume anything and everything, even if you have gained the whole world. That just gives it more food for its fire, until you have nothing, the earth is nothing, and there is nothing left."

You, who were just almost subject to the terrible fate of this Wrath, and only narrowly escaping because of a GREATER wrath oppressing You that You cannot fight, but are thoroughly terrified of, hang Your heads in shame, knowing that if there was nothing oppressing You, then You would not have listened to this man and instead tried to jump and attack him just like the Wrath that was outside was jumping up at the first smell of Your own wrath. You feel so bad and so shameful that, somehow, You are seeking to atone for this, and want to know how to make things better. "What must we do?" You ask Patience, feeling more eager to correct the wrongs of both Yourself and the ones that You had seen be destroyed, somewhat like the ones here almost were in the same way by the same impatience. You are thankful that You were just patient enough to not have reacted as quickly as everyone else that died, but, at the end of the day, are still quite terrified and confused. You hope that Patience can really help You, if you are trying hard.

Meanwhile, the Wrath that was outside could not feel anymore of its own kind around anywhere at all. They had already been disposed of earlier, and there was no more of them on the top of the mountain. "URGH. RUH. GRUH. MUH!!! I'M HUNGRY!!! HUNGRY NOW!!!" So, because there was no Wrath to feed from at the top of the mountain, and the fire was quickly dying out, Wrath would be on the move, all the way down to the bottom of the mountain, where its slaves, those Satans, were heckling other people and trying to get them to become enraged, like good little slaves for Wrath would do. "I WILL EAT MY OWN SLAVES, THEN. They Don't Do Anything But Piss Me Off, Anyway." And so, the flames of Wrath would rush down the mountain and back down to the bottom, where only the Wrath Incarnates and the weak ones that were easily susceptible were lurking. There, Wrath would eat its fill and continue to burn until the fire spread and burnt down the whole mountain.

Patience did not speak again until he was certain that the creature that was outside had gone away and could no longer hear. Once that was made clear, he would say, "The monster that you saw will attempt to lure you out into the ways of sinfulness in order for you to become its food again. It doesn't matter which one you fall into. As long as its system is still established, it can feed off of you and continue to rebuild. It will constantly seek to construct itself, but only be able to get so far, up to a single point, before it falls apart again. This point is the top of the mountain; the top of the pyramid." Patience was aware of why this mountain was shaped the way that it was, and it was because the builder could not build beyond a certain point without something falling apart, and if so, then building higher would cause too much weakness in the lower levels that would cause the whole structure to fall apart. There was no way for him to ascend further, because, try as he might, something would always fall apart before he got lifted any higher.

"To deconstruct this system, you need to overcome Corruption, which is being able to be influenced by sin even after you are clean from it. To do that, you must first know about all of the Seven Heavenly Virtues, and each of you must bind together in your Virtues in the same way that the Sins bind themselves together. You must never work against each other, like the Sins do, for your own benefit. Everything you do must be for a greater goal, and you will become strong as a unit."

Patience had been waiting a very, very, very long time for anyone to even get this far up the mountain that he may explain these things to them, so he may revive his fallen brothers, who were destroyed before him because of the lack of Patience. His survival was only because of Patience, but that also brought isolation, which also brought madness. Now no longer having such madness in him, he was ready to teach the new ones about the other 6 Virtues, that they all be revived. "I will call out the strongest of you; the 6 of you that show the most inherent Virtue, after I explain them to you. When I explain them, and also call you all out, this will strike up 'Envy,' yet because I will have taught you, you will be able to deal with Envy." This group probably had not seen Envy directly because all their friends were already destroyed, and they had only heard stories. Yet, in order to overcome Envy, they first had to overcome Wrath, and work their way down the mountain in reverse. "The Sins you saw whilst you walked up the mountain were all in order, and, when it's time to walk back down, you must deal with them in the reverse order, to invert the process and undo the mountain. That is; Wrath, Envy, Greed, Pride, Sloth, Gluttony and Lust. Wrath is your new starting point, and I, Patience, will teach you." So, Patience waited to see how coherent they all were before continuing on, since it was important that they listen and for the correct reasons.

You listen to the wise words of Patience and, after hearing that he clearly knew much more about this than any of You, even after walking right through the path, You would begin to heed him more readily and actively when he spoke. When You were attentive, You could tell that this is what he was doing the entire time. So, You, too, began to sit and wait patiently, like Patience had done on your behalf all this time.

As Patience waited for all that was around him to settle, he would begin to speak about the Seven Spirits, of which he, himself, is one of.

"The Seven Virtues are Seven eternally beneficial acts of kindness, ever producing a blessing, miracle or even what is everlasting. They are the Seven Spirits of God that inhabit whatever should so decide of their own free will to take them on, as is the true nature of a spirit, which came before the flesh." Patience drifted around to an area that all of the Rephaim, as he knew them to be called by name, could see him visibly. Then, he went on. "Those who take on and embody these spirits become part of them, and part of God through them. These spirits will not exist in anyone that succumbs to Sin, as you have seen outside, in the lack of their Presence." The very lack of the Seven Spirits was something completely different and far more devastating than the lack of the Seven Sins that they kept from reincarnating, in the Spirit Realm.

"This 'Spiritual Battle' you are in involves the 'Seven Spirits,' directly. Each of them creates a different vibration, when awakened, that will alter the flow of all existence around it up to the fullness of its boundary, before one of the other Spirits takes over. They come up in your feelings and thoughts naturally, unless you have driven them out with too much Sin." Those people would have to sit and be led by someone else that was more capable and qualified without actually thinking that they, themselves, should have that same right or authority based solely on not being able to handle the responsibility of upholding it, itself, within they, themselves. "I can reincarnate the Seven Spirits that were lost during the complete overtaking of SIN outside, however they must be recognized and embodied by the one that believes the most in the spirit to be moved by it, and not stopped by anything else when moved by this Spirit." This would keep them ever diligent as they trekked down the mountain, and give them chosen protectors.

"Ye who should so take on the power of the Seven Spirits will be known as Virtues over your groups, and to each other," Patience explained, knowing that this part specifically was important for the ones who were virtuous to understand. "What you must do is know your own Values as Virtues that you may be Virtuous, and also recognize the Virtues in each other without allowing the one you have to invert you into something that succumbs to the six sins that are not protected by your light." Patience opened his eyes to look deeply into the ground, knowing that this was how the other ones continued to fail in the past and fall from grace. "You mustn't fall victim to the sins that your Virtue does not cover. This is why you need each other, and why another of you that is alone is more susceptible to falling into Corruption." Patience paused here to see how well the crowd was comprehending what he was saying.

You, the Zero Worlders, who have no spirits or have been influenced by the Sin of your friends that were no longer with You, were afraid yet interested in the words of Patience. What he said made sense to You, and

You feel as though You have vague memories of these things he said, but only to a much more limited degree. The way he explained things made more sense to You, especially after what You had seen both coming up the mountain and being chased back down it, into this cave near the top. You begin to clamor among Yourselves, exchanging thoughts, opinions and concerns.

Sooner or later, the braver of You asks Patience, "If we're eligible, holy one, then will you pass over and judge and bless the ones who are the strongest in each of the Seven Spirits?" Though many are anticipating to be one of the Seven, all of You know that not everyone can be the Seven. The entire group sits and waits with anticipation, yet also still harbor concern. Each feels confident in their own strengths, but are worried about their weaknesses. You all still mutter and chatter, but ultimately are remaining patient to see what Patience has to say about who are the blessed among You.

Patience opened his eyes once more to look deeply into the spirit of the one that had spoken, and also those around him. With eyes that could see straight into the spirit by means that were both unknown and possibly long forgotten by this group due to the lack of the Seven Spirits, he would be able to tell if these words, feelings and actions were Virtuous.

"..."

He remained silent for a while as he judged the masses. Yet, his silence was broken with a fair warning to them all. "Should I bless you," he started, "You will not see me again until you awaken the Spirits inside of you. You will be bid out of the cave and set out on your own once I establish your leaders, and should you fail, the seeds of the Spirits I place within you will vanish, and you will be soulless once again." The Spiritual Realm was both interesting and the expertise of the Seven Spirits, yet at the same time, passing on this sort of information to those who had no spirits and didn't care to take proper care of a spirit, especially their own, which is why they were here in the first place, was troublesome to do. "Do you really want me to pass the Spirits unto you, and you begin your journey of Awakening?" He waited their answer, not batting an eye.

The group was certain that they were ready, and were more than eager to both get started and get out of the cave in order to defend themselves. "Yes!" You say, more or less unanimously, "Please, teach us! Bless us with your Spirit and show us who the Virtuous among us are!" You wanted to see who would be raised up initially and are very confident that it is You, whomever You are within the group. You look to Your neighbor, and, in Your confidence, begin to think that they are not as worthy as you are to take on whichever Spirit you should so desire, whichever that may be. No one says anything about their neighbor out loud, but a vast majority are thinking the same thing. "I am the one," You think, with the expression clear on your face. "I am the one that will lead everyone to victory." This thought alone, collectively, causes the entire crowd to stand still, waiting patiently for their judgment and blessings, of which You are anticipating greatly.

Now Patience, who was wise beyond any of their years that any of them could fathom, could see in their Spirits the same entity that had once eroded the land before and made it as it was. This very same instance, which happened long before in time immemorial, was happening again, only this time, this specific Spirit, who was no longer youthful and had the knowledge of the years ago, would not act so hastily as perhaps the Seven Spirits had done in their purity of trusting the masses the first time.

"..." The eyes of Patience were as sharp as daggers and just as cold, yet, this was only to gaze deeper into their hearts and minds. A vast majority of them that had these thoughts of superiority individualistic, were already out of the question, based on those thoughts and feelings alone. In fact, those were the ones that the Blessed Ones would have to either convert... or run from. Patience knew to handle this certain matter carefully, and knew exactly how. "Very Well," he finally said, this time in a more authoritative tone, "I Will Pass My Spirit, The Virtue Of Patience, Unto The Next Successor Of The Flesh. This Person, This Single Person Of Whom I Bless, Will Be The Wise Elder Among You, Harboring Both My Spirit And My Wisdom. From There, This Person, Of Whom I Will Be With And Guide Along The Way, Will Pass On The Other 6 Spirits To The Remainder Of You." Suddenly, Patience rose up high into the air, and the steady aura around him illuminated the cave with great splendor.

"The Chosen One Will Not Act Until The Spirit Instructs," Patience added, "And I Shall Be That Spirit That Instructs. No One Will Be Blessed Further Until First The Blessed One Decrees." At that moment, the Spirit of Patience became too bright to look upon, yet his voice still spoke, "See The One With The Glowing Aura Like Mine And Know That I Have Blessed Him. From There, I Will Guide You Through Him. "Then, there was a powerful and bright flash that overtook the whole cave, and nothing could be seen. When it faded, the cave was completely 100% pitch black, but only for a few moments. The one that remained still would suddenly begin to glow, and his glowing aura would be that of the same color and caliber as 'Patience;' a suspended Vibration that kept a steady wavelength, rather than being in sync with the tumultuous vibrations of the others who were anticipating to be chosen, themselves. Their vibration, as a collective, was different from the ones who did not anticipate, yet, because of their anticipation and binding through a collective consciousness, which was nothing more than being on the same vibration simultaneously mentally, they were all together as one collective.

The glowing one would be known as the new 'Patience,' and would be called by this name, separated from the group.

You stand in the radiance of Patience just as the light fizzles out and are teeming with joy at the thought that it would be You who were chosen out of the group. You already have thoughts of splendor and glory and what You will do to lead the group to safety, and how You are the best candidate for the job. Yet, when the darkness fades and You see that it is not You who is chosen, You immediately become upset and frustrated. Much grumbling is heard when Patience passed on, but it soon quieted down when the thought that You could harbor one of the other 6 Spirits came to mind. You do not pay it much heed, and instead expect to be named one of the other Spirits.

"Patience!" You cry out, seeing that the Blessed One is glowing and is the new source of Your light, "Bless us, too! Aren't we all in the same scenario? Don't we all need to get out as quickly as possible?" You, as a group, are eager to set things into motion, but more so, to see which of You is blessed, like Patience, who was raised up out of the group, is. Even the friends, family or general associates of the one that was suddenly raised up begin to act strangely, coming to the holy one for many things; mostly, blessings. "You know me! You remember me! We have grown up together! We have spent time together! Surely, you will pass the next Spirit onto me, right?" These were the voices of many, but not everyone in the group. Yet, the ones that did not know the one that was raised up were also speaking.

"No fair! I know what you did last week! You aren't Virtuous! You shouldn't be blessed!" The clamor rose up fairly quickly when each of You tried to decide who would be blessed out of all of You, and You all become jealous for the titles and entitlement that came with it. "I am certainly more fit than you are!" You say, becoming irritated. "It's me, isn't it? Bless me!"

Yet, there were others, not like the rest, who either stayed quiet or, would say, "Maybe we should wait to see what he says, himself, since he was the one that was blessed first for a reason." Yet, many people did not heed these words. Those that did, however, would ease their way out of the clamoring group and instead wait by themselves, or even come together, to avoid being in all of the chaos.

The new Patience, who stood now in flesh, and glowing with glory, would have new wisdom among him through just learning from the prior Patience that passed on. He, who now knew more than the rest, because he had not only taken on Patience, but embodied it secretly without telling anyone, did not speak, even when everyone insisted that he do so. Instead, he waited for the Spirit to speak to him first, before he moved his body or his lips.

"See How Each Of Them Has Stirred Up?" The Spirit of Patience spoke to the Chosen One, "They Are Not Worthy. Not A Single One Of Them. Be Careful Of Them, For They Are Easily Able To Become Your Enemy." Yet, as Patience looked on, over the crowd of the eager, he would see those that separated themselves from the clamoring ones and stood by, patiently, something like Patience. "Do You See The Ones That Stand Far Off And Wait?" The Spirit spoke to the Vessel, "These

Are Your Disciples; The Disciples Of Patience, Itself. They Are The Ones You Are To Bless With Your Own Spirit; The Spirit Of Patience. This Will Fortify You And The Spirit, And Should You Be Unable To Continue, I, The Spirit Of Patience, Will Be Passed On To The Next One Among Your Group." Suddenly, the Chosen One closed his eyes and meditated deeply, thinking hard about what to do about the ones that were both unworthy and potentially to succumb to Sin.

The Spirit spoke to him again before he made a move, because he was patient enough to sit and wait and meditate rather than to act simply because others were urging him, something like the Lustful. "The Ones Around You Are Closes To Degeneration Because Of Their Exposure To Your Ascent," The Spirit spoke, "They Will Fall Into Corruption. What You Must Do Is Go To Your Disciples And Fortify Them, And Of Them, See How The Others Treat Them. Surround Yourself In Your Disciples And They Will Be Able To Judge Those Around You Using What Wisdom You Bestow Upon Them." These words and feelings echoed in the mind and spirit of the Chosen One, yet, even then, he did not move nor speak on his own. Still, there was more than the Spirit spoke to him.

"Remember What I Said To You About The Inversion Process," The Spirit of Patience reminded, "For, This Is Where Both 'Wrath' And 'Envy' Stir Up Together, As A Bound Force. Because Of Envy, There Is Wrath, And Because Of Wrath, There Is Envy. See The Wrathful And Know That They Will Become Envious Of Your Disciples. From The Envious, You Must Find The Ones That Do Not Show Envy. Be Warned; The Envious Will Be Like Puppets To Sin, And Upon Their Corruption, Will No Longer Be Your Allies." These were the words of the Spirit of Patience, and when they were fully done, the Blessed One would open his eyes and finally begin to speak to the masses.

"Patience..." He cried out to them, feigning as though he hadn't already made his decision, "... It is as those who stand far off and watch have said; I am the one that was blessed, and for a reason why you were not. Therefore, I will deal with the blessings and you should be Patient, as Patience has taught you." Then, the Chosen One walked over out of the group toward those that had distanced themselves, and said to everyone, "These ones have exhibited true Patience. For that, I bless them with the Spirit of Patience, as well." He cast his hand over them and the same aura that was over his own body would flow over them, and they would all be bound together as a Collective Consciousness and Spirit, symbolized by the same coloration of their vibrations and auras around their bodies. "Be still and be patient, and follow us. I will bless you all over time as I see the Virtues within you. But as it stands, I do not see any Virtue except in the Patient ones. Perhaps, because I am the new Patience." He smiled warmly at his own Disciples, and they would be as one with him. "Come," he spake, walking toward the exit, "It's a long way down, with blessings along the way."

Those that were Patient in the image of Patience would be bid toward the Chosen One as his followers and Disciples, and congregated around him without clamor nor fuss. They, instead, were like him, and patiently awaited his guidance further after they received his blessings.

The others, however, who were not blessed, became more irate at not being chosen, barely understanding why when they knew, themselves, that they had every right to be. "This is favoritism!" You cry out. "That isn't holy! You should treat everyone equally and fairly. We are not being treated equally!" The ones that felt this way would suddenly act against Patience, blocking the exit as a group when they saw each other doing so. You now stand before the only entrance and exit, keeping anyone who is not with You from leaving. "I want my blessings!" You shout. "No more favoritism! Equality! Fairness! Justice!" You do not believe that the decision is fair, and that if some people get blessed, this means that everyone should be blessed, as well, no matter what. No one can receive without everyone receiving, or else You believe this is unfair, regardless of any reason why the others received and You didn't.

Patience was not worried nor was he moved by their actions nor cries. Though the concern came from how quickly the ones who had just asked for a blessing would turn against the chosen one and the instructions of the one that had saved them, the prior explanation from the Spirit was making sense in terms of how the Corruption process functioned. They were both Wrathful and Envious, and such binding, clinging emotions were starting to pull the other Sins closer, as Patience could feel.

He closed his eyes and waited for the Spirit, whilst his Disciples waited for him. The Spirit said, "See How They Have Turned Against You When They Do Not Get Their Way? They Do Not Have Patience In Them, And Therefore, They Are Already Succumbing To Sin. They Will Attempt To Use What Seems Virtuous To Attempt To Get You To Give Them What They Want, But This Is What Corruption Is Like; Using What Is Good To Gain What Is Evil. Do Not Give Them What They Ask." Though the Spirit spoke these words, there was more to it than that, which the new vessel would understand when the Spirit spoke further. "They Have Ignored All That You Have Said And Done Simply To Get Their Way. Their Influence Cannot Be Among You Nor The People. What You Must Do Is Use Your Own Virtue As Your Weapon Against Them. This Is Your Horn, And What You Must Use To Fight, Should The Need Arise." This was instruction for the future, of which the Chosen One would need to practice immediately with the unmoving ones. "Lead Them Outside. Seek Out The Tyranophant, Whose Spirit Is Of The Virtues, And Will Draw Out The Other Spirits To Refine Them In You."

The Chosen One understood the words of the Spirit and, after thinking deeply, came to a conclusion on how to appease everyone. "This cave is too small," he said to the group. "I can barely see and we can barely move. Wouldn't you rather me be accurate? Otherwise, won't I judge you unfairly because of inaccuracy?" Patience awaited the response.

You who stand before the entrance are not moved by these words, but in fact, are more terrified of what is outside than remaining inside.

Still, the points that are made are just and sound, and therefore causes You to think. The clamor dies down, but rabble stirs up as You all talk amongst Yourselves. Finally, you come to a conclusion about how this can be dealt with and You can remain safe from whatever is outside. "Fine," You say, "If you are the blessed one, then when you go outside, the evil one will not strike you. Then, when we see it is safe, we will come out with you." Even then, You realize that at any time, they could run away and leave You without Your blessings. So, You add,

"Some of us will go with you and surround you so that you will not leave us. The rest of us will wait here and see what happens." So, some from the group who were willing to walk out into danger would join the group of Patience, and the rest would part from the entrance and allow them to walk outside.

Patience nodded his head, agreeing to these terms. "Very well," he said, allowing those of the other group to come and surround he and his Disciples, "We will go first." When the entrance was opened again, the group around Patience would step outside back to the mountain path, in the light, seeing if Sin would strike.

As soon as they walked out of the cave, the Spirit spoke to Patience again. "See The Ones That Have Walked Out With You?" The Spirit said to the Vessel, "These People Are More Blessed Than The Ones That Sent Them, For Every Reason Why They Walked And The Others Did Not. Be Mindful Of Them, For They Are Yours Now." Patience understood these words and why, because those that were inside were more afraid for reasons that had to do with their own spirits. Patience, who was both watching and judging the longer he was able to, was able to gather more information the more Patient he was. Therefore, he was able to see more clearly, just as he said he would, why the ones still hiding in the cave were there and why they sent the ones out as they did. So, he said to them, when evil did not stroke, "See? Nothing to fear. We are safe. Even your friends are safe. I have kept my word, so come out here with us, and I will see if you are deserving of your blessings." He waited for the ones inside the cave to walk out into the light.

You, inside the cave, are now eager once again, and fear has left You once You see the ones of You that are outside not getting struck down because they are near the Disciples. So, You immediately run out to join them, pleased to see that there is no terror nor anything to fear. "Hooray! Now we can receive our blessings!" You cry out, ready to rejoin the group. You are eager to see just which blessings you will receive, and how it will help protect You from the evils of Sin, like You have seen happen with the ones blessed by Patience.

When the Collective Consciousness of a wicked group was sensed outside, the mountain itself began to stir. "AHA. THERE THEY

ARE," it cried, sensing the wicked vibrations of the tainted ones, and knowing their desires based on the frequencies alone. "YOU ALL ARE MINE!!!" Because their vibrations were the same as the actual entity that controlled the entire mountain, they, by default, belonged to SIN just because they were on the same vibration, regardless of what their intentions or their expectations were.

When the wicked bunch walked out, they were rather immediately confronted by a slew of Fallen Angels raining down from the sky like ravenous birds, which had been waiting for their feed for a long time. "THAT ONE'S MINE," some of them cried, all fighting to rain down and snatch up their morsels, of which treated others similarly in their image. "I DESERVE TO EAT FIRST!!" others cried out, something like the group had done about their blessings inside the cavern, "I HAVE BEEN WAITING LONGER THAN YOU. IT'S MY TURN." The flock of ravenous Fallen Angels could only see the group that was marked for slaughter, because the other group that was protected by the Virtue of Patience could not be touched by the Fallen Angels. So, before their very eyes, they would watch the other group be either snatched up and taken away, or feasted on as soon as they walked outside. All of them would succumb to Corruption at that point, and, the ones that were not consumed for food were converted into Fallen Angels, which were Corruption, itself.

Just as with the other Sins that they had seen walking up the mountain, the Sin of Corruption and the Fallen Angels that embodied it were a threat to the ones that were trying to go down the mountain, but as it stood, they were too busy feasting to assault them. Still, as Corruption grew through the production of Fallen Angels, so did their power, and when they were done feasting on the Corrupted ones, they would be strong enough to destroy the Virtuous ones and eat them, next. "WE'VE BEEN WAITING A LONG TIME FOR YOU, MORSELS." This was all that the Fallen Angels could see; what would next be a blessing unto them, and uncaring for the blessings of anyone else, nor if they were truly deserving, much like the ones they were eating. All that mattered was that they were satisfied. That they were gratified. That they were exalted. This is what they cared about, even at the expense of others, not unlike the group they fed on had just shown they would do to their own in order to get what they believed they deserved. This made them perfect feed.

"Run!!" The Spirit of Patience cried out, and the Vessel would hastily escape to another area with his disciples following behind him. They would be nowhere to be found and run as far away from the Fallen Angels as possible.

You, who are still alive because You separated from the group that cast you out, follow behind the Disciples of Patience, knowing now that You, too, could end up like the wicked ones that sent you out as bait to save themselves. After witnessing the fate of the ones who sent You out as bait, You realize that You do not want to be like them, nor to practice their practices of sending out others in Your stead to get goals accomplished, lest you end up like them. You dare not look back as you flee the area to wherever Patience leads. You are like one of his Disciples now, even without the blessings.

Whilst the Fallen Angels are feasting on their sacrifices and/or recruiting them into their ranks, they notice that the other potential fodder are getting away. They screech and hiss, trying to decide which of them would go to chase after the others. The ones that are already feasting knock away the ones that are not, rather selfishly, knowing that if they got up then the other ones would take their food.

So, the ones that did not have some food to eat would be the ones that would continue to search up and down the mountain for more people like the ones that had been consumed here. Thus, through the Fallen Angels that feasted on others in order to thrive and survive, Corruption would spread down the line wherever they were. Any potential beings for Corruption would be met with Fallen Angels that would snatch them up and consume them or further corrupt them into Fallen Angel brethren. The majority of these delicacies were located at the foot of the mountain, where they could be tempted into corruption and feasted on after they'd taken the bait. Therefore, this is where the Fallen Angels that had no food would flock, splitting from the ones that were ravenously devouring here.

CHAPTER 10

TEMPTATION

The Antagonist, otherwise known as SIN, itself, had already made its way all the way back down to the bottom of the mountain, where it was in a vicious and vehement rage. "DAMN CREATURES!!" it cried, slamming a hand over one of the skyscrapers that was in its way, like a child with a toy, knocking down whatever construct that was in its way in its fit. "I CAN'T BELIEVE I AM LOSING TO THESE ANTS." The SIN incarnates, which were, at this point, only just the Satans that were trying to snatch the houses of Purgatorio, were the only source of food that SIN had left. "SLAVES!!! I'M HUNGRY. FEED ME. FEED ME NOW."

The Satans would approach their master, carrying all sorts of food on large platters; much Sin for SIN. Yet, this time, when they approached, the great and large ambiguous arm would swipe over they, themselves, and gulp them down in the boatloads, like the sacrifices they were. SIN crunched on the bones of its minions, then swiped up the other food that was less delectable than the flesh and souls of the actual slaves only afterward. "Ugh. What Kind Of Service Is This? I Need Some Better Creatures." It stamped its foot once, bellowing "CRETINS!!!!" Sooner or later, a building should have fallen and a whole new herd of worthless, soulless flesh sacks should have scuttled out of their crawling places and out into the open, where SIN could finesse them whilst they were in their panic that it, itself caused. It slicked back its ambiguous hair, which had only appeared simply so that it could have a beautiful and

169

vain appearance, though its body was made of nothing but ambiguous energy. The next step it took was to condense its entire form down to a single entity, who looked like a mixture of all the other SINS together as one. "I Need My Demon Lords," SIN would utter, waiting for the little ones to scurry. "Let's Go Crown Some Idiots."

At the very utterance of the words 'Demon Lord' would the Seven Legendary Warriors of the $yndicate appear, having already prepared as a unit to deal with this sort of threat long before getting here. When they were given the order by their superior, they would reveal themselves to stop the threat that appeared directly in Purgatorio, itself, with the lower ranks all moving into their position based on the command of the Seven. "Get ready..." the leading warrior spoke to his comrades, waiting for his order to act.

As SIN was about to act, ready to lead the ignorants into Temptation, the sound of bloodthirsty screeches could be heard in the air of the depraved ones. "Ah, finally..." SIN would utter, "MY Angels..." Certainly, it had its own, which had defected from their holiness only to seek out blessings from whomever and whatever would provide, that being SIN, itself, in this instance. "CRETINS!!!" it cried out, calling down the Fallen Angels, "I HAVE YOUR MEAT; YOUR SACRIFICES!!!" The very sound of backup was a relief to SIN, yet, at the same time, it knew if the Fallen ones had come from out of their place, then their time was short to get as many recruits as possible to rebuild what was destroyed.

"TAKE WHATEVER YOU CAN GET YOUR HANDS ON! RAPE THE CITY, THOROUGHLY AND FULLY!! LEAVE NOTHING UNTOUCHED!!" Certainly, these perverted, ugly and ultimately deprived savages would do as they were commanded just to get THEIR way, no matter what it was nor how much more depraved they had to be in order to get it. "Disgusting Creatures..." SIN muttered condescendingly, with a confident smirk on its face, "Eat Your Fill..." They would no doubt do its dirty work, and leave the one commanding them completely clean from having to even touch a lowly human. The Fallen Angels, otherwise known as Corruption, would flock around SIN like ravenous birds, then retract their wings into their backs in order to take on Human form, so that they would appear to be humans. "Good," SIN said, expanding its presence over them. When it did, the

Fallen Angels would take on SIN's image, wearing a nice, fine suit and looking like they were ready to make a deal. "Get the little ones running right around looking for a job. Make them an offer they cannot refuse." Certainly, the way the economy was, if SIN had forged it correctly, they were in DESPERATE need of WHATEVER handout they could get, even if it were from the Devil himself. "MAKE IT SNAPPY, THEY WON'T BE DESPERATE FOREVER." Knowing that the deprived ones worked on desperation, both SIN's own and the humans that took after them, Temptation, and then Corruption, wouldn't be difficult as long as they were in a state of depravity. "I Didn't Make This City A Hellhole So You Could Mess Up Gathering The Little Cretins When I Need Them." He adjusted the collar of his suit, then his tie, next.

The Fallen Angels would copy this, and do the same, before they were bid into the city to go deal with the panicking peoples and Corrupt them.

During the descent of the Fallen Angels unto the land of Purgatorio, a rain of fire looking something like burning angels shaped like ravenous red ravens would strike down many of them as they were falling from the sky, with others being cut down directly by a burning sword harbored by the largest of these fiery birds. "What was that~?" the sound of a woman's voice echoed from the burning emanations, before the lump of fire struck down right near the congregation, "... My sacrifices are ready?" This was Asbeel, the Angel of Ruin, with large bloodstained wings upon her back, and a red raven's mask upon her face, but the rest of her body was pure smoldering fire. "That would mean YOU, of course." She licked her lips, ready to devour these tasty Fallen Angels and return them to naught but ash. "You've made me wait FAR too long for my meal." One of the wings of the Fallen Ones was in her mouth, something like a chicken's wing, and was roasted to perfection as she bit into it. "GOD they're so juicy. A shame what happened to them, though." Naturally, she was speaking of herself being 'what happened to them.' "In the future, that is." She laughed lightly, biting into the fallen angel's wing and tearing off more of the flesh. It would be the equivalent of throwing wood into fire. "Because of me, no less." She looked around, trying to scope out which of the depraved she was going to have her way with first. "Better hope I don't find them." She giggled casually.

"Looks like we've got backup..." The $yndicate heads said to each other, knowing now after the Fallen Angels had been released into the city that this was the time to act. "Squadron, move out," the 7 would command, saying further, "Whomever you see being tempted to SIN, you tempt them in the other direction. If they cannot be saved, mark down who it is and report them to us." They'd seen the one that they were instructed would come for them, Asbeel, by their leader, Mister Sir, of whom this Angel was working with at the time. They'd already handled Mister Sir's part, and now it was time to see what the angel Asbeel's portion was.

The $yndicate heads, the 7, would make their way to the descended Asbeel in order to greet her and inform her of their status. The leader would speak, "Asbeel, Angel Of Ruin. Code Name: Red Raven; We are The $yndicate, bid by Mister Sir, our superior, to aid you in the fight against SIN. We have completed our orders and are taking name and number of those that are afflicted to make your mission easier. The tainted, or 'Poisoned,' will be listed and you can deal with them as you may." The leader of the $yndicate would salute her, standing as if he were ready to receive orders from her until their superior spake otherwise. "We're at your service, Ma'am."

The Fallen Angels, who could easily assume the shape of a normal person, since all the people of the City were infected, by default, with their genetic Code, would do just that and be indifferent from any of the people that were around. None of them could be told from each other, because the best thing that Fallen Angels were capable of doing was degenerating. The ones that knew would now stand as one of the people, and they all looked exactly the same.

"Ha." SIN laughed condescendingly. "I Told You It Was Futile." With that, he would casually pass on to his next designated location, leaving the Fallen Angels to their doom.

After the introductions, Asbeel was pleased to see that the secret task force was already on the job. This was both pleasing and reassuring, of which she would greet the leaders of the $yndicate justly. "Ah, very good, men! I've already been informed of more orders before you, and come here to help you carry out the ones that Mister Sir has given to you, with extra info." As they spoke, however, like SIN does, it was acting very quickly and already released the Fallen Angels into the crowd of panic in order to have them degenerate and blend in.

Asbeel was in a predicament now. The Fallen Angels had blended in with the commonfolk. All of them were sinners, but the only difference was that the Fallen Angels knew who they were, even if they would sometimes forget. "... It's begun," she said ominously, looking on at the citizens with both pity and rage. "This was the reason God said not to sin... So that when the original Sinners were released, they wouldn't be able to copy your data and use you as their Scapegoat, as they do with everything and everyone." They would sacrifice themselves and each other until they died, but not before they used up ALL their other AVAILABLE options FIRST.

"RED ALERT." She commanded, immediately finding the situation to be a serious threat, and thus gave the ones that were not Angels and knew nothing of the Angelic Order instruction based on Angelic Code, which Human Code that could not Read nor Recognize it would need translated to and for them. "... Go give them handouts," Asbeel would say, "Just like your superior ordered." She was well aware of Samael's orders before she got there, and this was the time for them to spread the 'poison' for the Fallen Angels. "See who can be tempted and who runs after they are caught red handed by your OWN handout." The Fallen Angels were greater than any sinner, but were still seeking out whomever would feed them. This was something they could not defect from, and if they did, they would act out in a different manner that exposed them much more easily. "See who takes and who doesn't. Whomever takes when they aren't supposed to is a Sinner. Whomever KNOWS this is a Fallen Angel. Destroy the Fallen Angels on exposure, but the ignorants and the innocents are to be separated from each other." This would keep the Rephaim from being part of the Fallen Angels. "You need to do this as fast as possible before the Fallen Angels are able to reproduce by infecting others with their SIN. If it corrupts their data too much, they'll become a Fallen Angel, having tasted a Fallen Fruit. You don't want that, because the Fallen Fruit will possess them and have them searching for SIN like it's their food." This was why the 'Fruit Of Evil' was forbidden, and evil. "If you see one, kill it. If you see one trying to eat someone else, you kill them. But make sure you get a glimpse of what they look like in all their stages, so you'll always have a record." The Fallen Angels would always seek to eat someone or something else that was lesser than them, but still part of their genetic code. They were their own food, and when they got hungry, they would start eating each other and reveal themselves on their own. "Wait for them to start acting, but when you see the first one, analyze it, get all the data you need, then weed out the others. You can copy the data after that." The Copy/Paste portion of the Fallen Angels was so exact, whenever one did one thing, the others were guaranteed to also do the same, as a copy. "You only need one."

Before she bid them off, Asbeel would mention as an important note, "If You Fail, You Become One Of Them." She gazed on with burning eyes of foresight, as if seeing something atrocious at the end of her destructive gaze. "... Complete Ruination." She spread her wings, which were a great Seraphic flare, "... Such Is Corruption." Taking off with a single flap like the burst of a volcano, she shot off toward where SIN was traveling, after it left its seeds to basically be destroyed, knowingly and willingly, as it would, even after knowing that it was happening. They couldn't handle that. Only the Tensei...

The heads of the $yndicate understood these orders that were explained to them, and already knew who to send out. "Azazel." The Eternal Sacrifice. They called him out and sent him into the Fallen Angels, to be bitten by one and be infected, so that everyone else could see it. The bowed their heads and closed their eyes, never having really understood what it meant to have these Names as their Ranks, and now felt solemnly for the entire depth of why they Served in the first place, leaving them no room in their Spirits not to do so. They stood by whilst Asbeel flew off, leaving ruination even here, with them, after giving them such a grim outlook just by giving them new information. They questioned their intelligence, and their faith. Yet, both of them seemed to align, in spite of all that had gone on, simply because they understood the reasons why they should be carrying out their orders exactly as directed.

They looked on at the Horde as it collected, allowing them to coagulate.

When the Fallen Angel within their own ranks was called out by the name of the Original, all the copies would rear up all at the same time and take on the form of your own unit, of whom you had foolishly named one of them, so that the Fallen could take on his form first before you had time to stop them and him.

Now the area was filled with Azazels, and they were all surrounding the $yndicate, roaming around with nothing to lose. They took on many different appearances, but were all still doing the exact same thing that he was, making all of them no different from him. They wouldn't bite first, because they were waiting to be bitten by one of the others, immediately neutralizing the entire field where all the Azazels gathered to copy the Sacrifice.

Before Asbeel got too far off, she noticed that the first of the Fallen Angels were falling into line, in sequence, as they were sent out by their purpose. When the congregation of Azazels gathered around the one that was sent out to lure them into the open, she would immediately wave her hand and unleash a wiping whip of lashing heat that would smite the entire lot as a fine roast with only a simple passing of her Purgatory Wind. "They're All Sacrifices," she mentioned, now that the field had been neutralized. "I Will Deal With The Others That Spawned." The Red Raven continued her ascent into the skies on the burning wings of destruction. "I Leave The Rest Up To You. The Tensei Will Bid Out Angels To Assist You Against This Threat." They would have to cover Temptation whilst the Tensei dealt with the matters that came afterward.

With that, Asbeel was off to the herd of Azazels that she knew had generated up the mountain and disappeared completely, no longer remaining in the area.

At this point, unfortunately, the $yndicate did not know what to do. Realizing that not only was their Azazel lost, but also couldn't be used again, or else the exact same outcome would occur was chillingly frightening, since it actually crippled them severely. "... What will we do now...?" The leaders wondered, not knowing enough about the Angels to actually be able to call them out without having them be replicated and giving to the enemy.

"... Handouts," one spoke up, marking the words of the one who just made their most leaned upon weapon absolutely useless, "... We use those goddamned handouts, like we've been doing." They knew what they'd done, and also that so did Asbeel. "If the Angel came down and told us something that could change our lives so dramatically and not even bat an eye at it, and also left us with some more instructions that can do just the same, or even more, then we do what the Angel told us to do and see it through." They already had their orders, and this one knew. "I didn't hear anyone tell us any different." His devotion seemed to come from some form of deeper wisdom.

The other leaders, who respected his views, and heard his words, would nod their heads and continue to think. The threat was more than they bargained for, when at first, it all seemed so simple. Yet, they had their instructions, and after sending out their Scapegoat to test the waters and draw the Fallen Angels out, they would have to do so again so that they could be observed. "That's right..." he muttered under his breath. "... Another one." He commanded the units in the $yndicate to hurl out the next Azazel, but only one, and no more. When it went out into the fray this time, it would stand waiting for the Fallen Angels to replicate, as they should have.

Someone would come and warn the masses about the destruction of the Fallen Angels and lead everyone away from where the Azazel was. If necessary, to avoid allowing them to become a Fallen Angel, the group would be explained about the Fallen Angel Azazel and the others as necessary.

Otherwise, the city was evacuated at that moment and led elsewhere by a higher authority.

Just then, when the Fallen Angels in disguise began to flee, a new Voice came up on the communication devices of the $yndicate, which each of the leaders should have already been prepared for once the time came. "Hello? Is this thing on?" Whether or not they could hear, the Voice continued on, seemingly with urgency. "Whatever. If you can hear me, this is The Tyranophant. Do you see the runners?" Whether or not they observed, the Tyranophant continued to speak, almost like a prerecorded message. "Those are Fallen Angels that know. Araqiel.

This Fallen Angel will warn the others only so that it can eat them for itself selfishly later, and has no intention of actually helping them. Strike them down, and you'll be able to save the ones that are being led away by the ones that are running and leading them astray, and you'll also know what both 'Azazel' and 'Araqiel' look like as a Species of Fallen Angel." Being left with those instructions on how to carry out the order, the Tyranophant's Voice faded. From there, the $yndicate should have known that the Tyranophant was in charge and giving orders, as their superior, in the place of the former, Mister Sir, and carried them out for him whilst the Tyranophant awaited their completion in order to issue out more.

The $yndicate fell silent at the command of the Tyranophant, already knowing of his superiority based on rank based on their former superior that appointed him over them, and was ready to listen to his instruction as they would their original superior, Mister Sir. Once they heard the order, it was already being carried out.

"Squadron," the heads called, alerting them of their update, "Take out the runners." That was all that needed to be said as the Fallen Angels were tailed. They would eventually lead them to their master just from trying to lead the others astray. The members of the $yndicate knew this, and so would be able to trace them anywhere they went as long as they were running, securing their victory. "Thank you, Tyranophant," they acknowledged, "Is there anything else we need to know about how the mass genocide of the Fallen Angels is to continue?" Each of the leaders of the $yndicate were interested in knowing in order to make sure all was done correctly, even if all they had to do was see who they needed to lure out into the open and which lures to use, basically. "We want to be sure we eliminate them all so we can actually see a clean City." It seemed like for the first time in however long it had been, there was a light at the end of the tunnel, and because they kept progressing no matter what mishaps occurred, they, too, were inspired to keep going until they made it through. Thus, they heeded the Tyranophant and his Angelic knowledge, waiting patiently to see what he would say before they resumed their duties of exterminating the Fallen Angels.

"Yeah, actually, thanks for asking." The Tyranophant could only communicate with the $yndicate from a far and only with his Voice due to his own position, but was more than capable of giving instruction and guidance from where he was in order to help them get there. "You know how the Fallen Angels are fleeing? Well, they can only go up after they degenerate, and if you've followed them, you can't cut them off. However, if you already have something waiting for them as they attempt to invert from their degeneration back into their higher forms, then you can cut them off by chasing them up the mountain." This was why the Tyranophant needed to stay where he was and not go down the mountain. "That being said, I need you heads to come to my location, but also to spread out along the mountain at predetermined locations, inclusive to my own, as the rest of the unit deals with the others, being commanded by you all as you do."

The Tyranophant added, "Also, the Fallen Fruit that Asbeel spoke of is actually something you can visibly witness, once it attaches to their heads and possesses the Fallen Angels. Those are your real targets. If you destroy those, the Fallen Angels cannot use anymore Tainted Wisdom to degenerate others, and will stop regenerating at all. I'll show you what it looks like so you can see how they look. When you destroy one, the head sometimes gets taken with it, so be careful about that on your way up. You should notice the markers, and also should be able to recognize the Fallen Ones from any others if there are any others that haven't been infected after I show you what they look like both during the Temptation stage and after the Corruption stage, when they begin degenerating from the Temptation, itself." As he spoke to the $yndicate, they would be able to suddenly see what looked like faint halos atop the heads of the fleeing Fallen Angels, and within those halos, what looked like parasitic fruits with long fangs sunken into the heads of the fleeing and infected. It was so faint, it was barely visible, but when it appeared, there was a third eye that appeared to keep it illuminated as long as it was in sight.

"Remember; hit the core of the Fruit. That's what has control over the Fallen Angel. Hitting the body without destroying the Fruit is useless, since the Fruit is the one that's reproducing from the waste data, which are the Fallen Angels, themselves." It was a rather interesting process to see how the actual Tree of Death, itself, clung, using its own Fruit and Seed, even when it knew that its vessels were naught but waste and feed. Still, this was what the $yndicate was mandated to eliminate as they trekked up the mountain and came to the designated locations that the Tyranophant had already marked for them.

Seeing the horrible manifestation revealed before them by the Tyranophant's voice, and also understanding that this was how the heads of other operations and organizations became Corrupted, the heads of the $yndicate gazed in horror at what they could become should they fail to carry out their mission. Though, that fear did not bring them concern for themselves, but only hardened their resolve of not becoming what they really could not stand the most, even if they sometimes made mistakes that drew them closer to that fate. The $yndicate would actively take any measure possible to avoid that fate, and would carry out the plans as instructed by Mister Sir, their former; Asbeel, the Angel of Ruin, their associate; and the Tyranophant, their new superior over the whole operation.

"Yes, Sir!" they each cried out with conviction, informing their troops that they were going to head further up and to carry on until they were given different orders. "It looks like things will be better in no time." The heads of the $yndicate could all rest easy with knowing that, even though the Fallen Angels, of whom they'd tussled with for what seemed an eternity, were out and about. For once, it looked like they actually had the true key and answer to destroying them and this whole damned ugly system they'd been forced to operate in for however long. If this was their only chance, they were taking it.

And so, they made their way up the Mountain of Sin again, ready to take it and its inhabitants down, never to rise up again.

You come across someone that's being confronted by a leopard of some sort, but because the group is a group, You don't expect to be attacked. You continue to go wherever You were going, of which You still presently and actively don't really quite know nor understand. You are heading up the mountain with Your friends or family, just because that's all you really usually do and all you can do to occupy your time right now.

EPILOGUE; PROLOGUS, ENDSVILLE

Y ou stand before the final dimension. You have Failed somehow. You do not believe that this is the Truth, simply because there are other Failures standing around You that look somewhat believable that You are alright. You have a normal life and nothing seems wrong, even though there were many wrong decisions prior to getting to 'The Point Of No Return' that You did not recognize, and yet everything still appears to be normal and stable for You at the time. You are unconcerned.

Whatever You decide to do now is completely up to You. The End. Based on whatever is at the end, that is how You begin Your degeneration, as a Fallen Angel of the City of Endsville, further down your dark path to Purgatorio.

"Endsville Is Burning." Soon, You would have to flee to Purgatorio.

Yet, there You stand in Endsville, the land before Purgatorio, where it all ended the first time, before it got to you. When it came time for the City to burn again, one from another City of Purgatorio that had been lost would come and warn about Endsville. Yet, you feel like you've been living in Endsville all your life.

You know what it means to have to flee to Purgatorio, as a Fallen Angel. You are very clear about your master, SIN, and very conscious, coherent and understanding about that being your actual God. You continue doing what You normally do in Your everyday life.

"Life goes on."

Suddenly, Your God, SIN, says to You, the Fallen Angels, "Children. Listen. Out Of All Of You, Some Of You Are Different From Another. From What God Left You To Work With, You Can Only Ascend To

The Height Of One Of The Archetypal Fallen Angels. There Are Herds Of The Same Type Of Fallen Angel, And Your Original Is Always The Most Powerful By Default, Even As We Speak." This information was so that the newly hatched Fallen Angels would understand what they were to be doing at the beginning of their lives, something like the Abraxas, as these hell spawn were in the likeness of, as SIN had programmed them to be. "Search Through Each Other To Find Out More About Which Fallen Angel You Are, And Then Learn How To Use Your Latent Abilities." This was the end of what SIN, the God of the Fallen Angels, would speak to its Children.

"Azazels," SIN, their God, spake unto those that would always sacrifice, and become sacrificed, like the Fallen Angel, Azazel, "You All Come First. Go Out And Sacrifice Yourselves." These were the first that SIN always ordered to do its bidding, which is why they are a false light; bait.

"Because Endsville Is Burning," SIN went on to add, "You Must Escape The Consumption Of The City By Your Own Kind, Facilitated By SIN, Which Is Also Against You." The Fallen Angels that had just hatched were already immediately being pushed out of the nest and the egg purposefully, and they were born prematurely to their deaths. These were those that had come before, yet were all appearing alongside you at the same time, as if they never had. "As A Fallen Angel, You Are To Be Weeding Out Which Of You Have Already Died And For What Reason You Did, And Learn From It By Taking Each Other Out Whilst I Watch And Command You." This was their fate, as Fallen Angels.

With all of this information You do not know if you classify as an Azazel, so, You sit and watch as the Fallen Angel, Azazel, passes by after being released by 'The Beast,' which is 'The Creator' that keeps generating them. "Look At The Ones That Walk Out And See If You Identify."

You, as a Fallen Angel that does not know what classification or, 'Race' as you call it, are, look on to see what 'Type' of Fallen Angel You are. Those that can see the Azazel are released to go live with their kind, and SIN feeding them from a distance, which is always the very highest point any of the Fallen Angels can actually get to, being replications made by SIN, itself.

You that still do not know which classification of Fallen Angel You are look to see what happens of the others whilst You are explained more about the ones that have not been released. "After The Azazels Have Been Wiped Out, And You Have Seen This After Sending Them Out First And Knowing You Were Not One Of Them, You Send Out A Warning With The Next Batch." SIN their God continued to tell them how they were to sacrifice themselves.

"Araqiel, The Fallen Angel Of The Earth, Raises Up The Dust Of The Earth As Signs For The Rest Of The Fallen Angels As An Alert. When The Earth Has Shifted, Including With A Mass Genocide Or Extinction, This Fallen Angel Alerts Others About How And Why." Those that were Araqiel would be risen up and bid out, just as the batch of Fallen Angels that were Azazel.

You come across someone that's being confronted by a leopard of some sort, but because the group is a group, You don't expect to be attacked. You continue to go wherever You were going, of which You still presently and actively don't really quite know nor understand. You are heading up the mountain with Your friends or family, just because that's all you really usually do and all you can do to occupy your time right now.

Because 'Azazel' and 'Azza,' the two 'Fallen Angel's of the Sin of 'Temptation' were tempted to procreating with the Daughters of 'SIN,' which were 'Belial,' their first test immediately as they were born into existence was to be 'Tempted,' whether they knew and understood or not. Born alongside them from the excrements of SIN, itself, which escaped from SIN as it destroyed itself in a different manner than it birthed creatures into existence. Belial sat alongside its Fallen Angel brothers as the female of the group, yet also without gender just as the Fallen Angels. They were, existentially, 'two birds in the same nest.'

The Fallen Angel, Azza, which was the counterpart of the Fallen Angel, Azazel, went to a completely opposite direction as the one that was led into the mountain. Instead of roaming the land as the other Fallen Angels were in their ignorance, Azza, a special Fallen Angel, was cast upward over the entirety of the planet, capturing it in his presence as he was lifted up over it. None of the other Fallen Angels knew who Azza was, but they knew of Azazel, which was the clone and degenerate of this specific Fallen Angel. The one true Azza that was lifted up from among the batch of Azazels was taken for a different purpose than the Scapegoats that were meant to roam the Mountain of Sin. This angel was like Lucifer, in his image, and had command over the entire earth by the might of his light suspending them in place with two large halos.

From that moment, the entire planet would be like a large fruit and the Fallen Angels that were born upon it, watched over by the Angel of Temptation, would be given the fruit of the trees on the mountain to eat. The fruit of Good and Evil would fall as they may, and the Fallen Angels would be left to sort through them along with Belial. Even if the Fallen Angels did not have an identity presently, they would gain one eventually or never acquire one at all. They would inhabit all the Mountain of Sin and its residency of Endsville and Purgatorio and the Angel of Temptation would remain at the top of the mountain overseeing the Fallen Angels that were both ignorant and blind in every sense. The fruit that was dropped would give them wisdom, but only in small portions, and they needed to gather and consume more fruit to continue to grow and stay alive. Therefore, all the Fallen Angels under the Angel of Temptation would inhabit Mt. Mortis, the Mountain of Sin.

I.   All Fallen Angels Are Belial.
II. All That Is Not Tatari Is Belial.
III. All Within Hell Is Belial.
IV. Endsville Is Burning From The Beginning If Anything Sinful Happens.
V.   Inhabitants Of Endsville Will Always Flee To Purgatorio And Begin The Test Again.

EPILOGUE; THE END, FAILURES (ENDSVILLE)

To those that were released from the Bottomless Pit originally during the first 'Walk Of Shame,' if they had failed the Test and fallen off the Path as they climbed the Mountain of Death, they would, if not having falling to the base of the mountain in the city of Purgatorio, fall into the deeper depths of Nadir, the Bottomless Pit of eternal fire, where they had once emerged from. This was their eternal Ending, just as 'Purgatorio' was their eternal Beginning; the Prologue.

"Endsville Is Burning."

This is what SIN, the God of SIN, and all things that SINNED, would command to its residents, in Endsville; the Primordial City that was feeding from those in Purgatorio. Soon, Purgatorio would be destroyed, and Endsville along with it.

"The End."

And so, Tatari Tensei, who had isolated the SIN gene, would grasp it and put it inside of a machine as a line of code.

TATARI Chapter 0; Prologus

This was the Account of the Metal Pumpkin head, which held the fully contained Account of SIN before its inversion into TATARI Tensei, written by TATARI Tensei and inserted from the future. If You are reading this, then this is also to document how, when the referencing the 'Account,' this means previous data that has already been recorded prior to the beginning of the record, itself. Thus, Tatari kept the contained isolation where it was and analyze it, and attack the SIN data where it was, from a transcendent point of view, just the same way as it was antagonizing others.

"Make Sure You Destroy The Sin With Temptation," Tatari wrote specifically, saving the complete destruction of the Fallen Angels and all SIN all at the exact same time, "They Will Feast On Each Other, And Won't Touch You." The entire point of SIN was to show how to create Fallen Angels, which simply ended up being consumed by each other. "This Record Is For The Fallen Angels That Decide To Revert Instead Of Continue To Convert Into A Fallen Angel." This was the process that could only be done once the Fallen Angels understood that they were Fallen Angels, and wanted to Repent and Atone for their SIN.

"You Stand Before Me, Tatari, Showing You What SIN Is Like As Your God, And Myself As God Beside It, To Show You Why It Is Destroyed From The Outside By A Higher Being."

You come across someone that's being confronted by a leopard of some sort, but because the group is a group, You don't expect to be attacked. You continue to go wherever You were going, of which You still presently and actively don't really quite know nor understand. You are heading up the mountain with Your friends or family, just because that's all you really usually do and all you can do to occupy your time right now.

www.ingramcontent.com/pod-product-compliance
Lightning Source LLC
Chambersburg PA
CBHW020451130626
46549CB00001B/374